Praise for *Evaluating Software Architectures*

"The architecture of complex software or systems is a collection of hard decisions that are very expensive to change. Successful product development and evolution depend on making the right architectural choices. Can you afford not to identify and not to evaluate these choices? The authors of this book are experts in software architecture and its evaluation. They collected a wealth of ideas and experience in a well-organized and accessible form. If you are involved in the development of complex systems or software, you will find this book an invaluable guide for establishing and improving architecture evaluation practice in your organization."
    —Alexander Ran, Principal Scientist of Software Architecture, Nokia

"Software engineers must own this book. It is a well-written guide to the steps for evaluating software architecture. It argues for the inclusion of architecture evaluation and review as a standard part of the software development lifecycle. It introduces some new and innovative methods for analyzing important architecture characteristics, like extensibility, portability, and reliability. I believe these methods will become new engineering cornerstones for creating good software systems."
    —Joe Maranzano, AT&T Bell Labs Fellow in Software Architecture (1990), and former head of the Bell Labs Software Technology Center

"Experience and teamwork are the only approaches I know of to deliver products faster, cheaper, and yet to delight your customers. In their first book, *Software Architecture in Practice*, Paul and Rick (and Len Bass) helped me match my experience with theory. Their invaluable approaches and case studies changed my practice and the way I proceed to design systems and software architectures. This second book, with Mark, covers what I will look at before I feel good about an architecture. It is about how I can tap other people's experience to produce an improved outcome, using other people's feedback. I have used many of the concepts explained in this book for my customers' benefit. Using this book, you—architects, developers, and managers—will develop a common language and practice to team up and deliver more successful products."
    —Bertrand Salle, lead architect with a major telecommunications company

"If architecture is the foundation of system construction, architectural evaluation is part of the foundation of getting to a 'good' architecture. In this book, the authors put their considerable expertise to one of the most pressing issues in systems development today: how to evaluate an architecture prior to system construction to ascertain its feasibility and suitability to the system of interest. The book provides a practical guide to architecture evaluation using three contemporary evaluation methods. It should prove valuable to practitioners and as a basis for the evolution of architectural evaluation as an engineering practice."
—Rich Hilliard, Chief Technical Officer, ConsentCache, Inc.,
and technical editor, *IEEE Recommended Practice for Architectural Description of Software-Intensive Systems*

"Too many systems have performance and other problems caused by an inappropriate architecture. Thus problems are introduced early, but are usually detected too late—when the deadline is near or, even worse, after the problem makes the headlines. Remedies lead to missed schedules, cost overruns, missed market windows, damaged customer relations, and many other difficulties. It is easy to prevent these problems by evaluating the architecture choices early, and selecting an appropriate one."
—Connie U. Smith, Ph.D., principal consultant, Performance Engineering Services Division, L&S Computer Technology, Inc.,
and coauthor of the new book, *Performance Solutions: A Practical Guide to Creating Responsive, Scalable Software*

"The ATAM [an evaluation method described in this book] is the natural quality-gate through which a high-level design should pass before a detail design project is initiated. Why use the ATAM to evaluate an architecture? Mitigation of design risk is a major reason, but more importantly, the ATAM provides an interactive vehicle that can give key development and user stakeholders architectural visibility—visibility that can lead to an important 'early buy-in.' "
—Rich Zebrowski, Software Technology Manager, Motorola, Inc.

"Caterpillar's experience with architecture reviews includes SAAM, ATAM, ARID, and ADR [evaluation methods described in this book, the first three in detail]. These reviews ensured that the needs of the user community were being met, and they exposed the architecture to others in the organization helping with understanding and organizational buy-in. The SAAM- and ATAM-based evaluations worked well to expose the architecture early in the development cycle to a broad range of people. The ARID- and ADR-based evaluations facilitated the exposure of technical details of the architecture later in the development cycle. As the architect of the pilot project for ARID, I observed that this review even served as an architecture training session before the architecture was fully documented."
—Lee R. DenBraber, former Lead Software Architect, Caterpillar, Inc.

"We've heard all the management hype about harnessing the innovative creativity of our teams, establishing integrated customer-developer-product teams, and better targeting our systems to meet end user needs. The ATAM techniques described in this book give technical managers, system architects, and engineers proven tools for breaking down the communications barriers that impede our ability to realize these goals. We have successfully integrated the ATAM techniques throughout our lifecycle, including development and maintenance, and have found that they provide the strong technical basis we need to evaluate the many difficult trades required by a system as large as EOSDIS."

—Mike Moore, Deputy Manager, Science Systems
Development Office, Earth Observing System Data
Information System (EOSDIS) Project,
NASA Goddard Space Flight Center

"If you know how difficult architecture reviews are, you will be amazed how effective ATAM evaluations can be. For example, an ATAM evaluation we conducted on an important software product line identified a major architectural risk, which we subsequently were able to avoid—a benefit we expect to continue seeing. Moreover, ATAM techniques have enabled us to explain such risks to stakeholders far more clearly than by any other review method."

—Stefan Ferber, Corporate Research, Robert Bosch GmbH

Carnegie Mellon
Software Engineering Institute

The SEI Series in Software Engineering represents a collaboration between the Software Engineering Institute of Carnegie Mellon University and Addison-Wesley to develop and publish a body of work on selected topics in software engineering. The common goal of the SEI and Addison-Wesley is to provide the most current software engineering information in a form that is easily usable by practitioners and students.

For more information point your browser to www.awprofessional.com/seiseries

Dennis M. Ahern, et al., *CMMI® SCAMPI Distilled.* ISBN: 0-321-22876-6

Dennis M. Ahern, et al., *CMMI® Distilled, Second Edition.* ISBN: 0-321-18613-3

Dennis M. Ahern, et al., *CMMI® Distilled: A Practical Introduction to Integrated Process Improvement, Third Edition.* ISBN: 0-321-46108-8

Christopher Alberts and Audrey Dorofee, *Managing Information Security Risks.* ISBN: 0-321-11886-3

Julia H. Allen, et al., *Software Security Engineering: A Guide for Project Managers.* ISBN: 0-321-50917-X

Len Bass, et al., *Software Architecture in Practice, Second Edition.* ISBN: 0-321-15495-9

Marilyn Bush and Donna Dunaway, *CMMI® Assessments.* ISBN: 0-321-17935-8

Carnegie Mellon University, Software Engineering Institute, *The Capability Maturity Model.* ISBN: 0-201-54664-7

Mary Beth Chrissis, et al., *CMMI®, Second Edition.* ISBN: 0-321-27967-0

Paul Clements, et al., *Documenting Software Architectures.* ISBN: 0-201-70372-6

Paul Clements, et al., *Evaluating Software Architectures.* ISBN: 0-201-70482-X

Paul Clements and Linda Northrop, *Software Product Lines.* ISBN: 0-201-70332-7

Bill Curtis, et al., *The People Capability Maturity Model®.* ISBN: 0-201-60445-0

William A. Florac and Anita D. Carleton, *Measuring the Software Process.* ISBN: 0-201-60444-2

Brian P. Gallagher, et al., *CMMI®-ACQ: Guidelines for Improving the Acquisition of Products and Services.* ISBN: 0321580354

Suzanne Garcia and Richard Turner, *CMMI® Survival Guide.* ISBN: 0-321-42277-5

Hassan Gomaa, *Software Design Methods for Concurrent and Real-Time Systems.* ISBN: 0-201-52577-1

Elaine M. Hall, *Managing Risk.* ISBN: 0-201-25592-8

Hubert F. Hofmann, et al., *CMMI® for Outsourcing.* ISBN: 0-321-47717-0

Watts S. Humphrey, *Introduction to the Personal Software Process^SM.* ISBN: 0-201-54809-7

Watts S. Humphrey, *Managing the Software Process.* ISBN: 0-201-18095-2

Watts S. Humphrey, *A Discipline for Software Engineering.* ISBN: 0-201-54610-8

Watts S. Humphrey, *Introduction to the Team Software Process^SM.* ISBN: 0-201-47719-X

Watts S. Humphrey, *Winning with Software.* ISBN: 0-201-77639-1

Watts S. Humphrey, *PSP^SM: A Self-Improvement Process for Software Engineers.* ISBN: 0-321-30549-3

Watts S. Humphrey, *TSP^SM—Leading a Development Team.* ISBN: 0-321-34962-8

Watts S. Humphrey, *TSP^SM—Coaching Development Teams.* ISBN: 0-201-73113-4

Robert C. Seacord, *Secure Coding in C and C++.* ISBN: 0-321-33572-4

Robert C. Seacord, *The CERT® C Secure Coding Standard.* ISBN: 0321563212

Jeannine M. Siviy, et al., *CMMI® and Six Sigma: Partners in Process Improvement.* ISBN: 0321516087

Richard D. Stutzke, *Estimating Software-Intensive Systems.* ISBN: 0-201-70312-2

Sami Zahran, *Software Process Improvement.* ISBN: 0-201-17782-X

Evaluating Software Architectures

Methods and Case Studies

Paul Clements

Rick Kazman

Mark Klein

✦✦ Addison-Wesley

Boston • San Francisco • New York • Toronto • Montreal
London • Munich • Paris • Madrid
Capetown • Sydney • Tokyo • Singapore • Mexico City

Carnegie Mellon
Software Engineering Institute

The SEI Series in Software Engineering

Many of the designations used by manufacturers and sellers to distinguish their products are claimed as trademarks. Where those designations appear in this book, and Addison-Wesley, Inc. was aware of a trademark claim, the designations have been printed with initial capital letters or in all capitals.

CMM, Capability Maturity Model, Capability Maturity Modeling, Carnegie Mellon, CERT, and CERT Coordination Center are registered in the U.S. Patent and Trademark Office.

ATAM; Architecture Tradeoff Analysis Method; CMMI; CMM Integration; CURE; IDEAL; Interim Profile; OCTAVE; Operationally Critical Threat, Asset, and Vulnerability Evaluation; Personal Software Process; PSP; SCAMPI; SCAMPI Lead Assessor; SCE; Team Software Process; and TSP are service marks of Carnegie Mellon University.

The publisher offers discounts on this book when ordered in quantity for bulk purchases and special sales. For more information, please contact:

U.S. Corporate and Government Sales
(800) 382-3419
corpsales@pearsontechgroup.com

For sales outside of the U.S., please contact:

International Sales
(317) 581-3793
international@pearsontechgroup.com

Visit Addison-Wesley on the Web: www.awprofessional.com

Library of Congress Cataloging-in-Publication Data

Clements, Paul, 1955–
    Evaluating software architectures : methods and case studies / Paul Clements, Rick Kazman, Mark Klein.
        p. cm. — (SEI series in software engineering)
    Includes bibliographical references and index.
    ISBN 0-201-70482-X
    1. Computer software—Evaluation. 2. Computer architecture—Evaluation. I. Kazman, Rick. II. Klein, Mark. III. Title. IV. Series.

QA76.754.C47 2002
005.1—dc2
                                            2001045880

ISBN 0-201-70482-X

Text printed in the United States on recycled paper at Courier Westford in Westford, Massachusetts.
11th Printing, December 2014

Contents

Chapter 5   Understanding Quality Attributes   109

Chapter 6   A Case Study in Applying the ATAM   127

List of Figures

List of Tables

Preface

The foundation of any software system is its architecture, that is, the way the software is constructed from separately developed components and the ways in which those components interact and relate to each other. If the system is going to be built by more than one person—and these days, what system isn't?—it is the architecture that lets them communicate and negotiate work assignments. If the requirements include goals for performance, security, reliability, or maintainability, then architecture is the design artifact that first expresses how the system will be built to achieve those goals. The architecture determines the structure of the development project. It is the basis for organizing the documentation. It is the first document given to new project members, and the first place a maintenance organization begins its work. Schedules, budgets, and workplans all revolve around it. And the senior, most talented designers are paid to create it.

A system's longevity—how viable it remains in the face of evolutionary pressure—is determined primarily by its architecture. Some architectures go on to become generic and adopted by the development community at large: three-tier client-server, layered, and pipe-and-filter architectures are well known beyond the scope of any single system. Today, organizations are recognizing the importance and value of architectures in helping them to meet corporate enterprise goals. An architecture can give an enterprise a competitive advantage and can be banked like any other capitalized asset.

The right architecture is the first step to success. The wrong architecture will lead to calamity. This leads to an important question: If your organization is betting its future—or at least a portion of it—on an architecture for a system or family of related systems, how can you be sure that you're building from the right architecture and not the wrong one?

The practice of creating an architecture is maturing. We can identify causal connections between design decisions made in the architecture and the qualities and properties that result downstream in the system or systems that follow from it. This means that it is possible to evaluate an architecture, to analyze architectural decisions, in the context of the goals and requirements that are levied on systems that will be built from it.

And yet even though architecture is regarded as an essential part of modern system development, architecture evaluation is almost never included as a standard part of any development process. We believe it should be, and this book is an attempt to help people fill that gap.

The time has come for architecture evaluation to become an accepted engineering practice for two reasons. First, architecture represents an enormous risk in a development project. As we've said, the wrong one leads to disaster. It makes good sense to perform an evaluation on such a pivotal artifact, just as you would plan risk-mitigation strategies for other sources of uncertainty. Second, architecture evaluation can be remarkably inexpensive. The methods described in this book add no more than a week to the project schedule, and some abridged forms require no more than a day or two. Architecture evaluation represents a very cheap insurance policy. Compared to the cost of a poor architecture, the modest expense of a software architecture evaluation makes all the sense in the world. What has been lacking up to this point is a practical method for carrying it out, which is where this book comes in.

This is a guidebook for practitioners (or those who wish to become practitioners) of architecture evaluation. We supply conceptual background where necessary, but the intent of the work is to provide step-by-step guidance in the practice of architecture evaluation and analysis. To help put the methods into practice, we have included sample artifacts that are put into play during an architecture evaluation: viewgraph presentation outlines, scenarios, after-action surveys, final report templates, and so forth. The goal is that after reading this book, you will feel confident enough to try out the methods on an architecture in your own organization. We have tried to help answer the question, during an evaluation, "What should I do now?"

While the book is written from the point of view of the evaluator, there are others involved in an evaluation—project managers, architects, other stakeholders—who will gain valuable insights by reading this book. They will come to understand how their products will be evaluated and thus can position themselves to make those products fare better with respect to the evaluation criteria. This is rather like scoring well on a test because you've seen an early copy of the test, but in this case it isn't cheating but rather sound management and engineering practice. But know that when we use the word *you* in the text, we are speaking to the evaluator.

The techniques in this book are based on actual practice in government and industry. Most of the methods were developed by ourselves and others at the Software Engineering Institute and applied by ourselves and others to our customers' and collaborators' systems. Other material was gleaned by holding industrial workshops whose participants were experts in the analysis and evaluation of architecture. In short, we have learned by doing, and we have learned from others' doing.

This book will not teach you how to become a good architect, nor does it help you become fluent in the issues of architecture. We assume that you already have a good grasp of architectural concepts that comes from practical experience. This book will not help you assess the job performance of any individual architect nor a project's architecture (or development) process. What it will do is show you how to evaluate an architecture with respect to a broad spectrum of important quality attributes having to do with the architecture and the future system(s) that will be built from it.

Finally, we should say a word about *software* versus *system* architecture—that is, the architecture of software-intensive systems. This is a book about the evaluation of software architectures, but we often hear the question, "Well, what about the architecture of the system, not just the software? It's just as vital." We couldn't agree more. System architectures embody the same kinds of structuring and decomposition decisions that drive software architectures. Moreover, they include hardware/software tradeoffs as well as the selection of computing and communication equipment, all of which are completely beyond the realm of software architecture. System architectures hold the key to success or failure of a system every bit as much as the software architecture does for the software. Hence, they deserve to be evaluated every bit as much and for exactly the same reasons.

The methods presented in this book will, we believe, apply equally well to system architectures as to software architectures. If modifiability is a concern, the methods can be used to gauge the expense of making changes over the system's lifetime; if performance is a concern, the methods can be used to spot bottlenecks and problem areas in the system as well as the software; and so forth.

Why, then, do we call it a book about *software* architecture evaluation? Because that is the realm in which the methods were invented, developed, tested, and matured. In the remainder of this book when we speak of *architecture*, you can always safely prefix it with *software*. You can prefix it with *system* depending on how applicable you feel the methods are to system architectures and how confident you are about our intuition in the matter.

As a final word, we invite you to share your experiences with us. We would be keenly interested in knowing what you discover works well and what doesn't work so well. Writing a book is an opportunity to share lessons, but more importantly to us, it is an opportunity to gather new ones.

PCC	RK	MHK
Austin, Texas	Pittsburgh, Pennsylvania	Pittsburgh, Pennsylvania

Acknowledgments

This book describes work that is the product of many people. The Architecture Tradeoff Analysis Method (ATAM) evolved from the Software Architecture Analysis Method (SAAM), which was largely the brainchild of Len Bass, Gregory Abowd, and two of the authors. We owe some of the ideas about the mechanics and practicalities of evaluation to a series of workshops on architecture evaluation held at the Software Engineering Institute (SEI). These workshops led to useful technical reports co-authored by Gregory Abowd, Len Bass, Linda Northrop, and Amy Moormann Zaremski; we are grateful to them as well as to the industrial participants at those workshops who unselfishly shared their expertise with us.

Attribute-based architectural styles (ABASs), a concept which the ATAM uses, were the subject of a working group at the SEI, which (in addition to the authors) included Mario Barbacci, Len Bass, Jeromy Carriere, Rick Linger, Howard Lipson, Tom Longstaff, and Chuck Weinstock. Peter Feiler and Kurt Wallnau also participated.

We owe debts of gratitude to all of our colleagues, resident affiliates, and visiting scientists at the SEI who helped apply the ATAM, the SAAM, and ARID to real systems and brought home experience and countless ways to make the methods better. These include Felix Bachmann, Mario Barbacci, Len Bass, Joe Batman Jeromy Carriere, Gary Chastek, Sholom Cohen, Pat Donohoe, Matt Fisher, Brian Gallagher, David Garlan, John Goodenough, Bonnie John, Larry Jones, Tony Lattanze, Reed Little, Marta Lopez, Bob Krut, Robert Nord, Linda Northrop, Liam O'Brien, Judy Stafford, Christoph Stoermer, Chuck Weinstock, Bill Wood, and Dave Zubrow.

Special thanks are owed to the organizations who allowed us to pilot these methods before they were fully cooked, and who willingly joined with us to explore the ins and outs of architecture evaluation. These include the US Air Force, the US Army, Allied Signal, Boeing, Caterpillar, Robert Bosch, and Siemens.

We especially thank our careful reviewers, who include Gary Chastek, Pat Donohoe, Larry Jones, Martin Simons, and the anonymous reviewers engaged by the publisher. This book isvery much improved because of the time they devoted to give us high-quality insightful comments. Thanks to Mario Barbacci for writing the sidebar "Quality Attribute Workshops," to Tony Lattanze for writing the sidebar "My Experiences with the ATAM", and to Robert Nord for writing the sidebar "Making the Most of Evaluators' Efforts." Thanks to Stephan Kurpjuweit for helping to write the chapter "Introducing the SAAM and Using It to Evaluate an Example Architecture." Thanks to Joe Batman for contributing the questions that populate the checklist shown in Figure 6-3, "Checklist of questions the architect should plan to answer.

Thanks to Linda Northrop, the director of the SEI's Product Line Systems Program, home to the methods in this book. Linda supported the work that led to this book, promoted the work inside and outside of the SEI, secured funding on an ongoing basis, organized workshops for testing and exploring new ideas, offered technical advice, and carefully and tirelessly fostered the customer collaborations that allowed the methods to be used on real projects. These collaborations—with real customers in real settings—greatly accelerated the maturity and community acceptance of the analysis methods.

Special thanks to Mike Moore of NASA's Goddard Space Flight Center for his enthusiasm in applying the ATAM to the system described in Chapter 6, for his review of that chapter, and for his willingness to let us write about it. Special thanks also to everyone associated with the ECS program who participated in that ATAM exercise.

We thank the professionals at Addison-Wesley for their usual first-class work. Peter Gordon was once again the taskmaster with the velvet whip. Thanks to Bob Fantazier of the SEI for his superb work producing the figures in this book. Thanks to Sheila Rosenthal for her hard work in tracking down the sources for some elusive quotations.

Finally, thanks go to the Inn Above Onion Creek in Kyle, Texas, for providing the inspirational setting and the peaceful environment that helped us complete this book. Their library was a delight, and rich enough to provide sources for many of the chapter-opening quotations in this book.

Reader's Guide

We assume that you are fluent in the issues of architecture but not in the practices of architecture evaluation. The chapters in this book cover the following topics.

- Chapter 1 provides a short introduction to the topic of software architecture to establish a common conceptual starting point and terminology for the remainder of the book.

- Chapter 2 lays the groundwork for evaluating a software architecture. It discusses why and when to evaluate an architecture, who is involved, the costs and the benefits, and what tangible results you can expect an evaluation to produce.

- Chapter 3 introduces the Architecture Tradeoff Analysis Method (ATAM), the first of three methods presented in this book and the one covered in the most detail. This chapter describes the ATAM's major phases and steps.

- Chapter 4 is a short case study in applying the ATAM to a real system, so that you, having just learned the steps, can see them applied right away.

- Chapter 5 introduces some fundamental concepts that underlie the ATAM and related software architecture evaluation methods. These include quality attribute characterizations, their relationship to analysis questions, and attribute-based architectural styles (ABASs).

- Chapter 6 presents a detailed, in-depth application of the ATAM to a system operated by the National Aeronautics and Space Administration (NASA). This case study, like the one in Chapter 4, illustrates the method's steps, but here in far greater depth. This case study concentrates on practical details and provides experience-based guidance about what you can expect—and what to do when things don't go according to plan.

- Chapter 7 introduces the Software Architecture Analysis Method (SAAM), a specialized method used to evaluate architectures for modifiability (and its cousins portability, extensibility, maintainability, and the like) and functionality. It includes an authentic case study of applying the SAAM to a system.

- Chapter 8 introduces Active Reviews for Intermediate Designs (ARID), a method for testing the feasibility and suitability of a set of services provided by a portion of an architecture. ARID is useful for evaluating a partial design. This chapter also includes a case study of applying the method.
- Chapter 9 provides a comprehensive comparison of the ATAM, the SAAM, ARID, and several other architecture evaluation methods.
- Chapter 10 talks about growing a standing architecture evaluation capability in your organization, an important step in institutionalizing architecture-based software development.
- Chapter 11 offers conclusions and final thoughts.

The book is written to speak directly to evaluators, but customers and project representatives (especially architects) can also read it to learn what the process is for which they have signed up. In particular, this book is written with four kinds of readers in mind.

- *Evaluator:* someone who is planning to lead or serve on an architecture evaluation team. New evaluators should carefully read all chapters. Experienced evaluators should concentrate on the chapters that describe the evaluation methods (Chapters 3, 7, and 8) and the concepts underlying quality attributes (Chapter 5).
- *Client:* someone who is planning to commission an architecture evaluation and wishes to learn what will be involved. An evaluation client should read Chapters 1 and 2. If the client is not certain which method will best serve the project's needs, then skimming Chapters 3, 7, and 8 will provide an introductory tour of the methods. Chapter 9 will aid in the selection, after which the appropriate method chapter can be reread with care.
- *Project member:* a representative (such as the architect, manager, or other project member) of a project that is going to undergo an architecture evaluation who wishes to learn what to expect from the evaluation. Project members should read Chapters 1 and 2 lightly. Then they should read the chapter defining the method that will be used on their project (Chapters 3, 7, or 8). After that, they should read material containing a case study in applying that method. In the case of the ATAM, this includes Chapters 4 and 6. A special kind of project member is the architect, whose creation is going to be evaluated. In addition to the above, the architect should read Chapter 5 if the method to be used is the ATAM.
- *Evaluation unit manager:* someone who wishes to grow an architecture evaluation capability within his or her organization should be familiar with all of the chapters but especially Chapter 10. The case studies in Chapters

4, 6, 7, and 8 can also be used as source material to stage a team trial run exercise.

At various locations throughout the book we have included short, signed, visually distinguished sidebars written by one of us or by a guest author. These are intended to give background or perspective that is outside the normal flow of text.

Each chapter contains a set of discussion questions at the end. These are intended to help the book be used in a university class, an industrial training seminar, or simply a series of informal brown-bag-lunch discussions.

Finally, each chapter contains a For Further Reading section that describes where the reader can go to explore that chapter's topics in greater depth. A comprehensive list of references is at the end of the book.

1

What Is Software Architecture?

> You employ stone, wood and concrete, and with these materials you
> build houses and palaces. That is construction. Ingenuity is at work.
> But suddenly you touch my heart, you do me good, I am happy and
> I say "This is beautiful." That is Architecture.
>
> —Le Corbusier, 1923
> quoted in *Architecture: From Prehistory to Post-Modernism*

Software architecture is a burgeoning field of research and practice within software engineering. Or, to be more precise, the architecture of large, software-intensive *systems* has been the subject of increasing interest for the past decade. What accounts for this surge of interest in a field that was unheard of until about 1990?

To begin, the field did not spontaneously create itself in 1990, which was about when the term *software architecture* began to gain widespread acceptance and when the field first attracted substantial attention from both industry and the research community. The field was created out of necessity. Software systems were growing larger: systems of hundreds of thousands or even millions of lines of code were becoming commonplace. Clearly the foundations of the ideas underlying the field that is today called *software architecture* were laid by David Parnas, Fred Brooks, Edsger Dijkstra, and others in the 1960s through the 1980s—but what changed is that by the 1990s such large systems were becoming *common*. The pervasiveness of such systems meant that they needed to be understood and managed by ordinary engineers and were no longer solely the province of a select few virtuosos.

There are three reasons why software architecture is important to large, complex, software-intensive systems.

1

1. *It is a vehicle for communication among stakeholders.* Software architecture represents a common abstraction of a system that most if not all of the system's stakeholders can use as a basis for creating mutual understanding, forming consensus, and communicating with each other.

2. *It is the manifestation of the earliest design decisions.* The software architecture of a system is the earliest artifact that enables the priorities among competing concerns to be analyzed, and it is the artifact that has the most significant influence on system qualities. The tradeoffs between performance and security, between maintainability and reliability, and between the cost of the current development effort and the cost of future developments are all manifested in the architecture.

3. *It is a reusable, transferable abstraction of a system.* Software architecture constitutes a relatively small, intellectually graspable model for how a system is structured and how its components work together. This model is transferable across systems; in particular, it can be applied to other systems exhibiting similar requirements and can promote large-scale reuse and software product lines.

These reasons will be elaborated in the sections that follow. But first, what is a software architecture? Definitions abound (the Software Engineering Institute's Web site, where we collect definitions of software architecture, currently lists over 60 of them), but we will use the one that represents a reasonably centrist view:

> *The software architecture of a program or computing system is the structure or structures of the system, which comprise software components, the externally visible properties of those components, and the relationships among them. [Bass 98]*

There are some key implications of this definition.

- Architecture is an abstraction of a system or systems. It represents systems in terms of abstract components that have externally visible properties and relationships (sometimes called *connectors,* although the notion of relationships is more general than connectors and can include temporal relationships, dependencies, uses relationships, and so forth).

- Because architecture involves abstraction it suppresses purely local information; private component details are not architectural.

- Systems are composed of many structures (commonly called *views*). No single view can appropriately represent anything but a trivial architecture. Furthermore, the set of views is not fixed or prescribed. An architecture should be described by a set of views that supports its analysis and communication needs.

These points will be discussed in detail in the remainder of this chapter and will be used throughout the book.

The word *architecture* can be found in a bewildering number of terms. People talk about their business architecture, their enterprise architecture, their operational architecture, their information architecture, their process architecture, their technical architecture. By these uses of the term *architecture* they typically mean "structure" or "organizing principles" and nothing more formal than that. However, some uses of the term *are* related to the definition above. For example, a *reference architecture* is commonly found in many domains. A reference architecture is a set of domain concepts mapped onto a standard set of software components and relationships. For example, the domain of compiler construction has a well-known reference architecture, which details the gross chunks of functionality (lexical analysis, syntactic analysis, code generation, optimization, and so on) mapped onto a set of components arranged as a pipeline. Modern *information system architectures* consist of a database, business logic, and a user interface mapped onto a three-tier client-server structure.

1.1 Architecture as a Vehicle for Communication among Stakeholders

Architectures serve as a communication vehicle in two ways. First, they are a common abstraction of the system and so provide a convenient *lingua franca*— a language that all stakeholders can speak and understand. Stakeholders often have different backgrounds (they may be managers, users, customers, testers, implementors, administrators, operators, and so on) and so have widely different views on what the system is or will be and how they perceive and interact with it. Reviewing a software architecture with a large number of different stakeholders allows their concerns to be aired in a common understandable language, often for the first time.

Second, architecture serves as a communication vehicle by providing a technical "blueprint" for the system that is to be built, modified, or analyzed. We will return to this subject when we discuss architectural structures below.

1.1.1 Architecture and Its Effects on Stakeholders

An architecture is a technical description—an engineering blueprint—of a system. It affects everyone involved with the system. Each stakeholder of a system (user, customer, project manager, coder, tester, and so on) is concerned with different characteristics of the system that are affected by its architecture. For example, the user wants a system that is usable, reliable, and available; the customer is concerned about whether the architecture can be implemented on schedule and to budget; the manager thinks about (in addition to cost and schedule) how the architecture will allow development teams to work largely independently, interacting in disciplined and controlled ways; the developer worries about achieving all of those goals through coding; and the tester wants to prove (or disprove) that these goals will be met.

Architecture provides a common language in which different concerns can be expressed, negotiated, and resolved at a level that is intellectually manageable even for large, complex systems. Without such a language, it is difficult to communicate and comprehend such systems sufficiently to make the early decisions that influence both quality and usefulness.

1.1.2 Architectural Views

In a house, there are plans for the structure of the house, the layout of the rooms, electrical wiring, plumbing, ventilation, and so forth. Each of these plans constitutes a "view" of the house. These views are used by different people. The electrician primarily uses the wiring view. The carpenter primarily uses the structural view.

Each specialist uses his or her own view to achieve different qualities in the house. The carpenter is primarily interested in making the walls straight and square and in assuring that joists are of sufficient strength to support the floors. The electrician is primarily concerned with providing appropriate electrical capacity in convenient locations in a way that safeguards the house's occupants. But the specialists may need to consult views other than their primary ones: the electrician must ensure that when he drills a hole through a wall or joist that this hole doesn't compromise the structural properties of the house or interfere with a location where a water pipe might need to run.

As with houses, architectural views must be used as both a description and a prescription. Common architectural views include

- The functional view (sometimes called the logical view)
- The concurrency view (sometimes called the process or thread view)
- The code view
- The development view (sometimes called the implementation view)
- The physical view

To make the concept of views concrete in this chapter, we briefly illustrate these views below. For each one we note what its components and relationships are, who uses it, and what it's good for (what kind of reasoning it supports). Remember that these are not the only views available to the architect but rather are a representative sample.

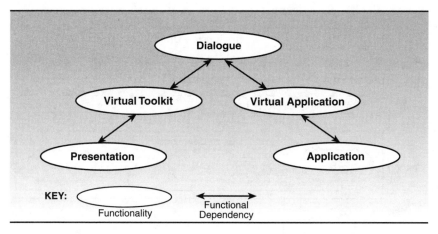

Figure 1.1 Functional View Example

Functional View

The functional view is an abstraction of system functions and their relationships. The components of the functional view are functions, key system abstractions, and domain elements. The relationships between components found in the view are dependencies and data flow.

The users of the view are domain engineers, product-line designers, and end users. These stakeholders think about this view in terms of what the functionality is, how data flow among the pieces, and what variability of functionality the architecture should support. The reasoning that it supports is, thus, decisions about what functionality should be in the architecture, the modifiability of the architecture (because part of modifiability depends on how functionality is partitioned with respect to anticipated future changes), product lines and reusability, tool support, and the allocation of work to various groups. For example, one might create a database group, a transaction management group, or a user interface group in response to identifying such functionality as important in this view.

An example of a purely functional view is shown in Figure 1.1. This is a decomposition of an interactive system into its functional elements.

Concurrency View

When a complex system is deployed, it is typically packaged into a set of processes or threads which are deployed onto some computational resources. The concurrency view is a necessary step for reasoning about what processes or threads will be created and how they will communicate and share (or compete for) resources.

The components of this view—processes and threads—interact with each other via data flow, events, and synchronization on shared resources. The users

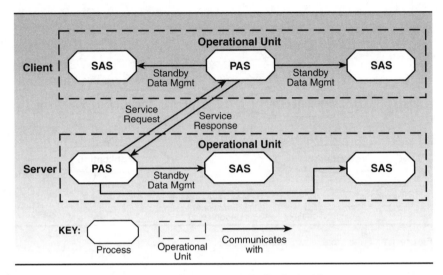

Figure 1.2   Concurrency View Example—An Air Traffic Control System

of this view are people who worry about deploying the system and those who are concerned with the performance and availability of the system, as well as integrators and testers. This view is used to reason about performance, availability, and deployment.

An example of a concurrency view is given in Figure 1.2. This view shows how a part of an air traffic control system is organized to provide high availability to the system. Processes are triply replicated and clustered into groups known as operational units. As it happens, each process in an operational unit is allocated to a different processor, but that information is *intentionally* omitted in this view. Operational units are organized into client-server relationships. Operational units consist of primary address space (PAS) processes and SAS (standby address space) processes. The primary process sends data by data management messages to its secondaries so that they are synchronized with its state. In the event of a failure, one of the SASs is "promoted" to become a PAS. Note that this view says nothing about what each operational unit's function is or how processes are allocated to processors. As mentioned, this separation of concerns is intentional.

Code View

The code view is what the programmer sees. Thus the components of this view are things like classes, objects, procedures, and functions and their abstraction/ composition into things like subsystems, layers, and modules. The relationships are again what a programmer sees—calls and method invocation—as well as containment relations like is-a-sub-module-of.

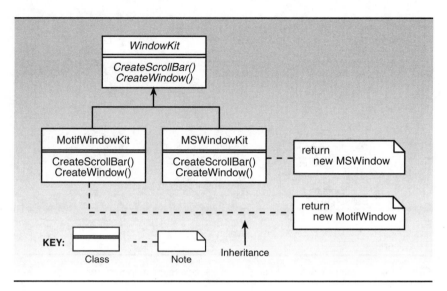

Figure 1.3   Code View Example—The Abstract Factory Design Pattern

The users of this view are programmers, designers, and reusers. They use this view to reason about modifiability/maintainability, portability, and subsetability (the ability to field a subset of the system's functionality without making major changes to its code).

An example of a pure code view is found in design patterns, as exemplified in Figure 1.3. Pure code views are sometimes found in practice. Code views typically show the mapping of functionality onto code structures.

Development View

The development view is another view that the developer sees, but it is distinct from the code view. It is a view of the structure of the source code as a *repository* that various users (programmers and maintainers) create, modify, and manage. The components of this view are typically files and directories (although other organizations are possible, such as keeping all source files in a database). The main relationship between these files and directories is containment. The users of the development view, in addition to programmers and maintainers, are managers and configuration managers. These stakeholders use the view to reason about the modifiability/maintainability of the system, to divide up the development and testing of the system, and to control configuration management and versions.

An example of the development view is shown in Figure 1.4. This view shows a greatly simplified view of the hierarchical structure of the directories and files comprising a physics simulation system. The top-level directory is Physics3D. Subdirectories are advection, chemistry, generator, hydro, io, and

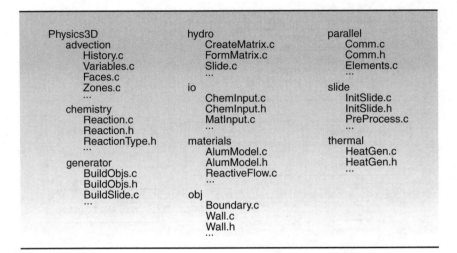

```
Physics3D              hydro                   parallel
   advection              CreateMatrix.c          Comm.c
      History.c           FormMatrix.c            Comm.h
      Variables.c         Slide.c                 Elements.c
      Faces.c             ...                     ...
      Zones.c          io                      slide
      ...                 ChemInput.c             InitSlide.c
   chemistry              ChemInput.h             InitSlide.h
      Reaction.c          MatInput.c              PreProcess.c
      Reaction.h          ...                     ...
      ReactionType.h   materials               thermal
      ...                 AlumModel.c             HeatGen.c
   generator              AlumModel.h             HeatGen.h
      BuildObjs.c         ReactiveFlow.c          ...
      BuildObjs.h         ...
      BuildSlide.c     obj
      ...                 Boundary.c
                          Wall.c
                          Wall.h
                          ...
```

Figure 1.4   Development View Example—A Physics Simulation System

so on. Each directory contains the source and the header files for that subsystem. This view provides a focus for the system's stakeholders when determining division of labor, testing, integration, and maintenance.

Physical View

The physical view of a system describes how the system is deployed in terms of its hardware resources. For small, trivial systems this description is equally trivial: there is a single computer on which all processing is done. But for large, complex systems there may be a myriad of sensors, actuators, storage devices, networks, and computers.

The components are things like CPUs, sensors, actuators, and storage. The relationships are typically networks or other communication devices (such as satellites or radio modems). The users of this view are hardware and system engineers who have to reason and worry about system delivery, installation, and upgrades (in some cases doing upgrades while the system is still running), as well as performance, availability, scalability, and security.

An example of a physical view, adapted from Bass et al. [Bass 98], is shown in Figure 1.5. This figure shows a plethora of computers and interfaces to hardware devices (in this case sensors such as radar and actuators such as missiles) all connected by a LAN which is replicated to ensure that there isn't a single point of failure in the communications network.

Summary of Views

Views are a mechanism to allow us to separate concerns while building or analyzing an architecture. They let us consider an architecture from different perspectives.

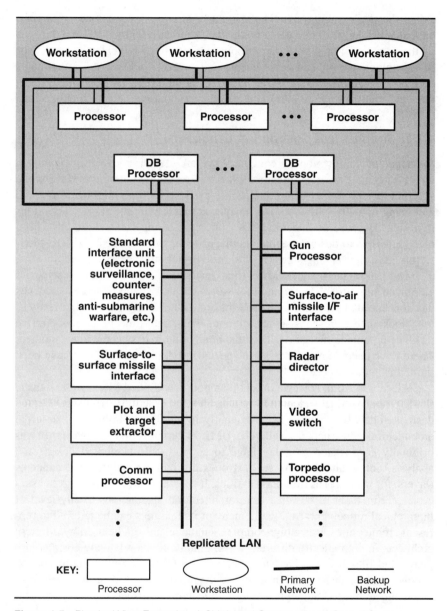

Figure 1.5   Physical View Example—A Shipboard Command and Control System

Useful information about an architecture is often conveyed not only by the views but also by merging or overlaying views. For example, a very useful piece of architectural documentation shows the allocation of processes (shown in the concurrency view) to processors (shown in the physical view). This hybrid is often called the deployment view. There is no "canonical" set of views, although there is no shortage of advice on the matter. Rational's Unified Process depends on the so-called 4+1 set of views proposed by Philippe Kruchten: logical, process, implementation, and deployment, augmented by a fifth "view" that maps each of the other four to a use-case-based set of requirements. You should select the views that convey the important information concerning your architecture.

1.1.3   Architecture Description Languages

We hope that by now you are convinced that architectural description is important. It is central to an architecture's success in being communicated from one stakeholder to another, being analyzable by describing the right information, and being actually built from the blueprints that the architectural descriptions represent. Because architectural description is so important, there have been many attempts to design specific languages to support this task. In fact, architectural description languages (ADLs) have been both successes and failures.

They have been successes in that many ADLs have been created and employed in both academic and real-world projects. Each of these languages has concentrated on a different facet of architectural description and analysis (deadlock detection, consistency, completeness, real-time properties, and so on). The notable failure of ADLs is that none of them has been widely adopted. There have been some successes in specialized domains, but these have been limited islands of success.

All of this work, however, might be moot. The Unified Modeling Language (UML) is being widely adopted by organizations to describe their object-oriented designs and is being extended (frequently in an ad hoc fashion) to describe architectural constructs as well. The UML is certainly not a panacea. It was originally constructed as a language to support object-oriented design and analysis, not as an ADL. As such, it does not include architectural concepts (layers, for instance) as first-class entities. It does not naturally support the successive refinement of designs, from architectural abstractions to any level of hierarchical refinement. And while many of its facilities can be tailored to represent architectures, it is a big, complex language and can be used by different architects in dramatically different ways. Finally, it is a relatively abstract language and thus it is not easy to communicate UML designs to nontechnical people. Despite these problems, it is receiving a great deal of attention from practicing architects, and representing architectural constructs in a more straightforward way is a major concern of those working on UML's next revision.[1]

---

1. In this book, we have used UML in some but not all of our figures. None of the methods in this book depends upon representing the architecture in a particular notation, UML or otherwise. We have used other notations to show alternative representation possibilities, in situations where using UML would be awkward, or in case studies to re-create the actual slides presented during the evaluations.

1.2 Architecture as the Manifestation of the Earliest Design Decisions

A software architecture is a coherent, justified collection of a system's earliest set of design decisions. These decisions will affect much of what the system will become.

First, the early design decisions of architecture will allow or preclude nearly all of the system's quality attributes. For example, if your system has stringent performance requirements, then as an architect you need to pay attention to intercomponent communication and component execution times. If you have modifiability goals for your system, then you need to pay attention to the encapsulation properties of your module components. If security is a consideration, then you need to pay attention to intercomponent communication and data flow and perhaps introduce special components (such as secure kernels or encrypt/decrypt functions) or impose authentication protocols between processes. If reliability is important, then the architecture needs to provide redundant components with warm or hot restart protocols among them. All of these approaches to achieving quality attributes are architectural in nature, having to do with the decomposition of the total system into parts and the ways in which those parts communicate and cooperate with each other to carry out their duties.

Even functionality—the doing of whatever it is that the system does—is carried out by the architecture, through the various components doing their part of the job. Functionality can be understood in terms of how the architectural pieces interact and cooperate with each other to perform the system's work. These decisions will impose constraints on an implementation; for example, all interprocess communication is to be done via TCP/IP. These decisions will affect how system resources are allocated and arbitrated, and they will affect the tradeoffs made by designers that any system must necessarily make.

Second, the architecture will affect the organization. There is almost always a strong correspondence between architectural structures and organizational ones. Why is this? Because architectural structures define coherent groupings of functionality and coherent sets of concerns. The concurrency view may suggest the need for a separate team that does performance planning, modeling, and tuning. Or it may suggest the need for a team that worries about how system failures are detected and managed. Each of these teams might do their own specific analyses and require specialized tools, training, and knowledge. The code and development views also dictate system structure in terms of modules, subsystems, and layers. These once again influence organizational structure. A module, subsystem, or layer represents a highly coherent set of functionality which suggests high internal coupling and low coupling to external entities. Conway's law states that this must match the organizational structure because otherwise you will have information flows in the system that don't match those of the organization. For example, the members of the database team typically know a great deal about each other's code and internal interfaces. They likely see only the externally published interfaces from the user interface team or the telecommunications team. Human separation of concerns must match the software separation of concerns. To do otherwise is to burden the development team with the need to know too much about the details of the system. Thus organizational structure must match the architectural structures.

Third, early design decisions made in the architecture result in constraints on an implementation. One such constraint is the choice of commercial components that can be easily integrated. Although interoperability protocols exist, for the most part choosing any commercial component will affect the choice of which other components may be employed. For example, choosing Microsoft's DNA (Distributed interNet Architecture) set of components will preclude or at least make costly the use of CORBA- or Enterprise JavaBeans–compliant components. Also, the choice of an architectural approach may make the use of some components difficult if they have widely divergent mechanisms for sharing data, passing control, and so on.

An architecture's earliest design decisions should center around the forms of its infrastructure: how components communicate, how they pass or share data, how they initialize, shut down, self-test, report faults, and so on. When the computational structure—sometimes called a framework—for supporting these activities is built first, then many benefits accrue. For one thing, there can be a working version of the system early in its life cycle. The earliest version may do little other than start up and hum to itself, but it provides all the infrastructure for the subsystems to work together. Many of these subsystems can be implemented initially as stubs: simply reading their data from a file, always outputting the same values, or looking up their results from a table. As the system is developed, these stubs can be replaced by their fully functioning versions. This means that, over time, the system increases in fidelity. But having an early working version of the system is wonderful for team morale. It also increases customer confidence, allows for better estimation of progress by management, and means that integration and testing are continuous, rather than a risky "big-bang" activity late in the project.

1.2.1   Architectural Styles

Choosing a prevalent architectural style for a system is usually the earliest of the early design decisions. Just what are styles exactly? Early research in software architecture was motivated, in part, by the observation that certain styles crop up over and over in practice in response to similar sets of demands. These styles, similar to object-oriented design patterns but typically covering larger chunks of the architecture, capture a recurring solution to a recurring problem. A style

- Describes a class of architectures or significant architecture pieces
- Is found repeatedly in practice

- Is a coherent package of design decisions
- Has known properties that permit reuse

Shaw and Garlan [Shaw 96] published the first fairly comprehensive collection of architectural styles. Shaw and Garlan's initial list consisted of

- Independent components: communicating processes, implicit invocation, explicit invocation
- Data flow: batch sequential, pipe and filter
- Data-centered: repository, blackboard
- Virtual machine: interpreter, rule-based
- Call/return: main program and subroutine, object-oriented, layered

Others have augmented this collection. There is no complete list of styles and there is no unique, nonoverlapping list. Complex systems can exhibit multiple styles at once: styles overlap or can contain one another hierarchically. But each architectural style consists of at least the following information:

- A set of component types (for example, data repository, process, object)
- A set of connector types/interaction mechanisms (for example, subroutine call, event, pipe)
- A topological layout of these components (for example, star, ring, hierarchical topologies)
- A set of constraints on topology and behavior (for example, a data repository is not allowed to change stored values, pipelines are acyclic)
- An informal description of the costs and benefits of the style (for example, "Use the pipe and filter style when reuse is desired and performance is not a top priority")

Although we have introduced styles here, we will seldom talk about them in the remainder of this book because these concepts are not as widely embraced in industrial practice as they are in academia. While the ideas behind architectural styles pervade the software industry, the terms themselves are not common and are often misunderstood by both academics and practitioners. Instead, we use the more neutral term *architectural approaches.*

1.3 Architecture as a Reusable, Transferable Abstraction of a System

Architecture is a reusable model that can become the basis for an entire family of systems aimed at particular market segments and built using a common asset base—that is, a software product line. A software architecture is an asset an organization creates at considerable expense. This expense can and should be reused. In fact, while other forms of reuse have historically shown little success, architecture-based product lines are proving to be a significant commercial success for many organizations. In fact, economics dictates that products be built in different ways than they were ten or twenty years ago.

When creating a product line, new software engineering challenges are encountered that do not occur in single product developments. The creation and management of a set of core assets is both crucial to the success of the product line and a major challenge, since a great deal of work goes into deciding which assets should be "core" and which should be product specific. The other major challenge in creating a product line is using the core assets to create products. In particular, new products frequently require new functionality, and it must be determined if and how this functionality gets folded back into the core assets.

The specific *architectural* challenges for a product line are twofold: managing the realization of quality attributes across instances of the product line and managing the variation in functionality while maintaining just a single product-line architecture. The first problem challenges the architect to, for example, create a small, inexpensive, low-performance, uniprocessor version of a product and a large, expensive, high-performance, multiprocessor version using the same product-line architecture. The infrastructure to manage this variation cannot itself absorb too much of the system's processing power. The second problem forces the architect to be able to accommodate a wide variety of features and functions without changing the underlying model of how the system works.

While these issues are by no means solved, a great deal of research and practical industrial experience shows that architecture-based software product lines can yield order-of-magnitude improvements in productivity, time to market, and cost.

1.4 Summary

Architecture is first and foremost a key to achieving system understanding. As a vehicle for communication among stakeholders, it enables high-bandwidth, informed communication among developers, managers, customers, users, and others who otherwise would not have a shared language. As the manifestation of the earliest design decisions, it is the key to project organization and the expression of strategies put in place to design the system (often using the design vocabulary of architectural styles). As a reusable, transferable abstraction of a system, it enables understanding of future systems that share the same architecture. Once built, an architecture and the components that populate it can be one of an organization's key assets for many years. An artifact of such far-ranging, long-lasting importance deserves to be evaluated to make sure it will serve its organization as intended.

The next chapter begins the journey into the realm of architecture evaluation.

1.5 For Further Reading

The foundation for the entire field of software architecture was laid in the early 1970s by authors who pointed out that the structure of software matters as much as its ability to compute a correct result. Seminal papers include Dijkstra [Dijkstra 68] and Parnas [Parnas 72], required reading for every software architect.

Today, general books on software architecture are becoming plentiful. Bass, Clements, and Kazman [Bass 98]; Hofmeister, Nord, and Soni [Hofmeister 00]; Shaw and Garlan [Shaw 96]; Bosch [Bosch 00]; and Malveau and Mowbray [Malveau 01] provide good coverage.

Architectural views in general and the so-called 4+1 views in particular are a fundamental aspect of the Rational Unified Process for object-oriented software [Kruchten 98]. A good overview of views is given in Bass et al. [Bass 98] and Jazayeri et al. [Jazayeri 00]; a comprehensive treatment appears in [Hofmeister 00]. For the genesis of the concept of views, see Parnas [74].

Architectural styles are treated by Bass et al. [Bass 98] and Shaw and Garlan [Shaw 96], but for encyclopedic coverage see Buschmann et al. [Buschmann 96] and Schmidt et al. [Schmidt 00]. Design patterns, the object-oriented analog of styles, are covered in Gamma et al. [Gamma 95] as well as a host of on-line resources and conferences. Jacobson et al. devote an entire section to architectural styles for object-oriented systems designed with strategic reuse in mind [Jacobson 97]. Smith and Williams include three chapters of principles and guidance for architecting systems in which performance is a concern [Smith 01].

For software product lines, the book by Clements and Northrop [Clements 01] is the most comprehensive to date, although Jacobson et al. treat reuse from a product-line perspective [Jacobson 97]. In addition, Bass et al. [Bass 98] and Bosch [00] provide coverage of software product lines.

A number of researchers have begun seriously considering how to link business considerations with software analyses, employing methods from economics, such as portfolio theory and real-options theory [Sullivan 99]. Although this kind of analysis is still in the early research stage, some methods and case studies already exist [Kazman 00]. Conway's law, which deals with the organizational impacts of architectures, can be found in [Conway 68].

As software architecture has emerged as an important study topic, so has architecture-based design, or the process of developing an architecture in a systematic fashion and then using it in a disciplined, repeatable fashion to build software systems. As an example of a first attempt at this, the Attribute Driven Design (ADD) method proposes a method for transforming a set of customer requirements into an architecture for a system or a product line via a set of decompositions and refinements [Bachmann 00].

Part of architecture-based development is assuring that an implementation conforms to the architecture. One way to do this is by reverse-engineering the system's architectural structures from the constructs that are realized in code (procedure calls, method invocations, class definitions, interprocess communication, and so on). Reverse engineering also comes into play when trying to exploit a legacy base of code for which the architecture has been lost or its documentation hopelessly outdated. Toolsets to help with architecture reverse engineering include ManSART [Yeh 97], Dali [Kazman 99], the Philips toolset [Krikhaar 99], and the Software Bookshelf [Finnigan 97].

An architecture is only as good as its ability to be communicated, which brings us to architecture representation. Although the UML has been criticized for its inability to straightforwardly represent architectural constructs, it is the de facto standard for languages to express design. Rational's Web site (http://www.rational.com/uml) is the starting point, and there is no shortage of UML books available. Medvidovic and Taylor have published a comparison of a group of more conventional ADLs [Medvidovic 00]. Acme, an ADL specifically designed to be an architecture interchange language, a means for the many disparate ADLs to jointly describe an architecture and to jointly support many different kinds of analysis that are unique to specific ADLs, is described in Garlan et al. [Garlan 97].

Finally, the Software Engineering Institute's software architecture Web page [SEI ATA] provides a wide variety of software architecture resources and links.

1.6 Discussion Questions

1. Find four or five definitions of software or system architecture in books or on Web sites. See if you can distill their essential differences and their essential similarities. What do you like and dislike about each one?

2. List the stakeholders for a software architecture. How do project managers, chief technical officers, chief information officers, analysts, customers, and users fit into your list?

3. List the stakeholders or consumers for each architectural view listed in this chapter. For each view, name at least one kind of analysis about a system (or its development) for which you might use that view.

4. A deployment view is a process view overlaid onto a physical view. Try to imagine other hybrid views and how they might be used.

5. Some architecture writers have described a work assignment view that divides a system into areas of responsibility to be carried out by separate teams. Which view or views discussed in this chapter do you believe constitute the work assignment view?

6. Layered architectures are extremely popular and extremely useful. What view would you use to depict a layered architecture?

7. What view(s) would you choose to depict data flow in a system?

2

Evaluating a Software
Architecture

Marry your architecture in haste and you can repent in leisure.
—Barry Boehm
from a keynote address: *And Very Few Lead Bullets Either*

How can you be sure whether the architecture chosen for your software is the right one? How can you be sure that it won't lead to calamity but instead will pave the way through a smooth development and successful product?

It's not an easy question, and a lot rides on the outcome. The foundation for any software system is its architecture. The architecture will allow or preclude just about all of a system's quality attributes. Modifiability, performance, security, availability, reliability—all of these are precast once the architecture is laid down. No amount of tuning or clever implementation tricks will wring any of these qualities out of a poorly architected system.

To put it bluntly, an architecture is a bet, a wager on the success of a system. Wouldn't it be nice to know in advance if you've placed your bet on a winner, as opposed to waiting until the system is mostly completed before knowing whether it will meet its requirements or not? If you're buying a system or paying for its development, wouldn't you like to have some assurance that it's started off down the right path? If you're the architect yourself, wouldn't you like to have a good way to validate your intuitions and experience, so that you can sleep at night knowing that the trust placed in your design is well founded?

Until recently, there were almost no methods of general utility to validate a software architecture. If performed at all, the approaches were spotty, ad hoc, and not repeatable. Because of that, they weren't particularly trustworthy. We can do better than that.

This is a guidebook of software architecture evaluation. It is built around a suite of three methods, all developed at the Software Engineering Institute, that can be applied to any software-intensive system:

- ATAM: Architecture Tradeoff Analysis Method
- SAAM: Software Architecture Analysis Method
- ARID: Active Reviews for Intermediate Designs

The methods as a group have a solid pedigree, having been applied for years on dozens of projects of all sizes and in a wide variety of domains. With these methods, the time has come to include software architecture evaluation as a standard step of any development paradigm. Evaluations represent a wise risk-mitigation effort and are relatively inexpensive. They pay for themselves in terms of costly errors and sleepless nights avoided.

Whereas the previous chapter introduced the concept of software architecture, this chapter lays the conceptual groundwork for architectural evaluation. It defines what we mean by software architecture and explains the kinds of properties for which an architecture can (and cannot) be evaluated.

First, let's restate what it is we're evaluating:

The software architecture of a program or computing system is the structure or structures of the system, which comprise software components, the externally visible properties of those components, and the relationships among them. [Bass 98]

By "externally visible" properties, we are referring to those assumptions other components can make of a component, such as its provided services, performance characteristics, fault handling, shared resource usage, and so on. The intent of this definition is that a software architecture must abstract some information about the system (otherwise there is no point looking at the architecture—we are simply viewing the entire system) and yet provide enough information to be a basis for analysis, decision making, and hence risk reduction (see the sidebar What's Architectural?).

The architecture defines the components (such as modules, objects, processes, subsystems, compilation units, and so forth) and the relevant relations (such as calls, sends-data-to, synchronizes-with, uses, depends-on, instantiates, and many more) among them. The architecture is the result of early design decisions that are necessary before a group of people can collaboratively build a software system. The larger or more distributed the group, the more vital the architecture is (and the group doesn't have to be very large before the architecture is vital).

One of the insights about architecture from Chapter 1 that you must fully embrace before you can understand architecture evaluation is this:

Architectures allow or preclude nearly all of the system's quality attributes.

This leads to the most fundamental truth about architecture evaluation: If architectural decisions determine a system's quality attributes, then it is possible to evaluate architectural decisions with respect to their impact on those attributes.

What's Architectural?

Sooner or later everyone asks the question: "What's architectural?" Some people ask out of intellectual curiosity, but people who are evaluating architectures have a pressing need to understand what information is in and out of their realm of concern. Maybe you didn't ask the question exactly that way. Perhaps you asked it in one of the following ways:

- What is the difference between an architecture and a high-level design?
- Are details such as priorities of processes architectural?
- Why should implementation considerations such as buffer overflows be treated as architectural?
- Are interfaces to components part of the architecture?
- If I have class diagrams, do I need anything else?
- Is architecture concerned with run-time behavior or static structure?
- Is the operating system part of the architecture? Is the programming language?
- If I'm constrained to use a particular commercial product, is that architectural? If I'm free to choose from a wide range of commercial products, is that architectural?

Let's think about this in two ways.

First, consider the definition of architecture that we quoted in Chapter 1 of this book. Paraphrasing: A software architecture concerns the gross organization of a system described in terms of its components, their externally visible properties, and the relationships among them. True enough, but it fails to explicitly address the notion of context. If the scope of my concern is confined to a subsystem within a system that is part of a system of systems, then what I consider to be architectural will be different than what the architect of the system of systems considers to be architectural. Therefore, context influences what's architectural.

Second, let's ask, what is *not* architectural? It has been said that algorithms are not architectural; data structures are not architectural; details of data flow are not architectural. Well, again these statements are only partially true. Some properties of algorithms, such as their complexity, might have a dramatic effect on performance. Some properties of data structures, such as whether they need to support concurrent access, directly impact performance and reliability. Some of the details of data flow, such as how components depend on specific message types or which components are allowed access to which data types, impact modifiability and security, respectively.

So is there a principle that we can use in determining what is architectural? Let's appeal to what architecture is used for to formulate our principle. Our criterion for something to be architectural is this: It must be a component, or a relationship between components, or a property (of components or relationships) *that needs to be externally visible* in order to reason about the ability of the system to meet its quality requirements or to support decomposition of the system into independently implementable pieces. Here are some corollaries of this principle:

- *Architecture describes what is in your system.* When you have determined your context, you have determined a boundary that describes what is in and what is out of your system (which might be someone else's subsystem). Architecture describes the part that is in.

- *An architecture is an abstract depiction of your system.* The information in an architecture is the most abstract and yet meaningful depiction of that aspect of the system. Given your architectural specification, there should not be a need for a more abstract description. That is not to say that all aspects of architecture are abstract, nor is it to say that there is an abstraction threshold that needs to be exceeded before a piece of design information can be considered architectural. You shouldn't worry if your architecture encroaches on what others might consider to be a more detailed design.

- *What's architectural should be critical for reasoning about critical requirements.* The architecture bridges the gap between requirements and the rest of the design. If you feel that some information is critical for reasoning about how your system will meet its requirements then it is architectural. You, as the architect, are the best judge. On the other hand, if you can eliminate some details and still compose a forceful argument through models, simulation, walk-throughs, and so on about how your architecture will satisfy key requirements then those details do not belong. However, if you put too much detail into your architecture then it might not satisfy the next principle.

- *An architectural specification needs to be graspable.* The whole point of a gross-level system depiction is that you can understand it and reason about it. Too much detail will defeat this purpose.

- *An architecture is constraining.* It imposes requirements on all lower-level design specifications. I like to distinguish between when a decision is made and when it is realized. For example, I might determine a process prioritization strategy, a component redundancy strategy, or a set of encapsulation rules when designing an architecture; but I might not actually make priority assignments, determine the algorithm for a redundant calculation, or specify the details of an interface until much later.

In a nutshell:

To be architectural is to be the most abstract depiction of the system that enables reasoning about critical requirements and constrains all subsequent refinements.

If it sounds like finding all those aspects of your system that are architectural is difficult, that is true. It is unlikely that you will discover everything that is architectural up front, nor should you try. An architectural specification will evolve over time as you continually apply these principles in determining what's architectural.

—MHK

2.1 Why Evaluate an Architecture?

The earlier you find a problem in a software project, the better off you are. The cost to fix an error found during requirements or early design phases is orders of magnitudes less to correct than the same error found during testing. Architecture is the product of the early design phase, and its effect on the system and the project is profound.

An unsuitable architecture will precipitate disaster on a project. Performance goals will not be met. Security goals will fall by the wayside. The customer will grow impatient because the right functionality is not available, and the system is too hard to change to add it. Schedules and budgets will be blown out of the water as the team scrambles to back-fit and hack their way through the problems. Months or years later, changes that could have been anticipated and planned for will be rejected because they are too costly. Plagues and pestilence cannot be too far behind.

Architecture also determines the structure of the project: configuration control libraries, schedules and budgets, performance goals, team structure, documentation organization, and testing and maintenance activities all are organized around the architecture. If it changes midstream because of some deficiency discovered late, the entire project can be thrown into chaos. It is much better to change the architecture before it has been frozen into existence by the establishment of downstream artifacts based on it.

Architecture evaluation is a cheap way to avoid disaster. The methods in this book are meant to be applied while the architecture is a paper specification (of course, they can be applied later as well), and so they involve running a series of simple thought experiments. They each require assembling relevant stakeholders for a structured session of brainstorming, presentation, and analysis. All told, the average architecture evaluation adds no more than a few days to the project schedule.

To put it another way, if you were building a house, you wouldn't think of proceeding without carefully looking at the blueprints before construction began. You would happily spend the small amount of extra time because you know it's much better to discover a missing bedroom while the architecture is just a blueprint, rather than on moving day.

2.2 When Can an Architecture Be Evaluated?

The classical application of architecture evaluation occurs when the architecture has been specified but before implementation has begun. Users of iterative or incremental life-cycle models can evaluate the architectural decisions made during the most recent cycle. However, one of the appealing aspects of architecture evaluation is that it can be applied at any stage of an architecture's lifetime, and there are two useful variations from the classical: early and late.

Early.   Evaluation need not wait until an architecture is fully specified. It can be used at any stage in the architecture creation process to examine those architectural decisions already made and choose among architectural options that are pending. That is, it is equally adept at evaluating architectural decisions that have already been made and those that are being considered.

Of course, the completeness and fidelity of the evaluation will be a direct function of the completeness and fidelity of the architectural description brought to the table by the architect. And in practice, the expense and logistical burden of convening a full-blown evaluation is seldom undertaken when unwarranted by the state of the architecture. It is just not going to be very rewarding to assemble a dozen or two stakeholders and analysts to evaluate the architect's early back-of-the-napkin sketches, even though such sketches will in fact reveal a number of significant architecture paths chosen and paths not taken.

Some organizations recommend what they call a *discovery review*, which is a very early mini-evaluation whose purpose is as much to iron out and prioritize troublesome requirements as analyzing whatever "proto-architecture" may have been crafted by that point. For a discovery review, the stakeholder group is smaller but must include people empowered to make requirements decisions. The purpose of this meeting is to raise any concerns that the architect may have about the feasibility of *any* architecture to meet the combined quality and behavioral requirements that are being levied while there is still time to relax the most troubling or least important ones. The output of a discovery review is a much stronger set of requirements and an initial approach to satisfying them. That approach, when fleshed out, can be the subject of a full evaluation later.

We do not cover discovery reviews in detail because they are a straightforward variation of an architecture evaluation. If you hold a discovery review, make sure to

- Hold it before the requirements are frozen and when the architect has a good idea about how to approach the problem
- Include in the stakeholder group someone empowered to make requirements decisions
- Include a prioritized set of requirements in the output, in case there is no apparent way to meet all of them

Finally, in a discovery review, remember the words of the gifted aircraft designer Willy Messerschmitt, himself no stranger to the burden of requirements, who said:

You can have any combination of features the Air Ministry desires, so long as you do not also require that the resulting airplane fly.

Late. The second variation takes place when not only the architecture is nailed down but the implementation is complete as well. This case occurs when an organization inherits some sort of legacy system. Perhaps it has been purchased on the open market, or perhaps it is being excavated from the organization's own archives. The techniques for evaluating a legacy architecture are the same as those for one that is newborn. An evaluation is a useful thing to do because it will help the new owners understand the legacy system, and let them know whether the system can be counted on to meet its quality and behavioral requirements.

In general, when can an architectural evaluation be held? As soon as there is enough of an architecture to justify it. Different organizations may measure that justification differently, but a good rule of thumb is this: Hold an evaluation when development teams start to make decisions that depend on the architecture and the cost of undoing those decisions would outweigh the cost of holding an evaluation.

2.3 Who's Involved?

There are two groups of people involved in an architecture evaluation.

1. *Evaluation team.* These are the people who will conduct the evaluation and perform the analysis. The team members and their precise roles will be defined later, but for now simply realize that they represent one of the classes of participants.

2. *Stakeholders.* Stakeholders are people who have a vested interest in the architecture and the system that will be built from it. The three evaluation methods in this book all use stakeholders to articulate the specific requirements that are levied on the architecture, above and beyond the requirements that state what functionality the system is supposed to exhibit. Some, but not all, of the stakeholders will be members of the development team: coders, integrators, testers, maintainers, and so forth.

    A special kind of stakeholder is a project decision maker. These are people who are interested in the outcome of the evaluation and have the power to make decisions that affect the future of the project. They include the architect, the designers of components, and the project's management. Management will have to make decisions about how to respond to the issues raised by the evaluation. In some settings (particularly government acquisitions), the customer or sponsor may be a project decision maker as well.

    Whereas an arbitrary stakeholder says what he or she wants to be true about the architecture, a decision maker has the power to expend resources to *make* it true. So a project manager might say (as a stakeholder), "I would like the architecture to be reusable on a related project that I'm managing," but as a decision maker he or she might say, "I see that the changes you've identified as necessary to reuse this architecture on my other project are too expensive, and I won't pay for them." Another difference is that a project decision maker has the power to speak authoritatively for the project, and some of the steps of the ATAM method, for example, ask them to do precisely that. A garden-variety stakeholder, on the other hand, can only hope to influence (but not control) the project. For more on stakeholders, see the sidebar Stakeholders on page 63 in Chapter 3.

The client for an architecture evaluation will usually be a project decision maker, with a vested interest in the outcome of the evaluation and holding some power over the project.

Sometimes the evaluation team is drawn from the project staff, in which case they are also stakeholders. This is not recommended because they will lack the objectivity to view the architecture in a dispassionate way.

2.4 What Result Does an Architecture Evaluation Produce?

In concrete terms, an architecture evaluation produces a report, the form and content of which vary according to the method used. Primarily, though, an architecture evaluation produces information. In particular, it produces answers to two kinds of questions.

1. Is this architecture suitable for the system for which it was designed?
2. Which of two or more competing architectures is the most suitable one for the system at hand?

Suitability for a given task, then, is what we seek to investigate. We say that an architecture is suitable if it meets two criteria.

1. The system that results from it will meet its quality goals. That is, the system will run predictably and fast enough to meet its performance (timing) requirements. It will be modifiable in planned ways. It will meet its security constraints. It will provide the required behavioral function. Not every quality property of a system is a direct result of its architecture, but many are, and for those that are, the architecture is suitable if it provides the blueprint for building a system that achieves those properties.
2. The system can be built using the resources at hand: the staff, the budget, the legacy software (if any), and the time allotted before delivery. That is, the architecture is *buildable*.

This concept of suitability will set the stage for all of the material that follows. It has a couple of important implications. First, suitability is only relevant in the context of specific (and specifically articulated) goals for the architecture and the system it spawns. An architecture designed with high-speed performance as the primary design goal might lead to a system that runs like the wind but requires hordes of programmers working for months to make any kind of modification to it. If modifiability were more important than performance *for that system*, then that architecture would be unsuitable *for that system* (but might be just the ticket for another one).

In *Alice in Wonderland,* Alice encounters the Cheshire Cat and asks for directions. The cat responds that it depends upon where she wishes to go. Alice says she doesn't know, whereupon the cat tells her it doesn't matter which way she walks. So

> If the sponsor of a system cannot tell you what any of the quality goals are for the system, then any architecture will do.

An overarching part of an architecture evaluation is to capture and prioritize specific goals that the architecture must meet in order to be considered

Why Should I Believe You?

Frequently when we embark on an evaluation we are outsiders. We have been called in by a project leader or a manager or a customer to evaluate a project. Perhaps this is seen as an audit, or perhaps it is just part of an attempt to improve an organization's software engineering practice. Whatever the reason, unless the evaluation is part of a long-term relationship, we typically don't personally know the architect, or we don't know the major stakeholders.

Sometimes this distance is not a problem—the stakeholders are receptive and enthusiastic, eager to learn and to improve their architecture. But on other occasions we meet with resistance and perhaps even fear. The major players sit there with their arms folded across their chests, clearly annoyed that they have been taken away from their *real* work, that of architecting, to pursue this silly management-directed evaluation. At other times the stakeholders are friendly and even receptive, but they are skeptical. After all, they are the experts in their domains and they have been working in the area, and maybe even on this system, for years.

In either case their attitudes, whether friendly or unfriendly, indicate a substantial amount of skepticism over the prospect that the evaluation can actually help. They are in effect saying, "What could a bunch of outsiders possibly have to tell us about *our* system that we don't already know?" You will probably have to face this kind of opposition or resistance at some point in your tenure as an architecture evaluator.

There are two things that you need to know and do to counteract this opposition. First of all, you need to counteract the fear. So keep calm. If you are friendly and let them know that the point of the meeting is to learn about and improve the architecture (rather than pointing a finger of blame) then you will find that resistance melts away quickly. Most people actually enjoy the evaluation process and see the benefits very quickly. Second, you need to counteract the skepticism. Of course they are the experts in the domain. You know this and they know this, and you should acknowledge this up front. But you are the architecture and quality attribute expert. No matter what the domain, architectural approaches for dealing with and analyzing quality attributes don't vary much. There are relatively few ways to approach performance or availability or security on an architectural level. As an experienced evaluator (and with the help of the insight from the quality attribute communities) you have seen these before, and they don't change much from domain to domain.

Furthermore, as an outsider you bring a "fresh set of eyes," and this alone can often bring new insights into a project. Finally, you are following a process that has been refined over dozens of evaluations covering dozens of different domains. It has been refined to make use of the expertise of many people, to elicit, document, and cross-check quality attribute requirements and architectural information. This alone will bring benefit to your project—we have seen it over and over again. The process works!

—RK

suitable. In a perfect world, these would all be captured in a requirements document, but this notion fails for two reasons: (1) Complete and up-to-date requirements documents don't always exist, and (2) requirements documents express the requirements for a *system*. There are additional requirements levied on an architecture besides just enabling the system's requirements to be met. (Buildability is an example.)

The second implication of evaluating for suitability is that the answer that comes out of the evaluation is not going to be the sort of scalar result you may be used to when evaluating other kinds of software artifacts. Unlike code metrics, for example, in which the answer might be 7.2 and anything over 6.5 is deemed unacceptable, an architecture evaluation is going to produce a more thoughtful result.

We are not interested in precisely characterizing any quality attribute (using measures such as mean time to failure or end-to-end average latency). That would be pointless at an early stage of design because the actual parameters that determine these values (such as the actual execution time of a component) are often implementation dependent. What we are interested in doing—in the spirit of a risk-mitigation activity—is learning where an attribute of interest is affected by architectural design decisions, so that we can reason carefully about those decisions, model them more completely in subsequent analyses, and devote more of our design, analysis, and prototyping energies to such decisions.

An architectural evaluation will tell you that the architecture has been found suitable with respect to one set of goals and problematic with respect to another set of goals. Sometimes the goals will be in conflict with each other, or at the very least, some goals will be more important than other ones. And so the manager of the project will have a decision to make if the architecture evaluates well in some areas and not so well in others. Can the manager live with the areas of weakness? Can the architecture be strengthened in those areas? Or is it time for a wholesale restart? The evaluation will help reveal where an architecture is weak, but weighing the cost against benefit to the project of strengthening the architecture is solely a function of project context and is in the realm of management. So

> *An architecture evaluation doesn't tell you "yes" or "no," "good" or "bad," or "6.75 out of 10." It tells you where you are at risk.*

Architecture evaluation can be applied to a single architecture or to a group of competing architectures. In the latter case, it can reveal the strengths and weaknesses of each one. Of course, you can bet that no architecture will evaluate better than all others in all areas. Instead, one will outperform others in some areas but underperform in other areas. The evaluation will first identify what the areas of interest are and then highlight the strengths and weaknesses of each architecture in those areas. Management must decide which (if any) of the competing architectures should be selected or improved or whether none of the candidates is acceptable and a new architecture should be designed.[1]

2.5 For What Qualities Can We Evaluate an Architecture?

In this section, we say more precisely what suitability means. It isn't quite true that we can tell from looking at an architecture whether the ensuing system will meet *all* of its quality goals. For one thing, an implementation might diverge from the architectural plan in ways that subvert the quality plans. But for another, architecture does not strictly determine all of a system's qualities.

Usability is a good example. Usability is the measure of a user's ability to utilize a system effectively. Usability is an important quality goal for many systems, but usability is largely a function of the user interface. In modern systems design, particular aspects of the user interface tend to be encapsulated within small areas of the architecture. Getting data to and from the user interface and making it flow around the system so that the necessary work is done to support the user is certainly an architectural issue, as is the ability to change the user interface should that be required. However, many aspects of the user interface—whether the user sees red or blue backgrounds, a radio button or a dialog box—are by and large not architectural since those decisions are generally confined to a limited area of the system.

But other quality attributes lie squarely in the realm of architecture. For instance, the ATAM concentrates on evaluating an architecture for suitability in terms of imbuing a system with the following quality attributes. (Definitions are based on Bass et al. [Bass 98])

- *Performance:* Performance refers to the responsiveness of the system—the time required to respond to stimuli (events) or the number of events processed in some interval of time. Performance qualities are often expressed by the number of transactions per unit time or by the amount of time it takes to complete a transaction with the system. Performance measures are often cited using *benchmarks*, which are specific transaction sets or workload conditions under which the performance is measured.

- *Reliability:* Reliability is the ability of the system to keep operating over time. Reliability is usually measured by mean time to failure.

---

1. This is the last time we will address evaluating more than one architecture at a time since the methods we describe are carried out in the same fashion for either case.

- *Availability:* Availability is the proportion of time the system is up and running. It is measured by the length of time between failures as well as how quickly the system is able to resume operation in the event of failure.
- *Security:* Security is a measure of the system's ability to resist unauthorized attempts at usage and denial of service while still providing its services to legitimate users. Security is categorized in terms of the types of threats that might be made to the system.
- *Modifiability:* Modifiability is the ability to make changes to a system quickly and cost effectively. It is measured by using specific changes as benchmarks and recording how expensive those changes are to make.
- *Portability:* Portability is the ability of the system to run under different computing environments. These environments can be hardware, software, or a combination of the two. A system is portable to the extent that all of the assumptions about any *particular* computing environment are confined to one component (or at worst, a small number of easily changed components). If porting to a new system requires change, then portability is simply a special kind of modifiability.
- *Functionality:* Functionality is the ability of the system to do the work for which it was intended. Performing a task requires that many or most of the system's components work in a coordinated manner to complete the job.
- *Variability:* Variability is how well the architecture can be expanded or modified to produce new architectures that differ in specific, preplanned ways. Variability mechanisms may be run-time (such as negotiating on the fly protocols), compile-time (such as setting compilation parameters to bind certain variables), build-time (such as including or excluding various components or choosing different versions of a component), or code-time mechanisms (such as coding a device driver for a new device). Variability is important when the architecture is going to serve as the foundation for a whole family of related products, as in a product line.
- *Subsetability:* This is the ability to support the production of a subset of the system. While this may seem like an odd property of an architecture, it is actually one of the most useful and most overlooked. Subsetability can spell the difference between being able to deliver nothing when schedules slip versus being able to deliver a substantial part of the product. Subsetability also enables incremental development, a powerful development paradigm in which a minimal system is made to run early on and functions are added to it over time until the whole system is ready. Subsetability is a special kind of variability, mentioned above.
- *Conceptual integrity:* Conceptual integrity is the underlying theme or vision that unifies the design of the system at all levels. The architecture should do similar things in similar ways. Conceptual integrity is exemplified in an architecture that exhibits consistency, has a small number of data

and control mechanisms, and uses a small number of patterns throughout to get the job done.

By contrast, the SAAM concentrates on modifiability in its various forms (such as portability, subsetability, and variability) and functionality. The ARID method provides insights about the suitability of a portion of the architecture to be used by developers to complete their tasks.

If some other quality than the ones mentioned above is important to you, the methods still apply. The ATAM, for example, is structured in steps, some of which are dependent upon the quality being investigated, and others of which are not. Early steps of the ATAM allow you to define new quality attributes by explicitly describing the properties of interest. The ATAM can easily accommodate new quality-dependent analysis. When we introduce the method, you'll see where to do this. For now, though, the qualities in the list above form the basis for the methods' capabilities, and they also cover most of what people tend to be concerned about when evaluating an architecture.

2.6 Why Are Quality Attributes Too Vague for Analysis?

Quality attributes form the basis for architectural evaluation, but simply naming the attributes by themselves is not a sufficient basis on which to judge an architecture for suitability. Often, requirements statements like the following are written:

- "The system shall be robust."
- "The system shall be highly modifiable."
- "The system shall be secure from unauthorized break-in."
- "The system shall exhibit acceptable performance."

Without elaboration, each of these statements is subject to interpretation and misunderstanding. What you might think of as robust, your customer might consider barely adequate—or vice versa. Perhaps the system can easily adopt a new database but cannot adapt to a new operating system. Is that system maintainable or not? Perhaps the system uses passwords for security, which prevents a whole class of unauthorized users from breaking in, but has no virus protection mechanisms. Is that system secure from intrusion or not?

The point here is that quality attributes are not absolute quantities; they exist in the context of specific goals. In particular:

- A system is modifiable (or not) with respect to a specific kind of change.
- A system is secure (or not) with respect to a specific kind of threat.
- A system is reliable (or not) with respect to a specific kind of fault occurrence.
- A system performs well (or not) with respect to specific performance criteria.
- A system is suitable (or not) for a product line with respect to a specific set or range of envisioned products in the product line (that is, with respect to a specific product line *scope*).
- An architecture is buildable (or not) with respect to specific time and budget constraints.

If this doesn't seem reasonable, consider that no system can ever be, for example, completely reliable under all circumstances. (Think power failure, tornado, or disgruntled system operator with a sledgehammer.) Given that, it is incumbent upon the architect to understand under exactly what circumstances the system should be reliable in order to be deemed acceptable.

In a perfect world, the quality requirements for a system would be completely and unambiguously specified in a requirements document. Most of us do not live in such a world. Requirements documents are not written, or are written poorly, or are not finished when it is time to begin the architecture. Also, architectures have goals of their own that are not enumerated in a requirements document for the system: They must be built using resources at hand, they should exhibit conceptual integrity, and so on. And so the first job of an architecture evaluation is to elicit the specific quality goals against which the architecture will be judged.

If all of these goals are specifically, unambiguously articulated, that's wonderful. Otherwise, we ask the stakeholders to help us write them down during an evaluation. The mechanism we use is the *scenario*. A scenario is a short statement describing an interaction of one of the stakeholders with the system. A user would describe using the system to perform some task; these scenarios would very much resemble *use cases* in object-oriented parlance. A maintenance stakeholder would describe making a change to the system, such as upgrading the operating system in a particular way or adding a specific new function. A developer's scenario might involve using the architecture to build the system or predict its performance. A customer's scenario might describe the architecture reused for a second product in a product line or might assert that the system is buildable given certain resources.

Each scenario, then, is associated with a particular stakeholder (although different stakeholders might well be interested in the same scenario). Each scenario also addresses a particular quality, but in specific terms. Scenarios are discussed more fully in Chapter 3.

2.7 What Are the Outputs of an Architecture Evaluation?

2.7.1   Outputs from the ATAM, the SAAM, and ARID

An architecture evaluation results in information and insights about the architecture. The ATAM, the SAAM, and the ARID method all produce the outputs described below.

Prioritized Statement of Quality Attribute Requirements

An architecture evaluation can proceed only if the criteria for suitability are known. Thus, elicitation of quality attribute requirements against which the architecture is evaluated constitutes a major portion of the work. But no architecture can meet an unbounded list of quality attributes, and so the methods use a consensus-based prioritization. Having a prioritized statement of the quality attributes serves as an excellent documentation record to accompany any architecture and guide it through its evolution. All three methods produce this in the form of a set of quality attribute scenarios.

Mapping of Approaches to Quality Attributes

The answers to the analysis questions produce a mapping that shows how the architectural approaches achieve (or fail to achieve) the desired quality attributes. This mapping makes a splendid rationale for the architecture. Rationale is something that every architect should record, and most wish they had time to construct. The mapping of approaches to attributes can constitute the bulk of such a description.

Risks and Nonrisks

Risks are potentially problematic architectural decisions. Nonrisks are good decisions that rely on assumptions that are frequently implicit in the architecture. Both should be understood and explicitly recorded.[2]

Documenting of risks and nonrisks consists of

- An architectural decision (or a decision that has not been made)
- A specific quality attribute response that is being addressed by that decision along with the consequences of the predicted level of the response

---

2. Risks can also emerge from other, nonarchitectural sources. For example, having a management structure that is misaligned with the architectural structure might present an organizational risk. Insufficient communication between the stakeholder groups and the architect is a common kind of management risk.

- A rationale for the positive or negative effect that decision has on meeting the quality attribute requirement

An example of a risk is

The rules for writing business logic modules in the second tier of your three-tier client-server style are not clearly articulated (*a decision that has not been made*). This could result in replication of functionality, thereby compromising modifiability of the third tier (*a quality attribute response and its consequences*). Unarticulated rules for writing the business logic can result in unintended and undesired coupling of components (*rationale for the negative effect*).

An example of a nonrisk is

Assuming message arrival rates of once per second, a processing time of less than 30 milliseconds, and the existence of one higher priority process (*the architectural decisions*), a one-second soft deadline seems reasonable (*the quality attribute response and its consequences*) since the arrival rate is bounded and the preemptive effects of higher priority processes are known and can be accommodated (*the rationale*).

For a nonrisk to remain a nonrisk the assumptions must not change (or at least if they change, the designation of nonrisk will need to be rejustified). For example, if the message arrival rate, the processing time, or the number of higher priority processes changes in the example above, the designation of nonrisk could change.

2.7.2 Outputs Only from the ATAM

In addition to the preceding information, the ATAM produces an additional set of results described below.

Catalog of Architectural Approaches Used

Every architect adopts certain design strategies and approaches to solve the problems at hand. Sometimes these approaches are well known and part of the common knowledge of the field; sometimes they are unique and innovative to the system being built. In either case, they are the key to understanding whether the architecture will meet its goals and requirements. The ATAM includes a step in which the approaches used are catalogued, and this catalog can later serve as an introduction to the architecture for people who need to familiarize themselves with it, such as future architects and maintainers for the system.

Approach- and Quality-Attribute-Specific Analysis Questions

The ATAM poses analysis questions that are based on the attributes being sought and the approaches selected by the architect. As the architecture evolves, these questions can be used in future mini-evaluations to make sure that the evolution is not taking the architecture in the wrong direction.

Sensitivity Points and Tradeoff Points

We term key architectural decisions *sensitivity points* and *tradeoff points*. A sensitivity point is an architectural decision involving one or more architectural components (and/or component relationships) that is critical for achieving a particular quality attribute response measure. We call it this because the response measure is sensitive to changing the decision. For example:

- The level of confidentiality in a virtual private network might be sensitive to the number of bits of encryption.

- The latency for processing an important message might be sensitive to the priority of the lowest priority process involved in handling the message.

- The average number of person-days of effort it takes to maintain a system might be sensitive to the degree of encapsulation of its communication protocols and file formats.

Sensitivity points tell a designer or analyst where to focus attention when trying to understand the achievement of a quality goal. They serve as yellow flags: "Use caution when changing this property of the architecture." Particular values of sensitivity points may become risks when realized in an architecture. Consider the examples above. A particular value in the encryption level—say, 32-bit encryption—may present a risk in the architecture. Or having a very low priority process in a pipeline that processes an important message may become a risk in the architecture.

A *tradeoff point* is an architectural decision that affects more than one attribute and is a sensitivity point for more than one attribute. For example, changing the level of encryption could have a significant impact on both security and performance. Increasing the level of encryption improves the predicted security but requires more processing time. If the processing of a confidential message has a hard real-time latency requirement then the level of encryption could be a tradeoff point. Tradeoff points are the most critical decisions that one can make in an architecture, which is why we focus on them so carefully.

Finally, it is not uncommon for an architect to answer an elicitation question by saying, "We haven't made that decision yet." In this case you cannot point to a component or property in the architecture and call it out as a sensitivity point because the component or property might not exist yet. However, it is important to flag key decisions that have been made as well as key decisions that have not yet been made.

2.8 What Are the Benefits and Costs of Performing an Architecture Evaluation?

The main, and obvious, benefit of architecture evaluation is, of course, that it uncovers problems that if left undiscovered would be orders of magnitude more expensive to correct later. In short, architecture evaluation produces better architectures. Even if the evaluation uncovers no problems that warrant attention, it will increase everyone's level of confidence in the architecture.

But there are other benefits as well. Some of them are hard to measure, but they all contribute to a successful project and a more mature organization. You may not experience all of these on every evaluation, but the following is a list of the benefits we've often observed.

Puts Stakeholders in the Same Room

An architecture evaluation is often the first time that many of the stakeholders have ever met each other; sometimes it's the first time the architect has met them. A group dynamic emerges in which stakeholders see each other as all wanting the same thing: a successful system. Whereas before, their goals may have been in conflict with each other (and in fact, still may be), now they are able to explain their goals and motivations so that they begin to understand each other. In this atmosphere, compromises can be brokered or innovative solutions proposed in the face of greater understanding. It is almost always the case that stakeholders trade phone numbers and e-mail addresses and open channels of communication that last beyond the evaluation itself.

Forces an Articulation of Specific Quality Goals

The role of the stakeholders is to articulate the quality goals that the architecture should meet in order to be deemed successful. These goals are often not captured in any requirements document, or at least not captured in an unambiguous fashion beyond vague platitudes about reliability and modifiability. Scenarios provide explicit quality benchmarks.

Results in the Prioritization of Conflicting Goals

Conflicts that might arise among the goals expressed by the different stakeholders will be aired. Each method includes a step in which the goals are prioritized by the group. If the architect cannot satisfy all of the conflicting goals, he or she will receive clear and explicit guidance about which ones are considered most important. (Of course, project management can step in and veto or adjust the group-derived priorities—perhaps they perceive some stakeholders and their goals as "more equal" than others—but not unless the conflicting goals are aired.)

Forces a Clear Explication of the Architecture

The architect is compelled to make a group of people not privy to the architecture's creation understand it, in detail, in an unambiguous way. Among other things, this will serve as a dress rehearsal for explaining it to the other designers, component developers, and testers. The project benefits by forcing this explication early.

Improves the Quality of Architectural Documentation

Often, an evaluation will call for documentation that has not yet been prepared. For example, an inquiry along performance lines will reveal the need for documentation that shows how the architecture handles the interaction of run-time tasks or processes. If the evaluation requires it, then it's an odds-on bet that somebody on the project team (in this case, the performance engineer) will need it also. Again, the project benefits because it enters development better prepared.

Uncovers Opportunities for Cross-Project Reuse

Stakeholders and the evaluation team come from outside the development project, but often work on or are familiar with other projects within the same parent organization. As such, both are in a good position either to spot components that can be reused on other projects or to know of components (or other assets) that already exist and perhaps could be imported into the current project.

Results in Improved Architecture Practices

Organizations that practice architecture evaluation as a standard part of their development process report an improvement in the quality of the architectures that are evaluated. As development organizations learn to anticipate the kinds of questions that will be asked, the kinds of issues that will be raised, and the kinds of documentation that will be required for evaluations, they naturally preposition themselves to maximize their performance on the evaluations. Architecture evaluations result in better architectures not only after the fact but before the fact as well. Over time, an organization develops a culture that promotes good architectural design.

Now, not all of these benefits may resonate with you. If your organization is small, maybe all of the stakeholders know each other and talk regularly. Perhaps your organization is very mature when it comes to working out the requirements for a system, and by the time the finishing touches are put on the architecture the requirements are no longer an issue because everyone is completely clear what they are. If so, congratulations. But many of the organizations in which we have carried out architecture evaluations are not quite so sophisticated, and there have always been requirements issues that were raised (and resolved) when the architecture was put on the table.

There are also benefits to future projects in the same organization. A critical part of the ATAM consists of probing the architecture using a set of quality-specific analysis questions, and neither the method nor the list of questions is a secret. The architect is perfectly free to arm her- or himself before the evaluation by making sure that the architecture is up to snuff with respect to the relevant questions. This is rather like scoring well on a test whose questions you've already seen, but in this case it isn't cheating: it's professionalism.

The costs of architecture evaluation are all personnel costs and opportunity costs related to those personnel participating in the evaluation instead of something else. They're easy enough to calculate. An example using the cost of an ATAM-based evaluation is shown in Table 2.1. The left-most column names the phases of the ATAM (which will be described in subsequent chapters). The other columns split the cost among the participant groups. Similar tables can easily be constructed for other methods.

Table 2.1 shows figures for what we would consider a medium-size evaluation effort. While 70 person-days sounds like a substantial sum, in actuality it may not be so daunting. For one reason, the *calendar* time added to the project is minimal. The schedule should not be impacted by the preparation at all, nor the follow-up. These activities can be carried out behind the scenes, as it were. The middle phases consume actual project days, usually three or so. Second, the project normally does not have to pay for all 70 staff days. Many of the

Table 2.1 Approximate Cost of a Medium-Size ATAM-Based Evaluation

Participant Group ATAM Phase	Evaluation Team (assume 5 members)	Stakeholders	
		Project Decision Makers (assume architect, project manager, customer)	Other Stakeholders (assume 8)
Phase 0: Preparation	1 person-day by team leader	1 person-day	0
Phase 1: Initial evaluation (1 day)	5 person-days	3 person-days	0
Phase 2: Complete evaluation (3 days)	15 person-days	9 person-days + 2 person-days to prepare	16 person-days (most stakeholders present only for 2 days)
Phase 3: Follow-up	15 person-days	3 person-days to read and respond to report	0
TOTAL	36 person-days	18 person-days	16 person-days

stakeholders work for other cost centers, if not other organizations, than the development group. Stakeholders by definition have a vested interest in the system, and they are often more than willing to contribute their time to help produce a quality product.

It is certainly easy to imagine larger and smaller efforts than the one characterized by Table 2.1. As we will see, all of the methods are flexible, structured to iteratively spiral down into as much detail as the evaluators and evaluation client feel is warranted. Cursory evaluations can be done in a day; excruciatingly detailed evaluations could take weeks. However, the numbers in Table 2.2 represent what we would call nominal applications of the ATAM. For smaller projects, Table 2.2 shows how those numbers can be halved.

If your group evaluates many systems in the same domain or with the same architectural goals, then there is another way that the cost of evaluation can be reduced. Collect and record the scenarios used in each evaluation. Over time, you will find that the scenario sets will begin to resemble each other. After you have performed several of these almost-alike evaluations, you can produce a "canonical" set of scenarios based on past experience. At this point, the scenarios have in essence graduated to become a checklist, and you can dispense with the bulk of the scenario-generation part of the exercise. This saves about a day. Since scenario generation is the primary duty of the stakeholders, the bulk of their time can also be done away with, lowering the cost still further.

Table 2.2 Approximate Cost of a Small ATAM-Based evaluation

Participant Group ATAM Phase	Evaluation team (assume 2 members)	Stakeholders	
		Project Decision Makers (assume architect, project manager)	Other Stakeholders (assume 3)
Phase 0: Preparation	1 person-day by team leader	1 person-day	0
Phase 1: Initial evaluation (1 day)	2 person-days	2 person-days	0
Phase 2: Complete evaluation (2 days)	4 person-days	4 person-days + 2 person-days to prepare	6 person-days
Phase 3: Follow-up	8 person-days	2 person-days to read and respond to report	0
TOTAL	15 person-days	11 person-days	6 person-days

Table 2.3   Approximate Cost of a Medium-Size Checklist-based ATAM-Based Evaluation

Participant Group ATAM Phase	Evaluation Team (assume 4 members)	Stakeholders	
		Project Decision Makers (assume architect, project manager, customer)	Other Stakeholders (assume the customer validates the checklist)
Phase 0: Preparation	1 person-day by team leader	1 person-day	0
Phase 1: Initial evaluation (1 day)	4 person-days	3 person-days	0
Phase 2: Complete evaluation (2 days)	8 person-days	6 person-days	2 person-days
Phase 3: Follow-up	12 person-days	3 person-days to read and respond to report	0
TOTAL	25 person-days	13 person-days	2 person-days

(You still may want to have a few key stakeholders, including the customer, to validate the applicability of your checklist to the new system.) The team size can be reduced, since no one is needed to record scenarios. The architect's preparation time should be minimal since the checklist will be publicly available even when he or she begins the architecture task.

Table 2.3 shows the cost of a medium-size checklist-based evaluation using the ATAM, which comes in at about $\frac{4}{7}$ of the cost of the scenario-based evaluation of Table 2.1.

The next chapter will introduce the first of the three architecture evaluation methods in this book: the Architecture Tradeoff Analysis Method.

2.9 For Further Reading

The For Further Reading list of Chapter 9 (Comparing Software Architecture Evaluation Methods) lists good references on various architecture evaluation methods.

Zhao has assembled a nice collection of literature resources dealing with software architecture analysis [Zhao 99].

Once an architecture evaluation has identified changes that should be made to an architecture, how do you prioritize them? Work is emerging to help an architect or project manager assign quantitative cost and benefit information to architectural decisions [Kazman 01].

2.10 Discussion Questions

1. How does your organization currently decide whether a proposed software architecture should be adopted or not? How does it decide when a software architecture has outlived its usefulness and should be discarded in favor of another?

2. Make a business case, specific to your organization, that tells whether or not conducting a software architecture evaluation would pay off. Assume the cost estimates given in this chapter if you like, or use your own.

3. Do you know of a case where a flawed software architecture led to the failure or delay of a software system or project? Discuss what caused the problem and whether a software architecture evaluation might have prevented the calamity.

4. Which quality attributes tend to be the most important to systems in your organization? How are those attributes specified? How does the architect know what they are, what they mean, and what precise levels of each are required?

5. For each quality attribute discussed in this chapter—or for each that you named in answer to the previous question—hypothesize three different architectural decisions that would have an effect on that attribute. For example, the decision to maintain a backup database would probably increase a system's availability.

6. Choose three or four pairs of quality attributes. For each pair (think about tradeoffs), hypothesize an architectural decision that would increase the first quality attribute at the expense of the second. Now hypothesize a different architectural decision that would raise the second but lower the first.

3

The ATAM—A Method for Architecture Evaluation

There is also a rhythm and a pattern between the phenomena of nature which is not apparent to the eye, but only to the eye of analysis. . . .

—Richard Feynman
The Character of Physical Law

This chapter will present the first of three methods for architecture evaluation that are the primary subject of this book. It is called the Architecture Tradeoff Analysis Method (ATAM). The ATAM gets its name because it not only reveals how well an architecture satisfies particular quality goals but it also provides insight into how those quality goals interact with each other—how they *trade off* against each other.

Having a structured method makes the analysis repeatable and helps ensure that the right questions regarding an architecture will be asked early, during the requirements and design stages when discovered problems can be solved relatively cheaply. It guides users of the method—the stakeholders—to look for conflicts and for resolutions to these conflicts in the software architecture.

The ATAM can also be used to analyze legacy systems. This need arises when the legacy system needs to undergo major modifications, integration with other systems, porting, or other significant upgrades. Assuming that an accurate architecture of the legacy system is available (which frequently must be acquired and verified using architecture extraction and conformance testing methods), applying the ATAM results in increased understanding of the quality attributes of the system.

The ATAM draws its inspiration and techniques from three areas: the notion of architectural styles; the quality attribute analysis communities; and the Software Architecture Analysis Method (SAAM), which was the predecessor to the

ATAM. Styles and quality attribute analysis are introduced in this chapter but discussed more thoroughly in Chapter 5. The SAAM is presented in Chapter 7.

This chapter introduces the steps of the ATAM, then describes the steps in more depth, and concludes by discussing how the steps are arranged in phases carried out over time.

3.1 Summary of the ATAM Steps

The main part of the ATAM consists of nine steps. (Other parts of the ATAM, including preparation before and follow-up after an evaluation, are detailed later in this chapter.) The steps are separated into four groups:

- Presentation, which involves exchanging information through presentations
- Investigation and analysis, which involves assessing key quality attribute requirements vis-à-vis architectural approaches
- Testing, which involves checking the results to date against the needs of all relevant stakeholders
- Reporting, which involves presenting the results of the ATAM

Presentation

1. **Present the ATAM.** The evaluation leader describes the evaluation method to the assembled participants, tries to set their expectations, and answers questions they may have.
2. **Present the business drivers.** A project spokesperson (ideally the project manager or system customer) describes what business goals are motivating the development effort and hence what will be the primary architectural drivers (for example, high availability or time to market or high security).
3. **Present the architecture.** The architect describes the architecture, focusing on how it addresses the business drivers.

Investigation and Analysis

4. **Identify the architectural approaches.** Architectural approaches are identified by the architect but are not analyzed.
5. **Generate the quality attribute utility tree.** The quality attributes that comprise system "utility" (performance, availability, security, modifiability, usability, and so on) are elicited, specified down to the level of scenarios, annotated with stimuli and responses, and prioritized.

6. **Analyze the architectural approaches.** Based upon the high-priority scenarios identified in Step 5, the architectural approaches that address those scenarios are elicited and analyzed (for example, an architectural approach aimed at meeting performance goals will be subjected to a performance analysis). During this step architectural risks, nonrisks, sensitivity points, and tradeoff points are identified.

Testing

7. **Brainstorm and prioritize scenarios.** A larger set of scenarios is elicited from the entire group of stakeholders. This set of scenarios is prioritized via a voting process involving all the stakeholders.

8. **Analyze the architectural approaches.** This step reiterates the activities of Step 6 but uses the highly ranked scenarios from Step 7. Those scenarios are considered to be test cases to confirm the analysis performed thus far. This analysis may uncover additional architectural approaches, risks, nonrisks, sensitivity points, and tradeoff points, which are then documented.

Reporting

9. **Present the results.** Based upon the information collected during the ATAM evaluation (approaches, scenarios, attribute-specific questions, the utility tree, risks, nonrisks, sensitivity points, tradeoffs), the ATAM team presents the findings to the assembled stakeholders.

Sometimes there must be dynamic modifications to the schedule to accommodate the availability of personnel or architectural information. Although the steps are numbered, suggesting linearity, this is not a strict waterfall process. There will be times when an analyst will return briefly to an earlier step, or will jump forward to a later step, or will iterate among steps, as the need dictates. The importance of the steps is to clearly delineate the activities involved in the ATAM along with the output of these activities. The next section offers a detailed description of the steps of the ATAM.

3.2 Detailed Description of the ATAM Steps

3.2.1 Step 1: Present the ATAM

The first step calls for the evaluation leader to present the ATAM to the assembled stakeholders. This time is used to explain the process that everyone will be following, allows time to answer questions, and sets the context and expectations for the remainder of the activities. In particular, the leader will describe

- The ATAM steps in brief
- The techniques that will be used for elicitation and analysis: utility tree generation, architecture approach-based elicitation and analysis, and scenario brainstorming and prioritization
- The outputs of the evaluation: the scenarios elicited and prioritized, the questions used to understand and evaluate the architecture, a utility tree describing and prioritizing the driving architectural requirements, a set of identified architectural approaches, a set of risks and nonrisks discovered, and a set of sensitivity points and tradeoffs discovered

A standard set of slides is used to aid in the presentation; the outline of such a set is given in Figure 6.6.

3.2.2 Step 2: Present the Business Drivers

The evaluation's participants—the stakeholders as well as the evaluation team members—need to understand the context for the system and the primary business drivers motivating its development. In this step, a project decision maker (ideally the project manager or the system's customer) presents a system overview from a business perspective. An outline for such a presentation is given in Figure 3.1. The presentation should describe

- The system's most important functions
- Any relevant technical, managerial, economic, or political constraints
- The business goals and context as they relate to the project
- The major stakeholders

Business Context/Drivers Presentation (~12 slides; 45 minutes)

- Description of the business environment, history, market differentiators, driving requirements, stakeholders, current need, and how the proposed system will meet those needs/requirements (3–4 slides)

- Description of business constraints (e.g., time to market, customer demands, standards, cost, etc.) (1–3 slides)

- Description of the technical constraints (e.g., commercial off-the-shelf [COTS] products, interoperation with other systems, required hardware or software platform, reuse of legacy code, etc.) (1–3 slides)

- Quality attributes requirements and from what business needs these are derived (2–3 slides)

- Glossary (1 slide)

Figure 3.1   Example Template for the Business Case Presentation

- The architectural drivers (major quality attribute goals that shape the architecture)

3.2.3 Step 3: Present the Architecture

In this step, the lead architect (or architecture team) makes a presentation describing the architecture at an appropriate level of detail. What the "appropriate level" is depends on several factors: how much of the architecture has been designed and documented, how much time is available, and the nature of the behavioral and quality requirements. The architectural information presented will directly affect the analysis that is possible and the quality of this analysis. Frequently the evaluation team will need to ask for additional architectural information before a more substantial analysis is possible.

In this presentation the architect should cover

- Technical constraints such as an operating system, hardware, or middleware prescribed for use
- Other systems with which the system must interact
- Architectural approaches used to meet quality attribute requirements

Architectural views, as described in Chapter 1, are the primary vehicle that the architect should use to present the architecture. Which views the architect chooses to present will, of course, depend on what about the architecture is important to convey. Functional, concurrency, code, and physical views are useful in almost every evaluation, and the architect should be prepared to show those. Other views should be presented in addition if they contain information relevant to the architecture at hand, especially information relevant to achieving important quality attribute goals. As a rule of thumb, the architect should present those views that he or she found most important to work on during the creation of the architecture.

At this time the evaluation team begins its initial probing for and capturing of architectural approaches as a prelude to Step 4.

An outline for the architecture presentation is shown in Figure 3.2. Providing a template like this to the architect well in advance of the ATAM meeting helps ensure that he or she presents the right information and also helps to ensure that the exercise stays on schedule.

3.2.4 Step 4: Identify the Architectural Approaches

The ATAM focuses on analyzing an architecture by understanding its architectural approaches. In this step they are captured by the evaluation team but are not analyzed. The team will ask the architect to explicitly name any identifiable approaches used, but they will also capture any approaches they heard during the architecture presentation in the previous step.

Architecture Presentation (~20 slides; 60 minutes)

- Driving architectural requirements, the measurable quantities associated with these requirements, and any existing standards/models/approaches for meeting these (2–3 slides)

- High-level architectural views (4–8 slides)
  - Functional: functions, key system abstractions, and domain elements along with their dependencies, data flow
  - Code: the subsystems, layers, and modules that describe the system's decomposition of functionality, along with the objects, procedures, and functions that populate these and the relations among them (e.g., procedure call, method invocation, callback, containment)
  - Concurrency: processes, threads along with the synchronization, data flow, and events that connect them
  - Physical: CPUs, storage, and external devices/sensors along with the networks and communication devices that connect them

- Architectural approaches, styles, patterns, or mechanisms employed, including what quality attributes they address and a description of how the approaches address those attributes (3–6 slides)

- Use of commercial off-the-shelf (COTS) products and how they are chosen/integrated (1–2 slides)

- Trace of 1–3 of the most important use case scenarios, including, if possible, the run-time resources consumed for each scenario (1–3 slides)

- Trace of 1–3 of the most important growth scenarios, describing, if possible, the change impact (estimated size/difficulty of the change) in terms of the changed components, connectors, or interfaces (1–3 slides)

- Architectural issues/risks with respect to meeting the driving architectural requirements (2–3 slides)

- Glossary (1 slide)

Figure 3.2   Example Template for the Architecture Presentation

The ATAM concentrates on identifying architectural approaches and architectural styles[1] because these represent the architecture's means of addressing the highest priority quality attributes, that is, the means of ensuring that the critical requirements are met in a predictable way. These architectural approaches define the important structures of the system and describe the ways in which the system can grow, respond to changes, withstand attacks, integrate with other systems, and so forth.

---

1. As we mentioned in Chapter 1, we use the term *approaches* because not all architects are familiar with the language of architectural styles and so may not be able to enumerate a set of styles used in the architecture. But every architect makes architectural decisions, and the set of these we call *approaches*. These can certainly be elicited from any conscientious architect.

An architectural style includes a description of component types and their topology, a description of the pattern of data and control interactions among the components, and an informal description of the benefits and drawbacks of using that style. Architectural styles are important since they differentiate classes of designs by offering experiential evidence of how each class has been used along with qualitative reasoning to explain why each class has certain properties and when to use it.

For example, Figure 3.3 shows the Concurrent Pipelines style. This style consists of a set of pipelines, each of which consists of a sequence of processes. Each input message is incrementally transformed by each process in the appropriate sequence. Systems built like this have several benefits, many of which result in enhanced modifiability.

- The system can be understood easily as a sequence of data transformations.
- Each element of the pipeline can be modified or replaced, in principle, without affecting any of the other elements.
- Elements can be reused elsewhere.
- Evaluators can reason about this style in terms of its performance implications.

A style can be thought of as a set of constraints on an architecture—constraints on component types and their interactions—and these constraints define the set or family of architectures that satisfy them. By locating architectural styles in an architecture, the evaluators can see what strategies the architect has used to respond to the system's driving quality attribute goals.

A specialization of an architectural style, called *attribute-based architectural styles* (ABASs), is particularly useful in the ATAM. An ABAS is an architectural

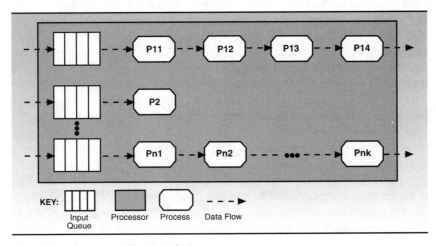

Figure 3.3 Concurrent Pipelines Style

style along with an explanation of how that style achieves certain quality attributes. That explanation in an ABAS leads to attribute-specific questions associated with the style. For example, a performance-oriented ABAS highlights architectural decisions in a style that is relevant to performance—how processes are allocated to processors, where they share resources, how their priorities are assigned, how they synchronize, and so forth. The derivative questions probe important architectural decisions such as the priority of the processes, estimates of their execution time, places where they synchronize, queuing disciplines, and so forth: in other words, information that is relevant to understanding the performance of this style. ABASs are discussed in Chapter 5.

3.2.5 Step 5: Generate the Quality Attribute Utility Tree

In this step the evaluation team works with the project decision makers (here, the architecture team, manager, and customer representatives) to identify, prioritize, and refine the system's most important quality attribute goals. This crucial step guides the remainder of the analysis. Lacking this guidance, the evaluators could spend precious time analyzing the architecture ad infinitum without ever touching on issues that mattered to its sponsors. There must be a way to focus the attention of all the stakeholders and the evaluation team on the aspects of the architecture that are most critical to the system's success. This is accomplished by building a utility tree.

The output of the utility tree–generation step is a prioritization of specific quality attribute requirements, realized as scenarios. The utility tree serves to make concrete the quality attribute requirements, forcing the architect and customer representatives to define the relevant quality requirements precisely.

Utility trees provide a mechanism for directly and efficiently translating the business drivers of a system into concrete quality attribute scenarios. For example, in an e-commerce system two of the business drivers might be stated as, "Security is central to the success of the system since ensuring the privacy of our customers' data is of utmost importance," and "Modifiability is central to the success of the system since we need to be able to respond quickly to a rapidly evolving and very competitive marketplace." Before the evaluation team can assess the architecture, these system goals must be made more specific and more concrete. Moreover, the team needs to understand the relative importance of these goals versus other quality attribute goals, such as performance, to determine where the team should focus its attention during the architecture evaluation. Utility trees help to prioritize and make concrete the quality goals. An example of a utility tree is shown in Figure 3.4.

The utility tree shown in Figure 3.4 contains *utility* as the root node. This is an expression of the overall "goodness" of the system. Quality attributes form the second level of the utility tree. Typically the quality attributes of performance, modifiability, availability, and security are the children of utility,

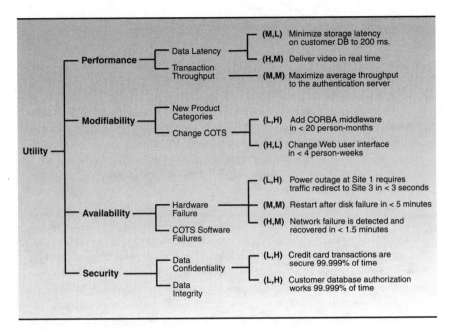

Figure 3.4   Sample Utility Tree

although participants are free to name their own quality attributes. Sometimes different stakeholder groups use different names for the same ideas (for example, some stakeholders prefer to speak of "maintainability"). Sometimes they introduce quality attribute names that are meaningful in their own culture but not widely used elsewhere. Whatever names the stakeholders introduce are fine, as long as the stakeholders are able to explain what they mean through refinement at the next levels.

Under each of these quality attributes are specific quality attribute refinements. For example, in Figure 3.4 performance is decomposed into "data latency" and "transaction throughput." This is a step toward refining the attribute goals into quality attribute scenarios that are concrete enough for prioritization and analysis. "Data latency" is then further refined into "minimize storage latency on customer database" and "deliver video in real time" because these are both kinds of data latency relevant to the system of the example.

These quality attribute scenarios (see the sidebar Scenarios) at the leaf nodes are now specific enough to be prioritized relative to each other and (equally important) analyzed. The prioritization may be on a 0 to 10 scale or may use relative rankings such as High (H), Medium (M), and Low (L). (We prefer the High/Medium/Low approach since we find that it works well for our purposes and takes less time than trying to assign precise numbers to an imprecise quantity.)

Scenarios

Typically the first job of an architecture evaluation is to precisely elicit the specific quality goals against which the architecture will be judged. The mechanism that we use for this elicitation is the *scenario*.

We use scenarios heavily in all three of our evaluation methods, and many other software and system analysis methods use them as well. They have been used for years in user interface engineering, requirements elicitation, performance modeling, and safety inspections. Why do so many fields rely on such a seemingly simple and innocuous device? The answer is threefold: they are simple to create and understand, they are inexpensive (it doesn't take much training to generate or work with them), and they are effective.

A scenario is a short statement describing an interaction of one of the stakeholders with the system. A *user* would describe using the system to perform some task; his or her scenarios would very much resemble *use cases* in object-oriented parlance. A *maintainer* would describe making a change to the system, such as upgrading the operating system in a particular way or adding a specific new function. A *developer*'s scenario might focus on using the architecture to build the system or predict its performance. A *product line manager's* scenario might describe how the architecture is to be reused for a second product in a product line.

Scenarios provide a vehicle for taking vague development-time qualities such as modifiability and turning them into something concrete: specific examples of current and future uses of a system. Scenarios are also useful in understanding run-time qualities such as performance or availability. This is because scenarios specify the kinds of operations over which performance needs to be measured or the kinds of failures the system will have to withstand.

Structure of Scenarios

Scenarios tell a very brief story about an interaction with the system from the point of view of a stakeholder. We ask stakeholders in evaluation exercises to phrase scenarios using a three-part format that helps keep the descriptions crisp and to make sure that the scenario provides enough information to serve as the basis for investigation. The three parts are stimulus, environment, and response.

The *stimulus* is the part of the scenario that explains or describes what the stakeholder does to initiate the interaction with the system. A user may invoke a function; a maintainer may make a change; a tester may run a test; an operator may reconfigure the system in some way; and so on.

The *environment* describes what's going on at the time of the stimulus. What is the system's state? What unusual conditions are in effect? Is the system heavily loaded? Is one of the processors down? Is one of the communication channels flooded? Any ambient condition that is relevant to understanding the scenario should be described. By convention, if the environment is simply "under normal conditions," then it is omitted.

The *response* tells us how the system—through its architecture—should respond to the stimulus. Is the function carried out? Is the test successful? Does the reconfiguration happen? How much effort did the maintenance change require?

The response is often the key to understanding what quality attribute the stakeholder who proposed the scenario is concerned about. If the response to a user-invokes-a-function stimulus is simply that the function happens, then the stakeholder is probably interested in the system's functionality. If the stakeholder appends "with no error" or "within two seconds" to the end, that indicates an interest in reliability and performance, respectively. By noticing the quality attribute of interest, the evaluation leader can prod the stakeholder to clarify or refine the scenario if necessary. Perhaps the stakeholder is interested in performance but left out a statement of the scenario's environment. The leader could ask about the ambient workload on the system to see if that played a part in the stakeholder's interest. Or the leader could ask whether the stakeholder was interested in worst-case, average, or best-case performance.

Ideally, all scenarios are expressed in this stimulus–environment–response form. In practice we don't usually achieve this ideal. In the heat of brainstorming we don't always pause to insist that every scenario be well formed. That's why the template in Figure 3.5 includes a place for the stimulus, environment, and response to be captured. That way, we can spend time structuring only those scenarios selected for analysis.

Types of Scenarios

In the ATAM we use three types of scenarios: *use case scenarios* (typical uses of the existing system, used for information elicitation), *growth scenarios* (anticipated changes to the system), and *exploratory scenarios* (extreme changes that are expected to "stress" the system). These different types of scenarios are used to probe a system from different angles, optimizing the chances of surfacing architectural decisions at risk. Examples of each type of scenario follow.

Use Case Scenarios

Use case scenarios describe a user's intended interaction with the completed, running system. For example:

1. The user wants to examine budgetary and actual data under different fiscal years without reentering project data (usability).
2. A data exception occurs and the system notifies a defined list of recipients by e-mail and displays the offending conditions in red on data screens (reliability).
3. The user changes a graph layout from horizontal to vertical and the graph is redrawn in one second (performance).
4. A remote user requests a database report via the Web during a peak period and receives it within five seconds (performance).

5. The caching system is switched to another processor when its processor fails, within one second of the failure (reliability).

6. There is a radical course adjustment before weapon release while approaching the target that the software computes in 100 ms. (performance).

Notice that each of the above use case scenarios expresses a specific stakeholder's desires. Also, the stimulus and the response associated with the attribute are easily identifiable. For example, in scenario 6 above, "radical course adjustment before weapon release while approaching the target," the stimulus and latency goal of 100 ms. is called out as being the important response measure. For scenarios to be well formed it must be clear what the stimulus is, what the environmental conditions are, and what the measurable or observable manifestation of the response is.

The quality attribute characterizations (which are discussed in Chapter 5) suggest questions that can be helpful in refining scenarios. Again consider scenario 6, which considers thse analysis questions:

- Are data sampling rates increased during radical course adjustments?
- Are real-time deadlines shortened during radical course adjustments?
- Is more execution time required to calculate a weapon solution during radical course adjustments?

Growth Scenarios

Growth scenarios represent typical *anticipated* changes to a system. Each scenario also has attribute-related ramifications, many of which are for attributes other than modifiability. For example, scenarios 1 and 4 below will have performance consequences and scenario 5 might have performance, security, and reliability implications.

1. Change the heads-up display to track several targets simultaneously without affecting latency.

2. Add a new message type to the system's repertoire in less than a person-week of work.

3. Add a collaborative planning capability with which two planners at different sites can collaborate on a plan in less than a person-year of work.

4. Double the maximum number of tracks to be handled by the system and keep to 200 ms. the maximum latency of track data to the screen.

5. Migrate to an operating system in the same family, or to a new release of the existing operating system with less than a person-year of work.

6. Add a new data server to reduce latency in use case scenario 5 to 2.5 seconds within one person-week.

7. Double the size of existing database tables while maintaining a one-second average retrieval time.

Exploratory Scenarios

Exploratory scenarios push the envelope and stress the system. The goal of these scenarios is to expose the limits or boundary conditions of the current design, exposing possibly implicit assumptions. Systems are seldom conceived and designed to handle these kinds of modifications, but at some point in the future these might be realistic requirements for change, so the stakeholders might like to understand the ramifications of such changes. For example:

1. Add a new three-dimensional map feature and a virtual reality interface for viewing the maps in less than five person-months of effort.

2. Change the underlying Unix platform to Macintosh.

3. Reuse the 25-year-old software on a new generation of the aircraft.

4. Reduce the time budget for displaying changed track data by a factor of ten.

5. Improve the system's availability from 98% to 99.999%.

6. Make changes so that half of the servers can go down during normal operation without affecting overall system availability.

7. Increase the number of bids processed hourly by a factor of ten while keeping worst-case response time below ten seconds.

Each type of scenario—use case, growth, and exploratory—helps illuminate a different aspect of the architecture, and together provide a three-pronged strategy for evaluation. Because scenarios are easy to formulate and understand, they are an excellent vehicle with which all stakeholders can communicate their architectural interests, and serve as the backbone for many evaluation methods.

—RK

Participants prioritize the utility tree along two dimensions: (1) by the importance of each scenario to the success of the system and (2) by the degree of difficulty posed by the achievement of the scenario, in the estimation of the architect. For example, "minimize storage latency on customer database" has priorities (M,L), meaning that it is of medium importance to the success of the system and the architect expects low difficulty to achieve, while "deliver video in real time" has priorities (H,M), meaning that it is highly important to the success of the system and the architect perceives the achievement of this scenario to be of medium difficulty.

Clearly the scenarios marked (H,H) are the prime candidates for scrutiny during the analysis steps of the ATAM. After those are handled, then either the (M,H) or (H,M) scenarios are attacked, depending on the consensus of the participants. After those, time permitting, will come the (M,M) scenarios. A scenario garnering an L rating in either category is not likely to be examined since it makes little sense to spend time on a case of little importance or little expected difficulty.

Refining the utility tree often leads to interesting and unexpected results. For example, Figure 3.4 came from an actual evaluation in which the stakeholders initially told us that security and modifiability were the key quality attributes. It turns out that another group of stakeholders thought that in fact performance and availability were the important drivers, and this discrepancy did not surface until the utility tree step. Creating the utility tree guides the key stakeholders in considering, explicitly stating, and prioritizing all of the current and future driving forces on the architecture.

The output of utility tree generation is a prioritized list of scenarios that serves as a plan for the remainder of the ATAM. It tells the ATAM team where to spend its (relatively limited) time, and in particular where to probe for architectural approaches and risks. The utility tree guides the evaluators to look at the architectural approaches involved with satisfying the high-priority scenarios at the leaves of the utility tree. Additionally, the utility tree serves to make the quality attribute requirements concrete, forcing the evaluation team and the customer to define their quality requirements precisely. Statements commonly found in requirements documents such as "The architecture shall be modifiable and robust" are untenable here because they have no operational meaning: they are not testable.

3.2.6 Step 6: Analyze the Architectural Approaches

At this point, there is now a prioritized set of concrete quality requirements (from Step 5) and a set of architectural approaches utilized in the architecture (from Step 4). Step 6 sizes up how well suited they are to each other. Here, the evaluation team can probe the architectural approaches that realize the important quality attributes. This is done with an eye to documenting these architectural decisions and identifying their risks, nonrisks, sensitivity points, and tradeoffs. The team probes for sufficient information about each architectural approach to conduct a rudimentary analysis about the attribute for which the approach is relevant. The goal is for the evaluation team to be convinced that the instantiation of the approach in the architecture being evaluated is appropriate for meeting the attribute-specific requirements for which it is intended.

Outputs of this step include

- The architectural approaches or decisions relevant to each high-priority utility tree scenario. The team should expect that all the approaches identified have been captured in Step 4; if not, the team should probe to find out the reason for the discrepancy. The architect should identify the approach and the components, connectors, and constraints involved.

- The analysis questions associated with each approach, geared to the quality attribute with which its scenario is associated. These questions might come from documented experience with approaches (as found in ABASs and their associated quality attribute characterizations, discussed in Chapter 5), from books on software architecture (see For Further Reading at the end of this chapter), or from the prior experiences of the assembled stakeholders. In practice all three areas are mined for questions.
- The architect's responses to the questions.
- The risks, nonrisks, sensitivity points, and tradeoff points identified. Each of these is associated with the achievement of one or more quality attribute refinements in the utility tree with respect to the quality attribute questions that probed the risk.

In effect, the utility tree tells the evaluation team where to probe the architecture (because this is a highly important factor for the success of the system), the architect (one hopes) responds with the architectural approach that answers this need, and the team can use the quality attribute–specific questions to probe the approach more deeply. The questions help the team to

- Understand the approach in detail and how it was applied in this instance
- Look for well-known weaknesses with the approach
- Look for the approach's sensitivity and tradeoff points
- Find interactions and tradeoffs with other approaches

In the end, each of these may provide the basic material for the description of a risk, and this is recorded in an ever-growing list of risks.

For example, assigning processes to a server might affect the number of transactions that server can process in a second. Thus the assignment of processes to the server is a sensitivity point with respect to the response as measured in transactions per second. Some assignments will result in unacceptable values of this response—these are risks. Finally, when it turns out that an architectural decision is a sensitivity point for more than one attribute, it is designated as a tradeoff point.

The analysis questions are not an end unto themselves. Each is a starting point for discussion and for the determination of a potential risk, nonrisk, sensitivity point, or tradeoff point. These, in turn, may catalyze a deeper analysis, depending on how the architect responds. For example, if the architect cannot characterize client loading and cannot say how priorities are allocated to processes and how processes are allocated to hardware, then there is little point in doing a sophisticated queuing or rate-monotonic performance analysis. If such questions can be answered, then the evaluation team can perform at least a rudimentary or back-of-the-envelope analysis to determine whether these architectural decisions are problematic or not vis-à-vis the quality attribute requirements they are meant to address. The analysis is not meant to be comprehensive and detailed. The key is to elicit enough architectural information to establish some link between the architectural decisions that have been made and the quality attribute requirements that need to be satisfied.

A template for capturing the analysis of an architectural approach for a scenario is shown in Figure 3.5.

For example, Step 6 might elicit from an architect the following information, shown in Figure 3.6, in response to a utility tree scenario that required high availability from a system.

As shown in Figure 3.6, based upon the results of this step the evaluation team can identify and record a set of sensitivity points and tradeoff points, risks and nonrisks. All sensitivity points and tradeoff points are candidate risks. By the end of the ATAM, each sensitivity point and each tradeoff point should be categorized as either a risk or a nonrisk. The risks, nonrisks, sensitivity points, and tradeoffs are gathered together in separate lists. The numbers R8, T3, S4, N12, and so on in Figure 3.6 simply refer to entries in these lists.

Analysis of Architectural Approach				
Scenario #: *Number*	**Scenario:** *Text of scenario from utility tree*			
Attribute(s)	*Quality attribute(s) with which this scenario is concerned*			
Environment	*Relevant assumptions about the environment in which the system resides, and the relevant conditions when the scenario is carried out*			
Stimulus	*A precise statement of the quality attribute stimulus (e.g., function invoked, failure, threat, modification . . .) embodied by the scenario*			
Response	*A precise statement of the quality attribute response (e.g., response time, measure of difficulty of modification)*			
Architectural Decisions	**Sensitivity**	**Tradeoff**	**Risk**	**Nonrisk**
Architectural decisions relevant to this scenario that affect quality attribute response	*Sensitivity Point #*	*Tradeoff Point #*	*Risk #*	*Nonrisk #*
. . .	. . .	. . .	. . .	. . .
. . .	. . .	. . .	. . .	. . .
Reasoning	*Qualitative and/or quantitative rationale for why the list of architectural decisions contribute to meeting each quality attribute requirement expressed by the scenario*			
Architectural Diagram	*Diagram or diagrams of architectural views annotated with architectural information to support the above reasoning, accompanied by explanatory text if desired*			

Figure 3.5 Template for Analysis of an Architectural Approach

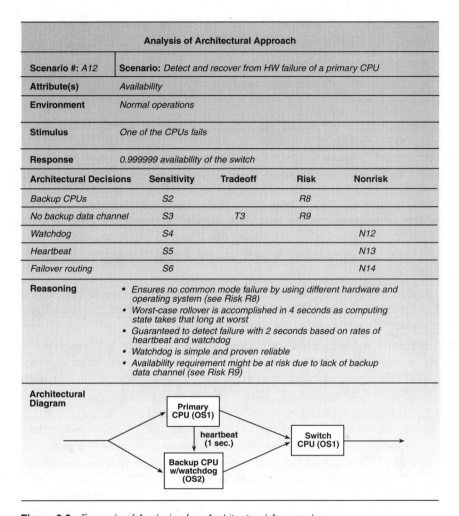

Analysis of Architectural Approach				
Scenario #: *A12*	**Scenario:** *Detect and recover from HW failure of a primary CPU*			
Attribute(s)	*Availability*			
Environment	*Normal operations*			
Stimulus	*One of the CPUs fails*			
Response	*0.999999 availablity of the switch*			
Architectural Decisions	**Sensitivity**	**Tradeoff**	**Risk**	**Nonrisk**
Backup CPUs	*S2*		*R8*	
No backup data channel	*S3*	*T3*	*R9*	
Watchdog	*S4*			*N12*
Heartbeat	*S5*			*N13*
Failover routing	*S6*			*N14*
Reasoning	• *Ensures no common mode failure by using different hardware and operating system (see Risk R8)* • *Worst-case rollover is accomplished in 4 seconds as computing state takes that long at worst* • *Guaranteed to detect failure with 2 seconds based on rates of heartbeat and watchdog* • *Watchdog is simple and proven reliable* • *Availability requirement might be at risk due to lack of backup data channel (see Risk R9)*			
Architectural Diagram				

Figure 3.6 Example of Analysis of an Architectural Approach

At the end of this step, the evaluation team should have a clear picture of the most important aspects of the entire architecture, the rationale for key design decisions that have been made, and a list of risks, nonrisks, sensitivity points, and tradeoff points.

At this point the team can now test its understanding of the architectural representations that have been generated. This is the purpose of the next two steps.

3.2.7 Step 7: Brainstorm and Prioritize Scenarios

Scenarios drive the testing phase of the ATAM. Generating a set of scenarios has proven to be a great facilitator of discussion and brainstorming, when greater numbers of stakeholders (see sidebar Stakeholders) are gathered to participate in the ATAM. Scenarios are used to

- Represent stakeholders' interests
- Understand quality attribute requirements

While utility tree generation is primarily used to understand how the architect perceived and handled quality attribute architectural drivers, the purpose of scenario brainstorming is to take the pulse of the larger stakeholder community. Scenario brainstorming works well in larger groups, creating an atmosphere in which the ideas and thoughts of one person stimulate others. The process fosters communication and creativity and serves to express the collective mind of the participants. The prioritized list of brainstormed scenarios is compared with those generated via the utility tree exercise. If they agree, great. If additional driving scenarios are discovered, this is also an important outcome.

In this step, the evaluation team asks the stakeholders to brainstorm three kinds of scenarios.

1. *Use case scenarios* represent the ways in which the stakeholders expect the system to be used. In use case scenarios the stakeholder is an end user, using the system to execute some function.

2. *Growth scenarios* represent ways in which the architecture is expected to accommodate growth and change in the moderate near term: expected modifications, changes in performance or availability, porting to other platforms, integration with other software, and so forth.

3. *Exploratory scenarios* represent extreme forms of growth, ways in which the architecture might be stressed by changes: dramatic new performance or availability requirements (order-of-magnitude changes, for example), major changes in the infrastructure or mission of the system, and so forth. Whereas growth scenarios provide a way to show the strengths and weaknesses of the architecture with respect to anticipated forces on the system, exploratory scenarios attempt to find more sensitivity and tradeoff points that appear at the stress points of the architecture. The identification of these points helps assess the limits of the system's architecture.

Stakeholders are encouraged to consider scenarios in the utility tree that have not been analyzed; those scenarios are legitimate candidates to put into the brainstorm pool. This gives the stakeholders the opportunity to revisit scenarios from Steps 5 and 6 that they might think received too little attention. This is in keeping with the spirit of Steps 7 and 8 as testing activities.

Once the scenarios have been collected, they must be prioritized. First, stakeholders are asked to merge scenarios that they believe represent the same behavior or quality concern. Then stakeholders vote for the scenarios they think are most important. Each stakeholder is allocated a number of votes equal to 30 percent of the number of scenarios,[2] rounded up. So, for instance, if there were eighteen scenarios collected, each stakeholder would be given six votes. These votes can be allocated in any way that the stakeholder sees fit: all six votes for one scenario, one vote each for six scenarios, or anything in between.

Each stakeholder casts his or her votes publicly; our experience tells us it's more fun that way, and the exercise builds unity among the participants. Once the votes are tallied, the evaluation leader orders the scenarios by vote total and looks for a sharp drop-off in the number of votes. Scenarios "above the line" are adopted and carried forth to subsequent steps. For example, a team might consider only the top five scenarios.

Figure 3.7 shows a few example scenarios from an evaluation of a vehicle dispatching system (only the top five scenarios of the more than thirty collected are shown here), along with their votes.

At this point in an evaluation, we pause and compare the result of scenario prioritization with the results of the utility tree exercise from Step 5 and look for agreement or disagreement. Using group consensus, each high-priority brainstormed scenario is placed into an appropriate leaf node in the utility tree. First, we agree on which quality attributes each scenario is addressing. In Figure 3.8, the highly ranked scenarios from Figure 3.7 are shown along with an indication of the quality attribute or attributes that each scenario affects most heavily; this helps to place the scenarios in appropriate branches of the utility tree.

When a brainstormed scenario is placed into the utility tree, one of three things will happen:

1. The scenario will match and essentially duplicate an already-existing leaf node.

#	Scenario	Votes
4	Dynamically replan a dispatched mission within 10 minutes	28
27	Split the management of a set of vehicles across multiple control sites	26
10	Change vendor analysis tools after mission has commenced without restarting system	23
12	Retarget a collection of diverse vehicles to handle an emergency situation in less than 10 seconds after commands are issued	13
14	Change the data distribution mechanism from CORBA to a new emerging standard with less than six person-months' effort	12

Figure 3.7 Examples of Scenarios with Rankings

---

2. This is a common facilitated brainstorming technique.

Scenario	# Votes	Quality Attributes
4	28	Performance
27	26	Performance, modifiability, availability
10	23	Modifiability
12	13	Performance
14	12	Modifiability

Figure 3.8   Highly Ranked Scenarios with Quality Attribute Annotations

2. The scenario will go into a new leaf node of an existing branch (or, if it addresses more than one quality attribute, it will be placed into the leaves of several branches after rewording to ensure its relevance to each particular quality attribute is clear).

3. The scenario will fit in no branch of the tree because it expresses a quality attribute not previously accounted for.

The first and second cases indicate that the larger stakeholder community was thinking along the same lines as the architect. The third case, however, suggests that the architect may have failed to consider an important quality attribute, and subsequent probing here may produce a risk to document.

From the introduction to this chapter, recall that Step 7 is the first of two so-called testing steps. The utility tree generation and the scenario brainstorming activities reflect the quality attribute goals, but via different elicitation means and from the point of view of different groups of stakeholders. The scenarios elicited in Step 5 are being tested against those representing a larger group of stakeholders.

The architects and key developers created the initial utility tree. The widest possible group of stakeholders is involved in the scenario brainstorming and prioritization. Comparing the highly ranked outputs of both activities often reveals disconnects between what the architects believe to be important system qualities and what the stakeholders as a whole believe to be important. This, by itself, can reveal serious risks in the architecture by highlighting entire areas of concern to which the architects have not attended. Table 3.1 highlights the differences between Step 5 and Step 7.

Before this step, the utility tree was the authoritative repository of all the detailed high-priority quality attribute requirements from all sources. After this step, when the high-priority brainstormed scenarios are reconciled with the utility tree, it still is.

Table 3.1 Utility Trees versus Scenario Brainstorming

	Utility Trees	**Scenario Brainstorming**
Stakeholders	Architects, project leader	All stakeholders
Typical group size	evaluators; 2–3 project personnel	evaluators; 5–10 project-related personnel
Primary goals	Elicit, make concrete, and prioritize the driving quality attribute requirements Provide a focus for the remainder of the evaluation	Foster stakeholder communication to validate quality attribute goals elicited via the utility tree
Approach	General to specific: begin with quality attributes, refine until scenarios emerge	Specific to general: begin with scenarios, then identify quality attributes they express

Stakeholders

A multitude of people have a stake in a system's architecture, and all of them exert whatever influence they can on the architect(s) to make sure that their goals are addressed. The users want a system that is easy to use and has rich functionality. The maintenance organization wants a system that is easy to modify. The developing organization (as represented by management) wants a system that is easy to build and will employ the existing work force to good advantage. The customer (who pays the bill) wants the system to come in on time and within budget.

The architecture is where these concerns converge, and it is the architect who must weigh them carefully and mediate their achievement. It can be a very daunting task.

First of all, many of these concerns are not expressed as actual requirements. Put another way, the requirements specification for a system conveys only a fraction of the constraints that an architecture must satisfy to be acceptable. The model taught in software engineering classes, wherein the requirements document comes sailing through the transom window and lands with a thud on the architect's desk, after which he or she can confidently design the system, is just not true. This model ignores the other stakeholders for the architecture who have concerns beyond the behavior and functionality. They also levy additional goals on the architecture, and although these goals are not quite requirements, the architecture will be as much of a failure if those goals are not met.

For example, the project manager may need to utilize an otherwise-idle staff who are experts in databases and may exert pressure on the architect to include a database in the system. The presence of a recently purchased tool environment, the cost of which the management is eager to justify, exerts pressure to develop with an architectural style that can be easily handled by that environment. The need to conform to new standards, to incorporate new kinds of peripheral devices, to migrate to new versions of the operating system, or to accommodate new functionality are architectural constraints that rarely make it into a requirements document in ways other than the vague and not-very-helpful dictum, "The system shall be easy to change."

And, as we have already seen, none of the concerns expressed as a generic quality (such as "The system shall be easy to use") can stand as the basis for any sort of design decision.

Worse, many of the stakeholders' wants and needs are likely to be in direct conflict with each other. Users' desire for speed may conflict with the maintainers' desire for modifiability, for instance. The architecture serves as the focal point for all of the often-conflicting pressures manifested by the different stakeholders' concerns. All of these wants and desires converge in the architecture, and the architect is often in the position of mediating the conflicts.

Therefore, a critical step of any architecture evaluation is to elicit exactly what the goals for the architecture in fact are, and the stakeholders who own those goals are the ones from whom they are elicited. The requirements specification, if it exists, is but a starting point. The other goals, and the stakeholders who champion them, must be taken into account. This leads to one of the most important principles about architecture evaluation:

Active participation by the architecture's stakeholders is absolutely essential for a high-quality evaluation.

The following table shows some of the architecture's stakeholders who might be involved in an architectural evaluation. Of course, not all are needed for every architecture evaluation; the specific context will determine which are appropriate and which are not.

Of course, it is often impractical to assemble this many people for a two- or three-day meeting. Many of the stakeholders may not even work for the organization in which the architecture is being developed. The goal is to have the important stakeholders' views represented. If, for example, the system is envisioned to have a long lifetime of evolution and modification, then you should recruit people who can speak to the kinds of modifications that the architecture should enable. And not all systems have the same set of stakeholders—perhaps performance is simply not a concern, or there will be no system administrator.

If you cannot assemble all of the architecture's stakeholders, then try to assemble people who can represent them. Having stakeholders missing or

Stakeholders for an Architecture Evaluation

Stakeholder	Definition	Interest
Producers of the System		
Software architect	Person responsible for the architecture of the system and responsible for making tradeoffs among competing quality pressures	Moderation and mediation all of the quality concerns of the other stakeholders
Developer	Coder or designer	Clarity and completeness of architecture description, high cohesion of parts, limited coupling of parts, clear interconnection mechanisms
Maintainer	Person making changes after initial deployment	Maintainability, ability to locate every place in the system that must change in response to a modification
Integrator	Developer responsible for integrating (assembling) the components	Same as developer
Tester	Developer responsible for testing the system	Integrated, consistent error-handling protocols; limited component coupling; high component cohesion; conceptual integrity
Standards expert	Developer responsible for knowing the details of standards (current and future) to which the software must conform	Separation of concerns, modifiability, interoperability
Performance engineer	Person who analyzes system artifacts to see if the system will meet its performance and throughput requirements	Understandability, conceptual integrity, performance, reliability
Security expert	Person responsible for making sure that the system will meet its security requirements	Security
Project manager	Person who allocates resources to teams, is responsible for meeting schedule and budget, interfaces with customer	Clear structuring of architecture to drive team formation, work breakdown structure, milestones and deadlines, etc.

(continued)

Stakeholders for an Architecture Evaluation (*continued*)

Stakeholder	Definition	Interest
Product-line manager or "reuse czar"	Person who has a vision for how this architecture and related assets can be (re-) used to further the developing organization's long-range goals	Reusability, flexibility
Consumers of the System		
Customer	Purchaser of the system	Schedule of completion, overall budget, usefulness of the system, meeting customers' (or market's) expectations
End user	User of the implemented system	Functionality, usability
Application builder (in the case of a product-line architecture)	Person who will take the architecture and any reusable components that exist with it and instantiate them to build a product	Architectural clarity, completeness, simple interaction mechanisms, simple tailoring mechanisms
Mission specialist, mission planner	Representative of the customer who knows how the system is expected to be used to accomplish strategic objectives; has broader perspective than end users alone	Functionality, usability, flexibility
Servicers of the System		
System administrator	Person running the system (if different from user)	Ease in finding the location of problems that may arise
Network administrator	Person administering the network	Network performance, predictability
Service representatives	People who provide support for the use and maintenance of the system in the field	Usability, serviceability, tailorability
Persons Interfacing or Interoperating with the Software		
Representatives of the domain or community	Builders or owners of similar systems or systems with which the subject system is intended to work	Interoperability

Stakeholders for an Architecture Evaluation (*continued*)

Stakeholder	Definition	Interest
System architect	Architect of the entire system; person who makes tradeoff decisions between hardware and software and who selects the hardware environment	Portability, flexibility, performance, efficiency
Device expert	Person who knows the devices with which the software must interface; can predict future trends in hardware technology	Maintainability, performance

represented with low fidelity exposes you to the risk that the architecture will not be analyzed (or will be analyzed with low fidelity) with respect to the missing stakeholders' concerns. The acceptability of that risk to you will determine whether or not you wish to proceed with the evaluation anyway.

The quality of a software architecture evaluation depends in very large part on the quality of the stakeholders whom you are able to assemble for it.

We wish to call out one stakeholder in the preceding in particular: the software architect. The next principle of sound architecture evaluations is this:

Insist on having the architect, or the architecture team, present at the evaluation.

Therefore, whenever crafting the list of stakeholders to be present during an evaluation, make sure the architect is first on the list.

Having the architect present is essential for several reasons. First of all, failure to identify an architect is a sure sign of trouble on a project. Second, an architecture evaluation will likely be the first time that an architect will have the luxury of having all of the stakeholders in the same room at the same time, articulating their goals for the architecture in a facilitated environment. If the architect is not there, the experience will be wasted. Third, the architect will be the one who will take away action items requiring attention in the architectural design. And fourth, somebody has to present the architecture to be evaluated and explain how it will meet the articulated goals. Who better than the architect?

Remember that you need to not just identify the *kinds* of stakeholders who should be present (or represented) but also to identify *names of specific individuals* who will serve the stakeholder roles. You can help the client identify the kinds (using the preceding table), but the client will have to assign names and ensure their participation. If the client cannot identify individuals and vouch for their participation in time for the evaluation, then you should call time-out until he or she can.

—PCC

3.2.8   Step 8: Analyze the Architectural Approaches

After the scenarios have been collected and analyzed, the evaluation team guides the architect in the process of carrying out the highest-ranked scenarios from Step 7 on whatever architectural descriptions have been presented. The architect explains how relevant architectural decisions contribute to realizing the scenario. Ideally this activity is dominated by the architect's explanation of scenarios in terms of previously discussed architectural approaches.

In this step the evaluation team performs the same activities as in Step 6, mapping the highest-ranked newly generated scenarios onto the architectural artifacts thus far uncovered. Assuming Step 7 didn't produce any high-priority scenarios that were not already covered by previous analysis, Step 8 is a testing activity: it is to be hoped that little new information will be uncovered.

3.2.9   Step 9: Present the Results

Finally, the collected information from the ATAM needs to be summarized and presented back to the stakeholders. This presentation typically takes the form of a verbal report accompanied by slides but might, in addition, be accompanied by a more complete written report delivered subsequent to the ATAM. In this presentation the evaluation leader recapitulates the steps of the ATAM and all the information collected in the steps of the method, including the business context, the driving requirements, the constraints, and the architecture. Most important, however, is the set of ATAM outputs:

- The architectural approaches documented
- The set of scenarios and their prioritization
- The set of attribute-based questions
- The utility tree
- The risks discovered
- The nonrisks documented
- The sensitivity points and tradeoff points found

These outputs are all uncovered, publicly captured, and catalogued during the evaluation. But in Step 9, the evaluation team produces an additional output: risk themes. Experience shows that risks can be grouped together based on some common underlying concern or systemic deficiency. For example, a

Sensitivities, Risks, and Nonrisks

The ATAM relies heavily on the identification of sensitivity points and risks in the architecture. It relies on sensitivity points to not only locate potential problems (risks) in the architecture but also to find the *strengths* of the architecture. One aspect of the method that is often overlooked is that we can find nonrisks as well as risks.

Recall that nonrisks, like risks, are related to architectural responses stemming from architectural decisions, based on some assumed stimuli. But with nonrisks we say that the architectural decision is appropriate—the way that the architecture has been designed meets the quality attribute requirements. We want to record this information, as we record information about risks, because if these architectural decisions ever change, we must examine their effect on the nonrisk to see if it still poses no risk. For example, we might choose to store some important shared system information in a flat file located on a centrally accessible server. We know that this poses no risk because the file is small, there are no security concerns associated with accessing the information in the file, and the various programs that need to use it never attempt to access it simultaneously. If any of these assumptions ever changed—for example, if the size of the file grew dramatically, or it began to hold confidential information, or if different programs might contend for exclusive access to the file—then we would have to revisit the architectural decision. Using a flat file might now be a risk.

As we stated in Chapter 2, a sensitivity point is a property of one or more components (and/or component relationships) that is critical for achieving (or failing to achieve) a particular quality attribute response. And as part of an ATAM effort every sensitivity point should be explicitly classified as a risk or a nonrisk, depending upon whether the desired response is achieved or not.

But there are other potential problems that we find during an ATAM exercise, and these can stem from factors beyond just architectural decisions. During the evaluation we might uncover potential problems that are managerial or process-related in nature. We might find supplier-related problems. We might discover that funding is insecure or schedules are unreasonable or that technical decisions are being made for political reasons. These findings are called *issues* and we record those separately (see the Issues sidebar in Chapter 4).

—RK

group of risks about inadequate or out-of-date documentation might be grouped into a risk theme stating that documentation is given insufficient consideration. A group of risks about the system's inability to function in the face of various kinds of hardware and/or software failures might lead to a risk theme about insufficient attention paid to backup capability or provision of high availability. For each risk theme, the evaluation team identifies which of the business drivers listed in Step 2 are affected. Identifying risk themes and then relating them to specific drivers precipitates two effects. First, it brings the evaluation full circle by relating the final results to the initial presentation. This provides a satisfying closure to the exercise. Second, it elevates the risks that were uncovered to the attention of management. What might otherwise have seemed to a manager like an esoteric technical issue is now identified unambiguously as a threat to something that manager cares about.

Because the evaluation team is systematically working through and trying to understand the architectural approaches, it is inevitable that, at times, the evaluation team sometimes makes recommendations on how the architecture might have been designed or analyzed differently. These mitigation strategies may be process related (for example, a database administrator stakeholder should be consulted before completing the design of the system administration user interface), they may be managerial (for example, three subgroups within the development effort are pursuing highly similar goals and these should be merged), or they may be technical (for example, given the estimated distribution of customer input requests, additional server threads need to be allocated to ensure that worst-case latency does not exceed five seconds). However, offering mitigation strategies is not an integral part of the ATAM. The ATAM is about locating architectural risks. Addressing them may be done in any number of ways.

Table 3.2 summarizes the nine steps of the ATAM and shows how each step contributes to the outputs that the ATAM delivers after an evaluation.

3.3 The Phases of the ATAM

Up to this point we have enumerated and described the steps of the ATAM. In this section we describe how the steps of the ATAM are carried out over time. The ATAM comprises four phases, corresponding to segments of time when major activities occur.

Phase 0 is a setup phase in which the evaluation team is created and a partnership is formed between the evaluation organization and the organization whose architecture is to be evaluated. Phase 1 and Phase 2, the evaluation phases of the ATAM, comprise the nine steps presented so far in this chapter. Phase 1 is architecture-centric and concentrates on eliciting architectural information and analyzing it. Phase 2 is stakeholder-centric and concentrates on eliciting stakeholder points of view and verifying the results of the first phase. Phase 3 is a follow-up phase in which a final report is produced, follow-on actions (if any) are planned, and the evaluation organization updates its archives and experience base.

The four phases are detailed next.

Table 3.2   Steps and Outputs of the ATAM, Correlated

Outputs of the ATAM:

Steps of ATAM:	Prioritized Statement of Quality Attribute Requirements.	Catalog of Architectural Approaches Used	Approach- and Quality-Attribute-Specific Analysis Questions	Mapping of Architectural Approaches to Quality Attributes	Risks and Nonrisks	Sensitivity and Tradeoff Points
1. Present the ATAM						
2. Present business drivers	*a				*b	
3. Present architecture		**			*c	*d
4. Identify architectural approaches		**	**		*e	*f
5. Generate quality attribute utility tree	**					
6. Analyze architectural approaches		*g	**	**	**	**
7. Brainstorm and prioritize scenarios	**					
8. Analyze architectural approaches		*g	**	**	**	**
9. Present results						

Key: ** = the step is a primary contributor to the output; * = the step is a secondary contributor.

a. The business drivers include the first, coarse description of the quality attributes.
b. The business drivers presentation might disclose an already-identified or long-standing risk which should be captured.
c. The architect may identify a risk in his or her presentation.
d. The architect may identify a sensitivity or tradeoff point in his or her presentation.
e. Many architectural approaches have standard risks associated with them.
f. Many architectural approaches have standard sensitivities and quality attribute tradeoffs associated with them.
g. The analysis steps might reveal one or more architectural approaches not identified in Step 4, which will then produce new approach-specific questions.

3.3.1   Phase 0 Activities

Phases 1 and 2 of the ATAM are where the analysis takes place and so are considered the "heart" of the method. But before Phase 1 can begin, a partnership must be established between the sponsor of the evaluation and the organization carrying it out. A statement of work must be signed and agreements arranged about times, dates, costs, and disposition of work. The evaluation team must be formed. This is the purpose of Phase 0.

Phase 0 includes all the groundwork that must be laid before an architecture evaluation can begin. Properly executed groundwork will ensure that the exercise will be a success. When the preparation phase is completed, you should be ready to begin the evaluation exercise with confidence that your client will understand what is involved, that the necessary resources will be at hand, and that the goals and outcomes of the evaluation are clear to all parties.

Phase 0 consists of two parts: establishing a partnership with the client and preparation for the evaluation phases.

Partnership

Phase 0 involves communication with the person(s) who commissioned the evaluation, whom we will refer to as the *client*. How you and the client make initial contact is beyond the scope of this book, as are any arrangement made concerning compensation for the work performed. Whatever the circumstances, we assume that you and the client have conversed about the possibility of performing an architecture evaluation. Now is the time to solidify the agreement.

The client needs to be someone who can exercise control over the project whose architecture is the subject of evaluation. Perhaps the client is a manager of the project. Or perhaps the client is someone in an organization who is acquiring a system based on the architecture. If the acquisition is a major one, the developing organization may well agree to having its architecture evaluated by outsiders. The client may or may not work for the same organization as the acquirer. In any case, it is assumed that the client has enough leverage to cause the development project to take the necessary time out so that the architecture can undergo the evaluation. It is also assumed that the client has access to a broad selection of stakeholders for the architecture.

The following issues must be resolved before the client gives the go-ahead for the evaluation to take place.

1. The client should have a basic understanding of the evaluation method and the process that will be followed. This can be handled by a briefing or by a written description of the method. This book is also a definitive source of information but may contain more than your client wishes to know. It is a good idea to make a videotape of a method briefing to give to prospective clients.

2. The client should describe the system and architecture being evaluated. This enables the evaluation leader to decide whether or not there is enough material present—that is, whether the architecture is far enough along—so that an ATAM-based evaluation will be useful. At this point, the evaluation leader will have to make a "go/no-go" decision.

3. Assuming the decision is "go," a contract or statement of work should be negotiated and signed. This lets both sides make sure that the following issues are understood:
   - Who is responsible for providing the necessary resources (such as supplies, facilities, a location, the attendance of stakeholders, the presence of the architect and other project representatives, and so on) for the evaluation
   - What is the period of performance for the evaluation a window in which the evaluation will be carried out
   - To whom will the final report be delivered and by when
   - What is the team's availability (or nonavailability) for follow-up work

4. Issues of proprietary information should be resolved. For example, the evaluation team might need to sign nondisclosure statements.

The negotiation phase is also a good time to talk to the client about the costs and benefits of architecture evaluation. Perhaps by the time the client has come to you, he or she already believes in the intrinsic value of the activity, but one of the goals of the premeeting is to share with the client any data you have about past benefits so that the client will feel confident about proceeding. Also, the client and the architect may belong to a different organization (such as when the client is acquiring the architecture from a separate development organization), in which case the client may be convinced of the value of the evaluation, but the architect and his or her organization may not be. Arming the client with cost/benefit data will help convince the developers of the value.

To increase client buy-in, you can do the following:

- Share with your client cost data and associated benefits from public sources, such as this book, and your own data from previous evaluations.
- As your repository of evaluations grows, share the (sanitized) comments about benefits with the client. Add them to your method overview presentation.
- Cite any instances you can of one organization asking for multiple evaluations.

Preparation

The preparation half of Phase 0 consists of

- Forming the evaluation team
- Holding an evaluation team kickoff meeting
- Making the necessary preparations for Phase 1

If your organization does not have a standing evaluation team, then you will have to form one. This means choosing individuals to take part in the exercise. Finding the individuals, scheduling their time, and clearing their participation with their respective supervisors are all part of forming the team.

Once you have assembled a team (or even if you have a standing team) you will need to assign each member a role in the upcoming evaluation. It is always a good idea to rotate the roles among team members from exercise to exercise; this way there are more people available to perform any given role in the event of a personnel shortage. The table below defines those roles and responsibilities for an architecture evaluation using the ATAM.

There is not necessarily a one-to-one correspondence between people and roles: a person may assume more than one role, or more than one person may

Table 3.3   Evaluation Team Individual Roles and Responsibilities

Role	Responsibilities	Desirable Characteristics
Team leader	Sets up the evaluation; coordinates with client; makes sure client's needs are met; establishes evaluation contract. Forms the evaluation team. In charge of seeing that final report is produced and delivered (although the writing may be delegated).	Well-organized, with managerial skills. Good at interacting with client. Able to meet deadlines.
Evaluation leader	Runs evaluation. Facilitates elicitation of scenarios; administers scenario selection/prioritization process; facilitates evaluation of scenarios against architecture. Facilitates on-site analysis.	Comfortable in front of an audience. Excellent facilitation skills. Good understanding of architectural issues. Practiced in architecture evaluations. Able to tell when protracted discussion is leading to a valuable discovery, or when it is pointless and should be redirected.
Scenario scribe	Writes scenarios on flip chart or whiteboard during scenario elicitation process. Carefully captures agreed-upon wording of each scenario and doesn't let discussion continue until exact wording is captured.	Good handwriting. Willingness to be a stickler about not moving on before an idea (a scenario) is captured. Able to quickly absorb and distill the essence of technical discussions.
Proceedings scribe	Captures the proceedings in electronic form on a laptop computer or in-room workstation. Captures the raw scenarios. Captures the issue(s) that motivated each scenario, as this is often lost in the wording of the scenario itself. Captures the resolution of each scenario when applied to architecture(s). Generates a printed list of adopted scenarios for hand-out to all participants.	Good, fast typist. Well-organized to allow rapid recall of information. Good understanding of architectural issues. Able to assimilate technical issues quickly. Must not be afraid to interrupt the flow of discussion (at opportune times) to test understanding of an issue, so that the appropriate information is captured.

(continued)

Table 3.3 Evaluation Team Individual Roles and Responsibilities (*continued*)

Role	Responsibilities	Desirable Characteristics
Timekeeper	Helps the evaluation leader stay on schedule. Helps control amount of time devoted to each scenario during evaluation phase.	Willingness to brazenly interrupt discussion to call time.
Process observer	Keeps notes on where the evaluation process itself could be improved or deviated from the plan. Usually a silent observer, but may make process-based suggestions to the evaluation leader, discretely, during the evaluation. After evaluation, reports on how the process went and what lessons were learned for future improvement. Also responsible for reporting experience to architecture evaluation team at large.	Thoughtful observer. Knowledgeable in the evaluation process. Should have previous experience in the architecture evaluation method.
Process enforcer	Helps the evaluation leader remember and carry out the steps of the evaluation method.	Should be fluent in the steps of the method. Willing and able to provide guidance to the evaluation leader in a discrete manner.
Questioner	Raises issues of architectural interest that perhaps the stakeholders have not considered.	Good architectural insights; good insights into needs of stakeholders. Experience with systems in similar domain. Not afraid to bring up possibly contentious issues and pursue them doggedly. Familiarity with attributes of concern.

collectively carry out a role. It is up to the evaluation team leader to assign people to roles (and roles to people). These rules of thumb may help.

- The minimum complement for an evaluation team should be four people.
- One person can usually carry out the process observer, timekeeper, and questioner roles simultaneously.
- The team leader's responsibilities occur primarily outside the evaluation exercise; hence, that person can double up on any other in-exercise role. The team leader is often the evaluation leader, because both tend to be senior people, but not always.

- Questioners should be chosen so that the appropriate spectrum of expertise in qualities of interest (performance, reliability, maintainability, and so on) can be brought to bear on the system being evaluated.

In Chapter 10, we will discuss setting up a standing evaluation team in which individuals are rotated on and off and trained so as to spread the expertise throughout the organization. This practice has many organizational benefits and is a major step in adopting mature architecture-based development processes within an organization. But more to the immediate point, it obviates the problem of recruiting individuals willing to serve on the team: the team is already formed.

After the team is formed, a kickoff meeting should be held in which all available knowledge about the evaluation should be shared and team roles assigned. Preparations for Phase 1 include taking care of the myriad logistical details to assure that everyone shows up at the right time and place prepared to work—this means the project's representatives in addition to the evaluation team.

3.3.2 Phase 1 Activities

In Phase 1, the ATAM team meets with a subset of the team whose architecture is being evaluated, perhaps for the first time. This meeting has two concerns: organization of the rest of the analysis activities and information collection. Organizationally, the manager of the architecture team needs to make sure that the right people attend the subsequent meetings, that people are prepared, and that they come with the right attitude—a spirit of nonadversarial teamwork.

With a small group of key people, Phase 1 concentrates on Steps 1 through 6. The evaluation team presents the ATAM method; a spokesperson for the project presents the business drivers; the architect presents the architecture. The group catalogs architectural approaches and builds the utility tree. The high-priority utility tree scenarios then form the basis for analysis.

Besides carrying out the six steps, the evaluation team has another purpose to fulfill during Phase 1. It needs to gather as much information as possible to determine

- Whether the remainder of the evaluation is feasible and should proceed. If not, then Phase 1 is an opportune cutoff point, before the larger group of stakeholders is assembled for Phase 2.
- Whether more architectural documentation is required and, if so, precisely what kinds of documentation and how it should be represented. If this is the case, the evaluation team can work with the architecture team during the hiatus between Phase 1 and Phase 2 to help them "catch up" so that Phase 2 can begin on a complete note.
- Which stakeholders should be present for Phase 2. An action item at the end of Phase 1 is for the evaluation's sponsor to make sure that the right stakeholders assemble for Phase 2. (See the Stakeholders sidebar on page 63.)

There is a hiatus between Phase 1 and Phase 2 in which ongoing discovery and analysis are performed by the architecture team, in collaboration with the evaluation team. As we described earlier, the evaluation team does not build detailed analytic models during this phase, but they do build rudimentary models that will give the evaluators and the architect sufficient insight into the architecture to make the Phase 2 meeting more productive. Also, during this hiatus the final composition of the evaluation team is determined, according to the needs of the evaluation, availability of human resources, and the schedule. For example, if the system being evaluated is safety critical, a safety expert might be recruited, or if it is database-centric, an expert in database design could be recruited to be part of the evaluation team.

3.3.3 Phase 2 Activities

At this point, the evaluation team will have understanding of the architecture in sufficient detail to support verification of the analysis already performed and further analysis as needed. The appropriate stakeholders have been identified and have been given advance reading materials such as a description of the ATAM, perhaps some scenario examples, and system documentation including the architecture, business case, and key requirements. These reading materials aid in ensuring that the stakeholders know what to expect from the ATAM. Now the stakeholders are gathered for Phase 2, which can involve as few as 3 to 5 stakeholders or as many as 40.[3]

Since there will be a broader set of stakeholders attending Phase 2 and since a number of days or weeks may have transpired between the first and second meetings, Phase 2 begins with an encore of Step 1: Present the ATAM. After that, Steps 2 through 6 from Phase 1 are recapped for the new stakeholders. Then the evaluation proceeds by carrying out Steps 7, 8, and 9.

Table 3.4 lists the steps and typical categories of attendees for Phase 1 and Phase 2.

A Typical ATAM Agenda for Phase 1 and Phase 2

In Figure 3.9 we show an example of a typical ATAM agenda for Phases 1 and 2. Each activity in this figure is followed by its step number, where appropriate, in parentheses. While the times here need not be slavishly followed, this schedule represents a reasonable partitioning of the available time in that it allows more time on those activities that experience has shown to produce more results (in terms of finding architectural risks).

---

3. Strive for about 10–15 stakeholders. A much larger crowd than that is feasible but will require excellent facilitation skills on the part of the evaluation leader and more time than is shown in the sample agenda in Figure 3.9.

Table 3.4 ATAM Steps Associated with Stakeholder Groups

Step	Activity	Participants for Phase 1	Participants for Phase 2
1	Present the ATAM	Evaluation team and project decision makers	Evaluation team, project decision makers, and all stakeholders
2	Present business drivers		
3	Present architecture		
4	Identify architectural approaches		
5	Generate quality attribute utility tree		
6	Analyze architectural approaches		
7	Brainstorm and prioritize scenarios	N/A	
8	Analyze architectural approaches		
9	Present results		

3.3.4 Phase 3 Activities

On the back end of the ATAM, the final report (if called for by the agreement between the evaluation organization and the evaluation client) must be written and delivered. But equally important from the point of view of maintaining an ATAM capability, repositories of artifacts must be updated, surveys and effort measures taken, and the evaluation team debriefed to try to identify ways in which the method could be improved. Phase 3 is the follow-up phase.

In Phase 3, the following tasks must be accomplished:

1. Produce the final report.
2. Collect data for measurement and process improvement.
3. Update the artifact repositories.

Producing the Final Report

If the contract with the client includes a written final report, it is produced during Phase 3. Producing the final report is a matter of cataloging (a) what you did, (b) what you found, and (c) what you concluded. By using a standard report template (such as the one outlined on page 203 in Chapter 6) and assigning responsibility for specific sections to team members at the start of the evaluation, writing the report can be accomplished quickly and efficiently.

Start	Activity	
8:30 am	Introductions/ATAM Presentation (Step 1)	
10:00	Present Business Drivers (Step 2)	
10:45	Break	
11:00	Present Architecture (Step 3)	
12:00	Identify Architectural Approaches (Step 4)	
12:30 pm	Lunch	**Phase 1**
1:45	Generate Quality Attribute Utility Tree (Step 5)	
2:45	Analyze Architectural Approaches (Step 6)	
3:45	Break	
4:00	Analyze Architectural Approaches (Step 6)	
5:00 pm	Adjourn	

Hiatus

Day 1		
8:30 am	Introductions/ATAM Presentation (Step 1)	
9:15	Present Business Drivers (Step 2)	
10:00	Break	
10:15	Present Architecture (Step 3)	
11:15	Identify Architectural Approaches (Step 4)	
12:00	Lunch	
1:00 pm	Generate Quality Attribute Utility Tree (Step 5)	
2:00	Analyze Architectural Approaches (Step 6)	
3:30	Break	
3:45	Analyze Architectural Approaches (Step 6)	
5:00 pm	Adjourn for the Day	
Day 2		**Phase 2**
8:30 am	Introductions/Recap ATAM	
8:45	Analyze Architectural Approaches (Step 6)	
9:30	Brainstorm Scenarios (Step 7)	
10:30	Break	
10:45	Prioritize Scenarios (Step 7)	
11:15	Analyze Architectural Approaches (Step 8)	
12:30 pm	Lunch	
1:30	Analyze Architectural Approaches (Step 8)	
2:45	Prepare Presentation of Results/Break	
3:30	Present Results (Step 9)	
5:00 pm	Adjourn	

Figure 3.9 A Sample ATAM Agenda for Phases 1 and 2

The Two Faces of the ATAM

The Strength of Scenarios

The predecessor of the ATAM is the SAAM (Software Architecture Analysis Method), which you will read about in Chapter 7. For a long while I thought SAAM was short for Scenario-based Architecture Analysis Method. It could have been, since scenarios are the root of its success.

The SAAM involves facilitating a scenario brainstorming session to generate a list of scenarios. A subset of the scenarios is then used to illuminate the architecture by identifying the components that would be involved if the architecture were actually able to execute the scenario. If the architecture cannot support the scenario, the exercise determines which components will have to change in order to execute the scenario. Some informal analysis is also performed, for example, by looking for components that are involved in "executing" many disparate scenarios but perhaps shouldn't be.

The SAAM is a successful method primarily for two reasons:

1. The brainstorming and prioritization of scenarios generally foster a level of stakeholder interaction and cooperative creative thinking that has never occurred before.

2. The generated collection of scenarios often is the best representation of system requirements that the stakeholders have seen up to that point.

The participating stakeholders generally feel that they learn something about the architecture and possibly each other. Moreover, in many cases, a SAAM-based evaluation is the first time that all of the stakeholders are assembled in the same place at the same time.

Clearly these were benefits that we wanted to retain when creating the ATAM. One of the faces of the ATAM is, in effect, the SAAM.

Putting "Analysis" in the Analysis Method

When we set out to create the ATAM, one of our goals was to strengthen the "analysis" aspect of the software evaluation. In fact, my attitude (despite the success of the SAAM) was that the ATAM should be predominantly about analysis and that scenario generation and stakeholder interaction was too touchy-feely. The real benefits accrue when you collect hard-core architecture data (process execution times, process priorities, details of encryption strategy, estimates of component failure rates, places where coupling between components is too strong, etc.) and then use some analytic methods to draw some firm engineering conclusions.

I then participated in my first ATAM-based evaluation exercise. Many stakeholders were present, but one "participant" was conspicuously absent: the architecture. However, what I found to be most amazing was that nobody seemed to miss it. Despite the absence of hard-core architectural information, we successfully executed the ATAM and the customer derived significant benefits from the experience. The participants felt that the discussion generated as a result of brainstorming scenarios and subsequently recalling (and sometimes creating) the architecture in real time was very valuable. Once again, scenarios carried the day. We had actually carried out a multi-attribute SAAM-based evaluation exercise under the guise of the ATAM.

Well, I became a believer in scenarios. However, the ATAM team still felt that the analysis aspects of the ATAM could and should be strengthened, but we needed additional methodological machinery that would enable us to carry out analysis in real time in the presence of many stakeholders.

Our solution was to incorporate the concept of architectural approaches (as discussed in Chapter 1) into the ATAM. The core of the idea was that approaches or patterns would be helpful in illuminating the "shape" of the architecture, whereas scenarios illuminated only selected paths through the architecture. We felt that understanding the shape (or shapes) of the architecture would be very helpful in analyzing its properties since different approaches are important for achieving different attribute-specific requirements. The new and improved method would work something like this:

- Identify the attributes that are key to the success of the system (using utility trees).
- Determine the architectural approaches that are used within the architecture to meet those attribute requirements.
- Ask attribute-specific questions (derived from the various attribute characterizations) to understand the extent to which those approaches are suitable for meeting the attribute-specific requirements.

Armed with our new methodological machinery, we tried out our new version of the ATAM. It proved to be somewhat successful. We found some approaches and many risks, but the analysis that we performed was cursory at best. Moreover, some of the stakeholders were confused, asking questions like:

- "What's an architectural approach and how do I go about finding one?"
- "Is portability an aspect of modifiability?"
- "Why don't we add manageability to the utility tree?"

Some of our other observations were:

- When generating the utility tree we found that the most vocal folks dominated the discussion.
- No one quite understood attribute-specific questions, so we ended up generating most of those ourselves.

- It wasn't clear why we needed both utility trees and scenarios. They seemed redundant.

This mode of operation was not amenable to large-group interaction and required more up-front preparation. It seemed better suited for a smaller group centered around the architects. Even with a more robust set of steps in our method, eliciting detailed architectural information and carrying out analysis in real time in the presence of many stakeholders was inherently awkward and difficult.

Two Faces Are Better Than One

We needed a new mode of interaction but didn't want to sacrifice the benefits of the old mode. That's when we decided that two faces are better than one. The same set of steps can be used at different times with different emphases. One face is very much architecture-centric and concentrates on eliciting architecture information and analyzing the architecture. The second face is very much stakeholder-centric and concentrates on eliciting stakeholder points of view and verifying the results of the first phase. These two modes of interaction are compared in the following table.

Two Faces of the ATAM

Face 1 for Phase 1	Face 2 for Phase 2
Few stakeholders (2–4)	Many stakeholders (10–15)
Architecture-centric	Stakeholder-centric
Solution-oriented	Problem-oriented
Analysis-oriented	Verification-oriented
Fosters an understanding of architecture	Fosters stakeholder interaction
Scenarios primarily used in creating utility tree	Scenarios primarily used to verify utility tree
High bandwidth, informal technical conversations	Organized meeting

—MHK

Collecting Data

Each evaluation provides a convenient, inexpensive opportunity to collect data so that you can improve your ideas about the costs and benefits of performing evaluations, and also to collect participants' impressions about what worked particularly well and what could stand to be improved.

Data comes from two sources: the evaluation team and the client. In both cases, you should collect improvement data (ideas about what worked particularly well and what could have been improved) and cost/benefit data. The client may not recognize benefits until well after the evaluation, so we recommend a follow-up survey to be taken about six months after the evaluation to gauge the longer-term effects.

We recommend sending out five short surveys:

1. An improvement survey to the participants, asking their impressions of the evaluation exercise
2. An improvement survey to the team members, asking for their impressions of the exercise
3. A cost survey to the client
4. A cost survey to the evaluation team
5. A long-term benefits survey to the client

It will help to categorize the cost data in terms of before-exercise activities, during-exercise activities, and post-exercise activities. Examples for many of these surveys may be found in Chapter 10.

Updating the Artifact Repositories

You should maintain repositories of the artifacts you used or produced during each previous evaluation. These will serve you during future evaluations.

In addition to recording the cost and benefit information, store the scenarios that you produced. If future systems that you evaluate are similar in nature, you will probably find that the scenarios that express the architecture's requirements will converge into a uniform set. This gives you a powerful opportunity to streamline the evaluation method: you can dispense with the scenario brainstorming and prioritization steps of the ATAM altogether and simply use the standard scenario set for your domain. The scenarios have in some sense graduated to become a checklist, and checklists are extremely useful because each architect in the developing organization can keep a copy of the checklist in his or her desk drawer and make sure the architecture passes with respect to it. Then an evaluation becomes more of a confirmation exercise than an investigatory one. Stakeholders' involvement becomes minimal—as long as you have confidence in the applicability and completeness of the checklist with respect to the new system under evaluation—thus reducing the expense of the evaluation still further.

Besides the scenarios, make a list of the analysis questions you used; these are the evaluation team's best tools, and growing your toolbox will make future evaluations easier and give you something to show to newly added team members as part of their training.

Add participants' comments to a repository as well. Future evaluation leaders can read through these and gain valuable insights into the details and idiosyncrasies of past evaluations. These exercise summaries provide excellent training material for new evaluation leaders.

Finally, keep a copy of the final report, sanitized if necessary to avoid identifying the system or cleansed of incriminating remarks. Future evaluation teams will appreciate having a template to use for the reports they produce.

3.4 For Further Reading

As this book was going to press, an initial draft of a training course on the ATAM was being alpha-tested. You can watch for details at the SEI's architecture tradeoff analysis Web site [SEI ATA].

The ATAM's analysis steps are based on questions about architectural approaches and quality attributes. The former come from descriptions of architectural styles in books [Bass 98, Shaw 96, Buschmann 96, Schmidt 00], and those chapters of Smith and Williams that deal with architecting performance-critical systems [Smith 01]. Quality attribute questions come from resources on performance evaluation [Klein 93, Smith 01], Markov modeling for availability [Iannino 94], fault tolerance [Jalote 94], reliability [Lyu 96], security [SEI NSS], and inspection and review methods (such as the SAAM, described in Chapter 7) for modifiability.

To read an interesting treatment of quality attribute requirements and their relationship to design decisions, see Chung et al. [Chung 00]. They refer to an early paper by Boehm et al. [Boehm 76] that presents a tree of software quality characteristics very similar to the utility trees presented in this chapter.

3.5 Discussion Questions

1. Prepare a short, informal presentation on the ATAM and present it to your colleagues.

2. Think of a software system in your organization whose architecture is of some interest. Prepare a presentation of the business drivers for this system, using the template given in this chapter.

3. What do you suppose the quality attributes of interest are for this system? Sketch a utility tree for the system. For each quality attribute of interest, write a refinement of it, and then write a scenario or two that make the concern concrete.

4. If you were going to evaluate the architecture for this system, who would you want to participate? What are the stakeholder roles associated with this system, and who could you get to represent those roles?

5. For each stakeholder role you identified, write a couple of scenarios that represent that role's point of view of the system.

6. How do the quality-attribute-focused scenarios you wrote for question 3 compare with the stakeholder-role-focused scenarios you wrote for question 5? Do they cover the same or different issues?

7. Pick a few of the scenarios you wrote for question 5 and try to understand how the architecture you've selected would respond to them. Use the analysis template given in this chapter.

8. Think of a system in your organization that is not yet ready for an architecture evaluation. What is it about the system that made you choose it? Can you generalize your answer to establish criteria for whether or not a project is ready for an architecture evaluation?

4

The Battlefield Control System—The First Case Study in Applying the ATAM

Example isn't another way to teach, it is the only way to teach.
—attributed to Albert Einstein

We now present a brief example of using the ATAM as it was realized in a real evaluation. Although some of the details have been changed for pedagogical reasons and to protect the identity and intellectual property of the client and developing organization, the architectural risks that we uncovered are not materially affected by these changes.

We call the evaluated system the Battlefield Control System (BCS). This system is to be used by army battalions to control the movement, strategy, and operations of troops in real time in the battlefield. This system is currently being built by a contractor, based upon government-furnished requirements.

In describing the BCS evaluation, we do not describe every detail of every step of the method. This is a simple first case study to familiarize you with the ATAM; to get the "big picture." In this case study we concentrate on the major activities of Phase 1 and Phase 2 and only briefly mention the activities in the other phases. We present a more thorough case study in Chapter 6.

4.1 Preparation

The story begins at Phase 0. Once we had agreed to perform an evaluation using the ATAM on the BCS, we arranged a meeting of the evaluation team leader, the key customer representatives, and the contractor's architects.

In this meeting the contractor presented the architecture, and the contractor and customer together described their initial quality attribute requirements and their initial set of scenarios. As a result of this meeting additional architectural documentation was requested. As is often the case when evaluating architectures, the initial documentation that was produced was far too vague and limited in scope to support any analysis. The documentation consisted of high-level data flows and divisions of functionality that had no clear mapping to software constructs. There was no discussion of architectural approaches in the provided documentation.

Owing to the paucity of available architectural information, we created an action plan to improve the architectural documentation for use in Phases 1 and 2. We requested specific additional architectural information to address the gaps in the documentation produced by the contractor. These requests were in the form of questions such as

- What is the structure of the message-handling software, that is, how is the functionality allocated to modules, functions, APIs (application program interface), layers, and so on?

- What facilities exist in the software architecture (if any) for self-testing and monitoring of software components?

- What facilities exist in the software architecture (if any) for redundancy, liveness monitoring, and failover? How is data consistency maintained so that one component can take over from another and be sure that it is in a consistent state with the failed component?

- What is the process and/or task view of the system, including mapping of these processes/tasks to hardware and the communication mechanisms between them?

- What functional dependencies exist among the software components? (This is often called a *uses* view.)

- What data is kept in the database? How big is it, how much does it change, and who reads/writes it?

- What are the anticipated frequency and volume of data being transmitted among the system components?

Between Phases 0 and 1 of the evaluation the contractor answered many of these questions and produced substantially more complete, more analyzable architectural documentation. This documentation formed the basis for the remainder of the evaluation.

4.2 Phase 1

4.2.1 Step 1: Present the ATAM

During this meeting we presented the ATAM to a large group of assembled stakeholders. They were then given time to ask any questions about the method, its outcomes, and its goals.

4.2.2 Step 2: Present the Business Drivers

The customer, in turn, presented the business drivers. The customer's business drivers were dominated by information on the sorts of battlefield missions that this system was to aid in fulfilling and the specific requirements of such missions. For example, the requirements state that the system supports a Commander node that commands a set of Soldier nodes and their equipment, including many different kinds of weapons and sensors. The system needs to interface with numerous other systems (such as command and control systems) that feed it commands and intelligence information. These external systems also periodically collect the BCS system's status with respect to its current missions. The business driver presentation also outlined a set of requirements (constraints, really) with respect to a standard set of hardware and software that was to be employed: the need for extreme levels of physical robustness, the need to adapt to frequent changes in message formats from the other systems with which it interacts, and a number of performance goals.

4.2.3 Step 3: Present the Architecture

Next, the contractor presented the architecture, and the contractor and customer together described their initial driving quality attribute requirements and their initial set of scenarios. The architectural documentation covered several different views of the system: a dynamic view, showing how subsystems communicated; a set of message sequence charts, showing run-time interactions; a system view, showing how software was allocated to hardware; and a source view, showing how subsystems were composed of objects. For the purpose of this example, we show just the highest-level hardware structure of the architecture.

This hardware architecture, shown in Figure 4.1, illustrates that the Commander node is central to the system. In fact, the Commander node acts as a server and the Soldier nodes are its clients, making requests of it and updating the server's database with their status. Internode communication between the clients and the server is only through encrypted messages sent via a radio modem. The radio modem uses a shared communication channel: only one node can be broadcasting at any moment.

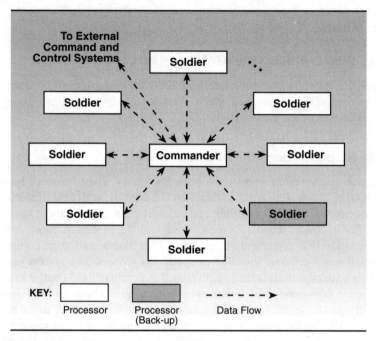

Figure 4.1   Hardware View of the BCS

4.2.4   Step 4: Identify the Architectural Approaches

We then elicited information on the architectural approaches. The architects presented approaches that were primarily aimed at addressing the modifiability, availability, and performance goals of the system. As stated above, the system was loosely organized around the notion of clients and servers. This dictated both the hardware architecture and the process architecture and affected the system's performance characteristics, as we shall see. In addition to this approach:

- A backup commander approach was described (which addressed meeting the system's availability requirements).
- A set of domain-specific design patterns were described (which were aimed at meeting the system's modifiability goals).
- An independent communicating components approach was described (which was supposed to support the system's performance goals).

Each of these approaches was probed for risks, sensitivities, and tradeoffs via our attribute-specific questions.

Issues

Architecture evaluations sometimes take on the air of a full-fledged project review. Stakeholders, God bless 'em, are not going to pass up the opportunity to air a concern of theirs in a room full of people with a vested interest in the system—potential allies in their cause—no matter whether or not that concern has anything to do with the architecture. Here are, after all, people with the power to change something about the system that the stakeholder doesn't like. And so, quite often, the ATAM facilitator is thrust into the position of facilitating a discussion that doesn't have very much to do with the architecture of the system per se.

What should happen at this point? The facilitator should steer the discussion back to architecture in no uncertain terms, that's what. But there's a way to do this that will let the person voicing the concern feel like he or she has been heard: record the complaint as an *issue* and make the list of issues part of the final report.

As an architecture evaluation proceeds, many things are recorded: the architecture that is presented, the scenarios that the stakeholders brainstorm, and the sensitivity and tradeoff points discovered during the course of analysis. Issues are usually none of these. Consider the following situation.

- A major university was buying a large financial management system and used an architecture evaluation of competing vendors' systems as a way to make an acquisition decision. Many of the stakeholders present were people who were going to use the new system. Their management had not gone out of its way to include them in the acquisition process, so they had very little idea about what capabilities either of the two competing systems would provide. That is, they didn't know if the new system would let them do their jobs. As a result, practically every scenario that they proposed was a use case, proposed as a way of asking the vendors exactly what their system did (and not as a way to discover its architecture). We finally recorded their concern as an issue, after which the brainstormed scenarios came to look much more architectural in nature.

- An architecture evaluation for an embedded vehicle control system came grinding to a halt because stakeholders kept proposing scenarios such as, "The system is developed with as few defects and as quickly as possible." They were voicing a concern about the lack of a mature development process in their organization. We recorded it as an issue and flagged it for management attention. After that, the scenarios they suggested were, again, much more about the architecture.

> • An architecture evaluation for a real-time, data-intensive command and control system was held up while a stakeholder argued that the architect had not availed himself of the latest academic results in the realm of real-time, object-oriented databases and was thus complicating the design by inserting a homegrown solution to an already-solved problem. The architect countered by essentially arguing that "academic" was a euphemism for "doesn't really work." By recording this as an issue, we were able to move on.
>
> Every evaluation is different, but one constant is that stakeholders will not be shy about using their "air time" to bring up whatever it is that they're worried about. And that's all right—one dedicated but off-the-wall stakeholder is better than any number of apathetic ones. The quality of any architecture evaluation depends upon how vested the stakeholders are in the process, so it's worth something to keep them tuned in. Recording off-the-subject issues lets the stakeholder feel heard, and listing the issues in the report brings them to the attention of management. If you don't record them, you're likely to have to deal with the same issue again and again until the stakeholder is satisfied some other way. Recording issues is cheap, it brings closure quickly, and it's the least confrontational way to bring a wandering stakeholder back in line.
>
> *—PCC*

4.2.5   Step 5: Generate the Quality Attribute Utility Tree

The stakeholders in this evaluation initially claimed that they were most interested in modifiability and performance. These were their greatest concerns when we began the exercise, as defined by their business drivers. Upon probing, however, they admitted that availability was also of great importance to them. This is a commonly seen benefit of the utility tree elicitation exercise: the issues that arise are often at odds with the "party line."

Based upon both the initially stated concerns of the stakeholder group and on our brainstorming exercise, a utility tree was created. A portion of this is shown in Figure 4.2. As part of our elicitation process we ensured that each of the scenarios in the utility tree had a specific stimulus and response associated with it.

4.2.6   Step 6: Analyze the Architectural Approaches

At this stage in the analysis we had in our possession a set of architectural documentation including some architectural approaches that had been identified, but we had little insight into the way that the architectural approaches actually performed to accomplish the BCS's mission. So we used a set of questions

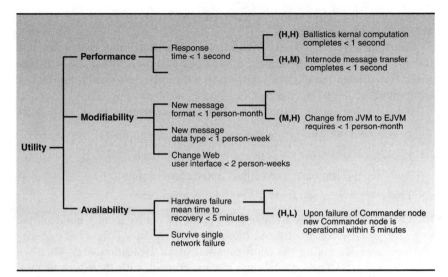

Figure 4.2 A Portion of the BCS Utility Tree

derived from our quality attribute characterizations (see Chapter 5) to flesh out our understanding of the approaches and to probe them for risks, sensitivity points, and tradeoffs. For example, for the backup commander approach (for availability) we generated a set of questions. The following is a subset of the questions applied to the approach for probing availability:

- How is the failure of a component detected?
- How is the failure of a communication channel detected?
- What is the latency for a spare component to be turned into a working replacement?
- By what means is a failed component marked for replacement?
- How are the system's working components notified that they should use the services of the spare?

These questions allowed us to probe the availability architectural approach and formed the basis for our analysis of this approach, as we show below.

By itself Figure 4.1 (or any similar representation of a software architecture view) tells us little about the system. However, when illuminated by a small number of scenarios and quality-attribute-based analysis questions, a view can become the focus for an in-depth understanding and analysis.

Recall that a sensitivity point for a quality attribute is defined as a decision in the architecture to which some measurable attribute is highly correlated; small changes in such decisions are likely to have significant effects on the measurable behavior of the system. For this reason we need to focus our attention on these points since they pose the highest risks to the system's success, particularly as the system evolves.

We find sensitivity points by first probing architectural approaches and eliciting information on how these approaches will meet the quality attribute goals. Based upon the elicited information we can begin to build informal or semiformal models of some aspect of a quality attribute.

As stated in Chapter 3, this elicited information helps us to

- Understand the approach in detail and how it was applied in this instance
- Look for well-known weaknesses with the approach
- Look for the approach's sensitivity and tradeoff points
- Find interactions and tradeoffs with other approaches

Our understanding of architectural approaches is frequently quite simple when we initially construct them; often we have time for only a back-of-the-envelope analysis during the short duration of an evaluation. But when we build even these simple models we can experiment with their architectural decisions until we determine which ones have substantial effects on a measurable attribute such as latency, throughput, or mean time to failure. The point of probing the approach is thus twofold: to find sensitivity points (not to precisely characterize a measurable attribute, for it is typically too early in the development process to do this with any rigor) and to gain insight into the architecture via the elicitation process.

For the BCS system we realized, via the utility tree construction process, that three quality attributes were the major architectural drivers for overall system quality: availability, modifiability, and performance. The next sections describe the analyses that we created when looking at the architectural approaches for availability and performance. The modifiability analysis was simply a SAAM analysis (see Chapter 7) and is not presented here. Each of these analyses was created by first eliciting an architectural approach and then applying quality-attribute-specific analysis questions to elicit information about the attribute in question.

Backup Commander Approach

A key quality attribute for the BCS was determined to be its steady state availability. Whenever we are considering the quality attribute of availability, the quality attribute characterization for availability leads us to a consideration of where resources are replicated (or not). The use of a client-server approach in this architecture made us suspicious of the server as a potential single point of failure. This turned out to be the case.

We determined that the system was considered to be working if there was a working Commander node and any number of Soldier nodes. When the Commander failed, the system had failed. Provisions had been made in the BCS architecture, however, to turn a Soldier into a Commander, that is, to convert a client into a server. The recovery time for the system was the time to turn a Soldier node into the Commander node and thus restore the system to operation. Failure of the Commander was detected via human-to-human communication.

As guided by the utility tree entry for availability, the key stimulus to model for the system was the failure of a node (specifically a Commander node) in the system due to attack, hardware failure, or software failure. The architecture of the BCS, as presented to us, statically specified a Commander node and a single backup selected from among the Soldier nodes, as indicated by the shaded Soldier node in Figure 4.1. In the existing design, *acknowledged* communication (state messages) took place between the Commander and the backup Soldier node to allow the backup to mirror the Commander's state. This allowed the backup to maintain a state of readiness in case of failure of the Commander. Upon failure of the Commander, the backup took over as the new Commander, converting from a client to a server.

However, there was no provision to have one of the surviving Soldier nodes promoted to become the new backup. That is, system availability was primarily affected by the failure rate of the Commander and the repair rate of the Commander (the time required to turn the backup into the Commander). The availability might also be affected by the repair rate of the backup, but in the BCS the repair rate of the backup was 0 since there was no provision for creating additional backups.

We determined that this was a risk: the lack of additional backups to the Commander could lead to the system not meeting its availability requirements. We could further probe the nature of this risk by building a simple model of the system's availability. Using this model we could determine the effects of changing the repair rate of the backup on the system's overall availability. Specifically, we could determine the amount of time required for a new backup to enter a readiness state (that is, where it could quickly become the Commander). This would, however, require a change to the architecture since the architecture statically specified only a single backup.[1]

An alternative architecture could allow multiple (perhaps all) Soldier nodes to monitor the Commander-to-backup communication and thus maintain a higher level of readiness. And these additional backups could either acknowledge communication with the Commander (requesting resends of missed packets) or could be silent receivers of packets, or some mixture of these schemes could be used (for example, the top *n* backups acknowledge receipt of packets, and the remaining *m* backups are passive). In the case where packets are not acknowledged, the state of the backups database would increasingly drift from that of the Commander, and if one of these backups were called upon to

---

1. Often when we are probing for risks in an evaluation we can see some obvious solutions to mitigate those risks. This isn't an explicit goal of the method but is a frequent beneficial by-product. This is what happened next.

become the Commander, it would need to engage in some negotiation (with the external systems and/or the other Soldier nodes) to complete its database.

Thus, there were three considerations for changing the BCS architecture to improve the data distribution to the backups:

1. A backup could be an acknowledging backup, which is kept completely synchronized with the Commander.

2. A backup might be only a passive backup and not ask for resends when it misses a message; this implies that it has the means for determining that it has missed a message (such as a message numbering scheme).

3. A backup, when it becomes the new Commander or when it becomes an acknowledging backup, could request any missed information from the upper-level command and control systems and/or the other Soldier nodes.

Each of these options has implications for both performance and availability. Option 1 will incur a small amount of performance overhead continually, but the backup will immediately be ready to assume Commander responsibilities when called upon. Option 2 will not have any negative performance consequences, but the backup may have incomplete information when it is called upon to become the Commander. Option 3 will not have any ongoing performance implications, but the backup will potentially need to download any data that it is lacking when it is called upon to become the Commander, thus lengthening the recovery time of the system.

The system does not need to choose a single option for its backups. It might have *n* acknowledging backups and *m* passive backups. Assuming that we have no control over the failure rate of the Commander, then the true sensitivities in this system with respect to availability are functions of the repair rates of the Commander and backups, which are themselves functions of the numbers of acknowledging and passive backups. Now we have a usable description of the architectural sensitivities—a correlation between some architectural decision and a measurable attribute:

$$Q_A = g(n, m)$$

where availability Q_A is a function of the number of acknowledging backups, n, and passive backups, m.

What were the issues in the choice of the number of backups to maintain and whether they acknowledged communications or not? We considered this issue in terms of the failure and recovery rates of the system under the various options. Clearly, the availability of the system increases as the number of backups is increased, because the system can survive multiple failures of individual nodes without failing its mission. The availability of the system is also increased by increasing the number of acknowledging backups, for two reasons: (1) acknowledging backups can be ready to assume the responsibilities of a Commander much more quickly because they do not need to negotiate with

Making the Most of Evaluators' Efforts

Robert L. Nord
Siemens Corporate Research

Over the years I've taken part in a number of architecture evaluations for which evaluators from outside of a project are brought in to provide an objective analysis. The evaluators are experts in architecture design and systems qualities, but not necessarily in the domain of the system to be evaluated. This raises the challenge of how to get the evaluators educated quickly about the requirements and design of the system, making efficient use of the available time to extract and review the necessary information. It is easy to spend the entire first day in presentations that go deep into the details of the system, but is that the best use of everyone's time? The evaluation team starts extracting information by asking questions, but do the questions address the most critical parts of the system? Getting a group of smart people together in a room to ask questions usually accomplishes the objectives, but after the flurry of activity one is often left wondering: Is there not a better way?

I have had the opportunity to participate in three architecture evaluations using the Architecture Tradeoff Analysis Method. These evaluated a data acquisition and analysis system, an IT system, and a tool integration system designed by my colleagues. My partners in each evaluation were the architect, project manager, marketer, and end-user stakeholders. I served on the evaluation teams in the questioner, process observer, and team leader roles. These evaluations gave my company perspectives from both sides of the evaluation process. I saw how the ATAM provided direction to the presentations and the questioning to get to the appropriate information in a goal-directed way. The project manager and architect were given examples to guide their presentations of the business goals and architecture approaches.

The evaluators' questions were based on scenarios captured during the construction of a utility tree. Building a utility tree from the business goals and working toward capturing scenarios for the system qualities provided a systematic approach to capturing the qualities that were important to the architect. It forced the team to consider the overall qualities and consciously choose which were important and which were not, quickly pruning away the lower-priority choices. Getting people to assign priorities was difficult at first. When asked to choose, project members said, "They are *all* important!" In one of the evaluations, after they were compelled to make choices, the project members were concerned that the final ranking did not reflect the most important qualities. They were asked to suspend their doubts to allow the process to continue. By the end of the evaluation, they were satisfied with the ranking; it turned out that what they had thought was the greatest risk (performance) was not so important while a new risk had surfaced concerning customer-specific customization policies across the product line.

At the conclusion of the evaluations, I heard members of the project team comment that the evaluation process was very worthwhile and that the most effective part of the exercise was prioritizing attributes and then identifying risks associated with high-priority attributes and possible solutions. This was an efficient way to get a group of outside reviewers to evaluate the architecture. The ATAM helped the development team better direct its risk-mitigation efforts and reduced the fear associated with unknown risks. Risks are more easily controlled when they are better understood. One of the project managers initialized his risk-tracking system based on the ATAM risk list and began to aggressively mitigate identified risks, and his program manager used the ATAM final presentation to justify investments for mitigating risks.

The ATAM is not a detailed technical design review but more of an architecture risk analysis. Design reviews still need to be performed. The ideal time to do an ATAM evaluation is when the architecture is well defined but still can be changed. Most designers are willing to spend a few days early in a project to identify architecture risks, especially when it's still possible to change the design. The ATAM provides a way to make the most of this opportunity for improvement.

other nodes for missed information, and (2) having more acknowledging backups means that there would not be an identifiable communication pattern between the Commander and the single backup, so the probability of two accurate incoming mortars disabling the system is reduced.

However, as the number of acknowledging backups is increased, the performance of the system is impacted since each of these acknowledgments incurs a small communication overhead. (This tradeoff is discussed further later in this chapter.) Collectively, this overhead was significant for the BCS because, as we discuss next, communication latency was the major contributor to overall system latency.

Independent Communicating Components Approach

Whenever we are considering the quality attribute of performance, the quality attribute characterization for performance leads us to a consideration of where resources are in contention (or not). The use of a client-server approach in the BCS architecture made us suspicious of the server as a potential bottleneck.

Through building a simple, back-of-the-envelope performance model of the system and varying the input parameters to the model (the various processing times and communication latencies), it became clear that the slow speed of radio modem communication between the Commander and the Soldiers (9600 baud) was the single most important performance driver for the BCS, swamping all other considerations. The performance measure of interest—average latency of client-server communications—was found to be relatively insensitive to all the other architectural performance decisions that we considered (for example, the time for the system to update its database, or to send a message internally to a process, or to do targeting calculations). But the choice of modem speed was given as a constraint, so our performance model was then focused on capturing those architectural decisions that affected message sizes and distributions. Note here that we did not, and did not need to, build a complex rate-monotonic analysis or queueing model to discover this correlation.

We thus began our investigation into message sizes by considering the performance implications and the communication requirements implied by the system's normal operations. We then looked at the system's operations under the assumption of some growth in the performance requirements. To do this we considered three situations stemming from use case scenarios provided by the stakeholders:

- Scenario A: Regular, periodic data updates to the Commander (consisting of various message sizes and frequencies)
- Scenario B: Turning a Soldier node into a backup; with a switchover requiring that the backup acquire information about all missions, updates to the environmental database, issued orders, current Soldier locations and status, and detailed inventories from the Soldiers.
- Scenario C: Doubling the number of weapons or the number of missions

For the purposes of illustration in this example, we present only the performance calculations for scenario B, turning a Soldier backup to Commander.

After determining that a switchover is to take place the Soldier backup needs to download the current mission plans and environmental database from the external command and control systems. In addition, the backup needs the current locations and status of all of the remaining Soldiers, inventory status from the Soldiers, and the complete set of issued orders.

A typical calculation of the performance implications of this situation must take into account the various message sizes needed to realize the activities, the 9600 baud modem rate (which we equate to 9600 bits/second), and the fact that there are a maximum of 25 Soldiers per Commander (but since one is now being used as a Commander, the number of Soldier nodes in these calculations is 24).

Downloading mission plans:
280 Kbits ÷ 9.6 Kbits/second ≅ 29.17 seconds

Updates to environmental database:
66 Kbits ÷ 9.6 Kbits/second ≅ 6.88 seconds

Acquiring issued orders (for 24 Soldiers):
24 × (18 Kbits ÷ 9.6 Kbits/second) = 45.0 seconds

Acquiring Soldier locations and status (for 24 Soldiers):
24 × (12 Kbits ÷ 9.6 Kbits/second) = 30.0 seconds

Acquiring inventories (for 24 Soldiers):
24 × (42 Kbits ÷ 9.6 Kbits/second) = 105.0 seconds

Total ≅ 216.05 seconds for Soldier to become backup

Note that since the radio modem is a shared communication channel, no other communication can take place while a Soldier/backup is being converted to a Commander.

Keeping each backup in a state of high readiness requires that they become acknowledging backups, or for a lower state of readiness they can be kept as passive backups. Both classes of backups require periodic updates from the Commander. From an analysis of scenario B, we calculated that these messages averaged 59,800 bits every 10 minutes. Thus, to keep each backup apprised of the state of the Commander requires 99.67 Kbits/second, or approximately 1 percent of the system's overall communication bandwidth. Acknowledgments and resends for lost packets would add to this overhead. Given this insight, we can characterize the system's performance sensitivities (Q_P) as follows:

$$Q_P = h(n, m, CO)$$

That is, the system is sensitive to the number of acknowledging backups (n), passive backups (m), and other communication overhead (CO). The main point of this simple analysis is to realize that the size and number of messages to be transmitted over the 9600 baud radio modem is important with respect to system performance and hence availability. Small changes in message sizes or frequencies can cause significant changes to the overall throughput of the system. These changes in message sizes may come from changes imposed upon the system from the outside.

4.3 Phase 2

4.3.1   Step 7: Brainstorm and Prioritize Scenarios

Scenarios are applied not only to determine whether the architecture meets a functional requirement but also for further understanding of the system's architectural approaches and the ways in which these approaches meet the quality attribute requirements such as performance, availability, modifiability, and so forth.

The scenarios for the BCS ATAM were collected by a round-robin brainstorming activity. Table 4.1 shows a few of the 40 growth and exploratory scenarios that were elicited in the course of the ATAM evaluation.

Scenario Prioritization

Prioritization of the scenarios allows the most important scenarios to be addressed within the limited amount of time (and energy) available for the evaluation. Here, "important" is defined entirely by the stakeholders. The BCS prioritization was accomplished by giving each stakeholder a fixed number of votes; 30 percent of the total number of scenarios has been determined to be a useful heuristic. Thus, for the BCS, each stakeholder was given 12 votes to use to vote for the scenarios in which he or she was most interested. Normally, the resulting totals provide an obvious cutoff point; 10–15 scenarios are the most that can be considered in a normal one-day session. For the BCS a natural cutoff

Table 4.1   Sample Scenarios for the BCS Evaluation

Scenario	Scenario Description
1	Same information presented to user, but different presentation (location, fonts, sizes, colors, etc.).
2	Additional data requested to be presented to user.
3	User requests a change of dialog.
4	A new device is added to the network, e.g., a location device that returns accurate GPS data.
5	An existing device adds additional fields that are not currently handled to existing messages.
6	Map data format changes.
7	The time budget for initialization is reduced from 5 minutes to 90 seconds.
8	Modem baud rate is increased by a factor of 4.
9	Operating system changes to Solaris.
10	Operating schedule is unpredictable.
11	Can a new schedule be accommodated by the OS?
12	Change the number of Soldier nodes from 25 to 35.
13	Change the number of simultaneous missions from 3 to 6.
14	A node converts from being a Soldier/client to become a Commander/server.
15	Incoming message format changes.

occurred at 12 scenarios, which we proceeded to map onto the architectural information that we had previously elicited.

4.3.2   Step 8: Analyze the Architectural Approaches

In the ATAM process, once a set of scenarios has been chosen for consideration, these are used as test cases of the architectural approaches that have been documented. In the case of a scenario that implies a change to the architecture, the architect demonstrates how the scenario would affect the architecture in terms of the changed, added, or deleted components, connectors, and interfaces. For the use case scenarios, the architect traces the execution path through the relevant architectural views.

Stakeholder discussion is important here to elaborate the intended meaning of a scenario description and to discuss whether the architectural approaches are suitable or not from the stakeholders' perspective. This process illustrates weaknesses in the architecture and its documentation or even missing architectural approaches.

For the BCS, each of the high-priority scenarios was mapped onto the appropriate architectural approach. For example, when a scenario implied a modification to the architecture, the ramifications of the change were mapped onto the source view, and scenario interactions were identified as sensitivity points. For availability and performance, use case scenarios describing the execution and failure modes of the system were mapped onto run-time and system views of the architecture. During this testing phase our understanding of the architectural approaches and their implications on performance, availability, and modifiability was further probed and refined. However, no new and significant risks or tradeoffs were found.

4.3.3   Step 9: Present the Results

As a result of these analyses we identified three sensitivities in the BCS system. Two of these were affected by the same architectural decision: the amount of message traffic that passes over the shared communication channel employed by the radio modems, as described by some functions of n and m, the numbers of acknowledging and passive backups, respectively. Recall that availability and performance, respectively, were characterized as

$$Q_A = g(n, m)$$

and

$$Q_P = h(n, m, CO)$$

These two parameters, n and m, control the tradeoff point between the overall performance of the system, in terms of the latency over its critical communication resource, and the availability of the system, in terms of the number of backups to the Commander, the way that the state of those backups is maintained, and the negotiation that a backup needs to do to convert to a Commander. To determine the criticality of the tradeoff more precisely, we can prototype or estimate the currently anticipated message traffic and the anticipated increase in message traffic due to acknowledgments of communications to the backups. In addition, we would need to estimate the lag for the switchover from Soldier to Commander introduced by not having acknowledged communication to the Solder backup nodes. Finally, all of this increased communication needs to be considered in light of the performance scalability of the system (since communication bandwidth is the limiting factor here).

One way to mitigate against the communication bandwidth limitation is to plan for new modem hardware with increased communication speeds. Presumably this means introducing some form of indirection into the modem communications software—such as an abstraction layer for the communications—if this does not already exist. This modifiability scenario was not probed during the evaluation.

While this tradeoff might seem obvious, given the presentation here, it was not so. The contractor was not aware of the performance and availability implications of the architectural decisions that had been made. In fact, in the business drivers discussion, not a single performance or availability scenario was generated by the stakeholders; these simply were not among their concerns. The stakeholders were most worried about the modifiability of the system, in terms of the many changes in message formats that they expected to withstand over the BCS's lifetime. However, the identified tradeoff affected the very viability of the system. If this tradeoff were not carefully reasoned, it would affect the system's ability to meet its most fundamental requirements.

4.4 Results of the BCS Evaluation

The evaluation that we performed on the architecture for the BCS revealed some potentially serious problems in the documentation of the architecture, the clarity of its requirements, its performance and availability, sensitivities and tradeoffs, and its architectural risks. We briefly summarize each of these problems in turn.

4.4.1 Documentation

The documentation provided at the inception of this project was minimal: two pages of diagrams that did not correspond to software artifacts in any rigorous way. This is, in our experience, not uncommon and is the single greatest

My Experiences with the ATAM

Tony Lattanze
Software Engineering Institute

I have participated in two ATAM-based evaluation exercises. In one I was assigned the role of questioner; in the second I was the evaluation leader. Although I had studied the ATAM method extensively before each exercise and thought I knew what to expect, both experiences held several surprises for me.

The first surprise was that, in both cases, the systems whose architectures we were evaluating were already built and in operation. I had expected to apply the ATAM during initial development. But the clients of these evaluations wanted to use the ATAM to determine the fitness of their respective architectures for evolving into the next generation of applications, so that's what we did. The ATAM worked in these situations without missing a beat.

The second surprise was that the architecture you see is not necessarily the one you get. In the first exercise, the architect confidently presented a veritable parade of box-and-line diagrams. However, we noticed immediately that the diagrams were lacking a key explaining precisely what the boxes and lines meant. Our experience with architectural views has taught us that diagrams lacking a key are often a sign that the architect is unclear about what the symbols mean or is unconsciously conflating one or more views. Simply asking the architect questions about the semantics of these objects forced him to think critically about the components and their relationships in greater detail. This resulted in more consistent and precise architectural renderings, which in turn led to new insights about the architecture and the design possibilities that it embodied—a major benefit of this particular exercise.

In the second exercise the architectural depictions were well done, replete with legends and accompanying details. However, we soon discovered that the architecture that was presented did not reflect the system's implementation. Therefore, any claims that the designers made about the system's quality attributes were unsupportable, if those claims were based upon the architectural depiction. Needless to say, many of the stakeholders were surprised. We were able to proceed by eliciting the as-built architecture from the development team, but uncovering the divergence turned out to be a major benefit of that exercise.

My third surprise about the ATAM was discovering how essential it is for the evaluation leader to be sensitive to the dynamics of the interactions among participants. The leader must promote a free flow of conversation and make participants feel at ease, yet stop unproductive discussions from detracting from the exercise. This sounds much easier than it really is, and in fact it takes a good deal of practice to do well. Facilitation training helps greatly in this regard. By keeping the proceedings moving on track and keeping the participants happy, it is not uncommon to document thirty or more risks during the course of an evaluation. A derailed evaluation or grumpy participants can substantially diminish the risks uncovered and hence the quality of the evaluation.

My fourth surprise concerned the social power of the final presentation. For the exercise in which I gave the results, all of the stakeholders were assembled to review the outputs of the exercise. They listened intently and I had the distinct impression that they felt ownership, and maybe some pride, in the results of the exercise. And rightly so: their participation had created those results. However, each stakeholder takes away his or her own personal message. The architect had a clearer understanding of how the decisions he made affected the ability of the marketing department to sell systems. The developers understood the importance and the role of their software in the overall organization. The marketers had a better understanding of what features they could safely promise to customers and what features would be more costly or problematic to deliver. The manager left with a deeper appreciation of the need for broader communication among the various stakeholders required to bring a product to market.

I can now see that each ATAM-based evaluation takes on its own special flavor despite the use of the same steps, the same roles, and the same process guidance. Each group of stakeholders and each software development situation has its own unique character. In the final analysis, despite this innate variability from one evaluation to the next, the ATAM is for me about breaking down the barriers between system stakeholders. The ATAM brings interested parties together under the aegis of architecture, empowers them, and opens productive and long-lasting communication channels. The result makes powerful use of a project's most important assets: its people.

---

impediment to having a productive architecture evaluation. Having a distinct Phase 1 and having the opportunity to request additional documentation from the contractor made the evaluation successful.

As a result of our interaction with the BCS contractor team, substantially augmented and higher-quality architectural documentation was produced. This improved documentation became the basis for the evaluation. The improvement in the documentation was identified by management as a major success of using the ATAM, even before we presented any findings.

4.4.2 Requirements

One benefit of doing any architectural evaluation is increased stakeholder communication, resulting in better understanding of requirements. Frequently, new requirements surface as a result of the evaluation. The BCS experience was typical, even though the requirements for this system were "frozen" and had been made public for over two years.

For example, in the BCS the only performance timing requirements were that the system be ready to operate in 300 seconds from power-on. In particular, there were no timing requirements for other specific operations of the system, such as responding to a particular order or updating the environmental database. These were identified as lacking by the questions we asked in building the performance model.

Furthermore, there was no explicit switchover requirement, that is, the time that it took for a Soldier to turn itself into a Commander was not identified as a requirement. This requirement surfaced as a result of building the availability model.

In addition, there was no stated availability requirement. Two well-aimed hits or two specific hardware failures would put the system we evaluated out of commission. By the end of the evaluation the stakeholders viewed this as a major oversight in the system's design.

4.4.3   Sensitivities and Tradeoffs

The most important tradeoff identified for the BCS was the communications load on the system, as it was affected by various information exchange requirements and availability schemes. The overall performance and availability of the system were highly sensitive to the latency of the (limited and shared) communications channel, as controlled by the parameters n and m. Not only should the current performance characteristics be modeled but also the anticipated performance changes in the future as the system scales in its size and scope.

4.4.4   Architectural Risks

In addition to the sensitivities and tradeoffs, we discovered, in building the models of the BCS's availability and performance, a serious architectural weakness that had not been previously identified: there existed the possibility of an opposing force identifying the distinctive communication pattern between the Commander and the backup and thus targeting those nodes specifically. The Commander and backup exchanged far more data than any other nodes in the system. An attacker could easily discern the distinctive pattern of communication between the Commander and the single backup, even without being able to decrypt the actual contents of the messages. Thus, it must be assumed that the probability of failure for the Commander and its backup would increase over the duration of a mission under the BCS architecture we evaluated.

This was a major architectural flaw that was revealed only *because* we were examining the architecture from the perspective of multiple quality attributes simultaneously. This flaw is, however, easily mitigated by assigning multiple backups, which would eliminate the distinctive communication pattern.

Therefore, the dominant risk theme for the BCS architecture was that the availability of the entire system was in jeopardy due to the limitations of the backup commander approach. The ability of the BCS to meet its mission objectives was severely hampered by this risk theme.

4.5 Summary

The point of this example is not to show which actions the contractor took, which alternatives the organizations chose, or precisely what lessons they learned. The point here is to show that the process of performing an ATAM evaluation on the BCS raised the stakeholders' awareness of critical risk, sensitivity, and tradeoff issues. This, in turn, focused design activity in the areas of highest risk and caused a major iteration within the spiral process of design and analysis.

An architecture analysis method, *any* architecture analysis method, is a garbage-in-garbage-out process. The ATAM is no different. It crucially relies on the active and willing participation of the stakeholders (particularly the architecture team); some advance preparation by the key stakeholders; an understanding of architectural design issues and analytic models; and a clearly articulated set of quality attribute requirements and a set of business goals from which they are derived.

4.6 Discussion Questions

1. What qualities do you think an evaluation leader should possess? What experience? Who in your organization would make a good one, and why?

2. What qualities do you think a scenario scribe should have? Who in your organization would make a good one, and why?

3. What qualities do you think a software architect should possess that will be important during a software architecture evaluation?

4. The major tradeoff identified in the BCS evaluation was between performance and availability. Pick other pairs of quality attributes and hypothesize architectural situations that would cause a tradeoff between the members of each pair.

5. Redundancy is a common technique used to achieve availability. The ATAM also uses its own form of redundancy. Explain how the ATAM exploits redundancy, and show how it helped to identify key risks in this case study.

5

Understanding Quality Attributes

If you don't know where you're going, you might not get there.
—Yogi Berra
When You Come to a Fork in the Road, Take It!

The quality attributes of any nontrivial system are determined by its architecture. This insight is one of the principal motivations for the study of software architecture as a field. If this were not the case, then the only motivation for architectural design would be functional completeness (and we would not be writing this book!). But architectural decisions have a profound impact on the achievement or nonachievement of quality attributes, so they are the focus of architecture evaluation.

For this reason, a prerequisite of an evaluation is to have a statement of the quality attribute requirements that are motivated by key business goals and a specification of the architecture that includes a clear articulation of the architectural design decisions. But this prerequisite is often not met in practice. It is not uncommon for quality attribute requirements and architecture documentation to be incomplete, vague, and ambiguous. Therefore, by necessity, two of the major goals of architecture evaluation are to:

1. Elicit and refine a precise statement of quality attribute requirements
2. Elicit and refine a precise statement of architectural design decisions

Given the quality attribute requirements and the design decisions, the third major goal of architecture evaluation is to:

3. Evaluate the architectural design decisions to determine if they address the quality attribute requirements

This chapter discusses the foundational technical concepts that support these goals, centering on a knowledge of quality attributes.

Since architecture evaluation focuses on quality attributes, it is important to have clear and informative characterizations for each quality attribute that is important to you—ones that lead a questioner to ask probing questions and uncover the architectural strategies used. These characterizations organize information surrounding the following aspects of each attribute:

- What are the stimuli to which the architecture must respond?
- What is the measurable response of the quality attribute by which its achievement is judged?
- What are the important architectural decisions that impact achieving the quality attribute requirement?

These classes of questions recur in every evaluation, irrespective of what quality attribute is the current focus of attention. Noting the recurring patterns of these questions we have developed an elicitation and analysis aid that helps us to organize the important characteristics of a quality attribute and its architectural manifestation. We call these aids *quality attribute characterizations.*

5.1 Quality Attribute Characterizations

Systematically codifying the relationship between architecture and quality attributes greatly enhances the design and analysis process. This will allow an engineer to reuse existing analyses and determine tradeoffs explicitly rather than on an ad hoc basis. Experienced designers do this intuitively but even they would benefit from codified experience. For example, during analysis, designers could recognize a codified structure and instantly know its impact on quality attributes. Codifying this relationship will also aid in reconfiguring architectures to provide specified levels of a quality attribute by enabling designers to replace one set of mechanisms for another when necessary.

For these reasons, the idea of documenting and characterizing the relationship between architecture and quality attributes is a worthy goal. A universally accepted premise of the software architecture community is that architecture determines attributes.

Every quality attribute is different. It is different in its stimuli: for modifiability we care about a change request; for performance we care about the arrival of events at the system; for availability we care about a fault occurring in some portion of the system. It is different in its responses: for modifiability we care about how many person-days or -months will be required to make a requested change; for security we care about how many intruders will break into the system and what resources they will be able to access. And it is different in the architectural decisions that designers use to plan for and accommodate it: for performance we worry about the allocation of processes to processors and preemptability and priorities; for availability we worry about replication and fault detection and failover protocols. What these quality attributes share is nothing inherent, but rather an approach to thinking about them, eliciting information about them, and documenting them.

To facilitate using the wealth of knowledge that already exists in the various quality attribute research communities, we have created characterizations for the quality attributes of performance, availability, and modifiability. These characterizations serve as starting points, which you should flesh out further in preparation for or while conducting an architecture evaluation.

Our goal in presenting these attribute characterizations is not to claim that we have created an exhaustive taxonomy for each of the attributes, but rather to suggest a framework for thinking about quality attributes. The frameworks facilitate eliciting the appropriate attribute-related information. Where do these frameworks come from? We created them from information in the literature, from books on quality attributes, and from our collected expertise and experience. In doing architectural analyses you could start with these and then grow your own.

As suggested above, each quality attribute characterization is divided into three categories: external stimuli, responses, and architectural decisions. *External stimuli* (or just *stimuli* for short) are the events that cause the architecture to respond or change. To evaluate an architecture for adherence to quality attribute requirements, those requirements need to be expressed in terms that are concrete and measurable or observable. These measurable/observable quantities are described in the *responses* section of the attribute characterization. *Architectural decisions* are those aspects of an architecture—components, relations, and their properties—that have a direct impact on achieving attribute responses.

5.1.1 Performance

Performance is the ability of a system to allocate its computational resources to requests for service in a manner that will satisfy timing requirements The system must do so in the presence of competing requests. Stimuli trigger a computation to be initiated. For performance the stimuli include (as shown in Figure 5.1) external events such as messages or user key strokes, internal events based on state changes, and clock interrupts. Performance architectural decisions include (as shown in Figure 5.2) various types of resources, resource arbitration and allocation policies, and resource consumption. Resource types comprise processors, networks, buses, and memory, for example. Resource arbitration, also known as scheduling, concerns policies for determining which

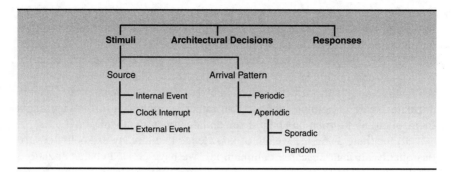

Figure 5.1 Performance Characterization—Stimuli

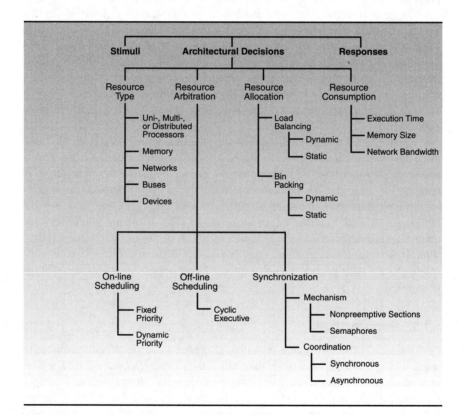

Figure 5.2 Performance Characterization—Architectural Decisions

of a set of pending resource requests (from entities such as processes and messages) will be served. Resource allocation concerns policies for moving resource demands in a manner that will achieve better throughput or minimize the number of necessary resources. Resource consumption is measured in terms such as execution time on processors or bandwidth for networks. Responses (as shown in Figure 5.3) are characterized by measurable quantities such as latency, throughput, and precedence.

These characterizations help to ensure proper understanding (and hence analysis coverage) of a quality attribute. But just as importantly they represent a guide for creating questions that elicit attribute-specific information. This information feeds our analyses, as we will show. Every node in the characterization can motivate an analysis question. For example, regardless of the architecture being analyzed we will always want to elicit information by asking questions such as those listed below.

- Performance-related stimuli:
  - What is the arrival pattern of external events? For example, do messages arrive periodically or aperiodically?
- Performance-related architectural decisions:
  - What resources (for example, CPUs and LANs) are being used?
  - What is the resource consumption (for example, execution time for CPU processes and bandwidth for LAN messages) for each resource?
  - What resource arbitration policy (for example, fixed priority scheduling of processes on the CPU) is being used?
- Performance-related responses:
  - What is the latency requirement associated with each message type?
  - How critical is it to meet the latency requirement? (In other words, what are the consequences of not meeting the latency requirement?)

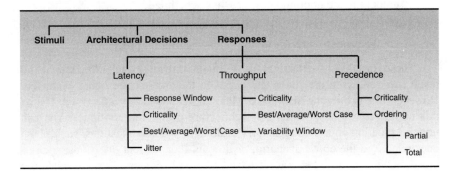

Figure 5.3 Performance Characterization—Responses

We want to capture the basis of this information in the quality attribute characterization so that it can be consistently reused and applied by analysts.

For example, if a stakeholder generates a scenario such as "Unlock all of the car doors within one second of pressing the correct key sequence" in an evaluation, the performance characterization will help us to create relevant questions. First, the structure of the characterization suggests that we parse the scenario to identify the stimulus and the response.

- Stimulus: "pressing the correct key sequence."
- Response: "unlock all of the car doors within one second."

Now we can take the generic performance questions suggested by the performance characterization and instantiate them for this scenario.

- Performance-related stimulus:
  - What happens if several "unlock the door" events occur quickly in succession before the system has had time to react to the first stimulus?
  - What if there are conflicting stimuli, such as someone using a physical key to unlock the door at the same time the key sequence is being entered on the keypad?
- Performance-related response:
  - What is the criticality of the one-second deadline, that is, what are the consequences of not meeting the one-second requirement? Is it simply user frustration or is there some other aspect of the system that relies on this deadline being met?

These questions help to probe and clarify the performance aspects of this scenario and quite naturally lead to questions concerning the architecture's ability to fulfill this scenario.

- Performance-related architectural decisions:
  - What processes are involved in responding to the *event* that initiates unlocking the door and how are they scheduled?
  - What are the execution times of those processes?
  - Do the processes reside on the same or different processors?

These questions are inspired by the quality attribute characterizations and result from applying the characterizations to the architecture being evaluated. However, this is only the beginning. Many more detailed questions will follow this initial set of questions as the architecture evaluation continues. You can imagine creating your own repository of domain-specific questions, such as the ones related to the above scenario, or domain-independent questions, such as those shown in Figure 5.4 that we have gathered from conducting architecture evaluations. In either case questions such as these become assets that can be used in future architecture evaluations.

Performance-Related Stimuli

What is the client loading in terms of the number of concurrent sessions?

How would you characterize the event model (periodic or stochastic)?

What internal state changes trigger computations?

Performance-Related Architectural Decisions

Are the server processors single- (nonpreemptable) or multithreaded (preemptable)?

How are (fixed or dynamic) priorities assigned to processes?

Are processes statically or dynamically allocated to hardware?

What is the physical distribution of the hardware and its connectivity?

What are the bandwidth characteristics of the network?

How is arbitration done in the network?

Do you use synchronous or asynchronous protocols?

What is the location of firewalls and their impact on bandwidth?

How are resources allocated to service requests?

If there are multiple processes/threads competing for a shared resource, how are priorities assigned to these processes/ threads and the process/thread controlling the shared resource?

Are there any relatively slow communication channels along an important communication path (e.g., a modem)?

Performance-Related Responses

What is the performance impact of a thin versus a thick client in terms of latency or throughput?

What are the performance characteristics of the middleware? What are the effects of load balancing and arbitration on throughput?

Are there any computations that must be performed in a specific order?

Figure 5.4 Sample Performance Questions

As you gain experience with specific quality attributes and with architecture evaluation you will find that the generation of new questions and the reuse of existing questions become a natural part of your process.

5.1.2 Availability[1]

The important stimuli in an availability characterization are faults, in both hardware and software. Such faults are the events that cause systems to fail. We measure the system's response by looking at measures such as reliability (the probability of not failing over a period of time), mean time to failure, and steady state availability. Another kind of response that we are often interested in understanding is levels of service. A system may offer several levels of service depending on the current condition of its hardware and software, and these should be enumerated and characterized.

---

1. Availability and reliability are closely related. Availability is concerned with the long-term proportion of time the system is working and delivering its services. Reliability is concerned with the probability a system will not fail over some specified interval of time. The attribute characterization in this section is relevant to both availability and reliability.

Architectural decisions principally involve how resources are replicated or backed up and how the system detects and recovers from these faults.

The availability characterization given in Figure 5.5 serves to inspire questions, such as those listed below, that probe availability requirements and architectural decisions that have been made (or not made, or not even considered!).

- Availability-related stimuli:
  - Has the architect made any provisions to sense or "trap" hardware or software faults?
- Availability-related architectural decisions:
  - What mechanisms are used to detect and recover from failures?
  - Is some form of redundancy in use?
- Availability-related responses:
  - How often do the various types of faults occur? Based on what evidence?
  - How long does it take to recover from a failure?
  - What is an acceptable level of reliability?

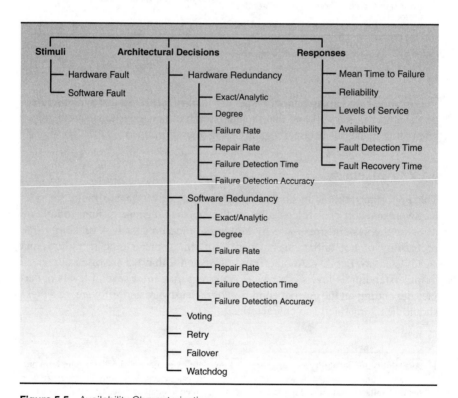

Figure 5.5 Availability Characterization

Again let us consider applying these types of questions to refine a scenario and probe an architecture with respect to this scenario: "A software failure prevents the door from being unlocked after the correct key sequence is entered. This causes a light around the door lock to flash, suggesting that the driver use the door key." We use the same strategy here that we used for the performance scenario by first identifying the stimulus and the response.

- Stimulus: "A software failure prevents the door from being unlocked after the correct key sequence is entered."
- Response: "This causes a light around the door lock to flash, suggesting that the driver use the door key."

Then we take the generic attribute questions suggested by the availability characterization as a starting point to refine the scenarios.

- Availability-related stimulus:
    - What types of software or hardware failures might prevent the electronic keypad from working? Have you accounted for all of these?
    - Could these failure modes prevent exit as well as entry?
    - Can this failure cause other failures to occur, for example, preventing the window from working or preventing the physical key and lock mechanism from working?
- Availability-related response:
    - How often do you predict that keypad failures can occur?
    - How long does it take to detect a keypad failure?
    - Is this failure noticed prior to a user trying the keypad or does it require the user to try typing the key sequence?

These questions help to probe and clarify the availability aspects of this scenario and lead to questions concerning the architecture's ability to fulfill this scenario.

- Availability-related architectural decisions:
    - What mechanisms are used to detect keypad failures?
    - Is there software involved with opening the door with a physical key?
    - How do the keypad and physical lock mechanisms interact?

Additional availability questions are shown in Figure 5.6. These questions, unlike those above, are generic. They are generated by the contemplation of the availability characterization and by recording questions that are asked during architecture evaluations. As with the performance questions, we recommend that an organization develop, capture, and refine its own sample questions.

Availability-Related Stimuli

How are hardware and software failures identified?

Can active as well as passive failures be identified?

If redundancy is used in the architecture, are there any common-mode failures?

Availability-Related Architectural Decisions

If redundancy is used in the architecture, what type of redundancy (analytic, replication, functional)?

If redundancy is used in the architecture, how long does it take to switch between instances of a redundant component?

If redundancy is used in the architecture, how many replicas of each critical component and connection are used?

How do you know that all critical components have been replicated?

If live redundant components are used in the architecture, how does the system choose when their results differ?

Does one component detect the failure of other components?

Is there any kind of system "heartbeat" used to detect dead components?

Availability-Related Responses

Are there different levels of service available? How are these characterized?

If a backing store is used, how quickly can a backup be made and how quickly can state be restored from the backup?

Figure 5.6   Sample Availability Questions

5.1.3   Modifiability

Modifiability is the ability of a system to be changed after it is implemented (and often deployed). In this case, the stimulus is the arrival of a change request; the response is the time or cost necessary to implement the change. Requests can reflect changes in functions, platform, and operating environment. They can reflect attempts to correct an existing problem with the system. A request can also modify how the system achieves its quality attributes. Responses might involve changes to the source code or data files. They can involve the addition, modification, and deletion of components, connectors, and interfaces.

Three very typical architectural strategies used for achieving modifiability, that is, for controlling "how far" the effects of a change will propagate, are indirection, encapsulation, and separation. *Indirection* involves using a mediator to allow producers and consumers of data to communicate without having direct knowledge of each other. Only the mediator knows who needs data from whom. Consequently additional producers or consumers can be added without changes to existing consumers or producers. *Encapsulation* is similar to indirection; an interface serves the role of the mediator, separating the implementation details that live inside a module from the clients that use the module. *Separation* isolates orthogonal aspects of an architecture from one another. For example, by separating data from views of the data, the creation of a new view can be independent of other existing views. Separating commands from data allows new commands to be added without affecting existing commands.

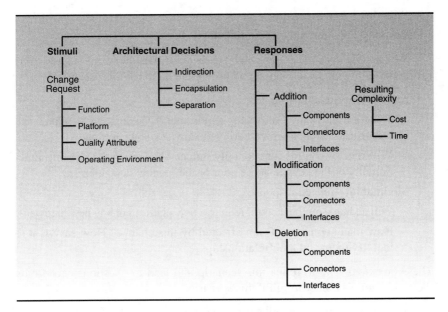

Figure 5.7   Modifiability Characterization

The modifiability characterization in Figure 5.7 can be used to inspire questions that will help determine what types of changes need to be considered and whether there are mechanisms in place to limit the propagation of change.

- Modifiability-related stimuli:
  - What types of changes do you anticipate having to make during the lifetime of the system?
  - Do you anticipate adding, changing, or deleting functionality, moving to a new platform, or changing quality attribute requirements?
- Modifiability-related architectural decisions:
  - What mechanisms do you have in place that prevent changes from propagating?
- Modifiability-related responses:
  - For each change that you anticipate, how many components, connectors, and interfaces need to be added, changed, or deleted?
  - Is it easy or difficult to trace coupling dependencies?

Questions such as those above can be used to probe scenarios. Consider: "Add the ability to enter a key sequence via remote control within three person-months." Using the same strategy we used for the performance and availability scenarios, we first identify the stimulus and the response.

- Stimulus: "Add the ability to enter a key sequence via remote control."
- Response: "within three person-months."

We can now take the domain-independent attribute questions suggested by the modifiability characterization and instantiate them for this scenario.

- Modifiability-related stimulus:
  - What are the quality attributes requirements, such as performance and security, associated with entering the key sequence remotely?
  - Will remote control functionality induce changes to the existing functionality of the keypad at the door or the manual door lock?
- Modifiability-related response:
  - Will adding a remote control require a new platform or any new hardware?
  - How many components are affected by this change? How easy is it to identify them and their relationships?

These questions help to refine this scenario and lead to questions concerning the architecture's ability to fulfill this scenario.

- Modifiability-related architectural decisions:
  - Is the interface to the door-locking hardware capable of handling multiple simultaneous requests for service?
  - Are all door locks handled by a single processor?
  - How is the remote control disabled while the car is running?

Additional modifiability questions are shown in Figure 5.8. They are generated by further contemplation of the modifiability characterization and by recording questions asked during architecture evaluations.

5.1.4   Characterizations Inspire Questions

Figures 5.4, 5.6, and 5.8 represent a small sampling of the types of questions that can be inspired by the attribute characterizations. As you have seen, these questions can be used to refine quality attribute scenarios, resulting in a clearer understanding of quality attribute requirements. These questions are also the starting point for examining your architecture to understand if and how it can fulfill important scenarios.

Clearly not everyone can be an expert in every quality attribute. These quality attribute characterizations allow most analysts to ask probing, relevant questions in an evaluation exercise. Different uses of the quality attribute characterizations require different levels of expertise. A beginner can make use of existing questions. It requires more expertise in a quality attribute to devise new questions from the characterizations. It requires still more expertise to understand how to respond to the questions.

Modifiability-Related Stimuli	Modifiability-Related Responses
What new functionality do you anticipate adding in future versions of the system?	How many interfaces will change as a consequence of a change to some functionality?
Do you anticipate the need for making your system more secure in the future?	Do changes to your user interface affect application modules?
How do you plan to handle migration to new releases of your operating system?	What changes will result from adding a source of data such as a new sensor or user input field?
Modifiability-Related Architectural Decisions	What is the impact of a change in functionality on the ability to meet performance requirements?
Do any components have access to the implementation details of global variables?	How many components, connectors, and interfaces will be affected by removing obsolete data from the data repository?
Do you use indirection mechanisms such as publisher/subscriber?	How much will it cost to change from a uniprocessor to a multiprocessor platform?
How do you handle the possibility of changes in message formats?	How long do you anticipate it will take to deploy your change?
Are implementation details or low-level services ever exposed to enhance performance?	

Figure 5.8   Sample Modifiability Questions

The next section discusses how we organize and begin to analyze the information elicited by these questions.

5.2 Using Quality Attribute Characterizations in the ATAM

While quality attribute characterizations can apply to any evaluation that focuses on quality attributes, the ATAM incorporates this notion as a foundation. As you know from the description of the ATAM, we begin by eliciting quality attribute requirements in the form of the utility tree. The attribute characterizations help us generate and refine scenarios at the leaves of the utility tree.

Once we elicit the utility tree and its scenarios in the ATAM we apply the scenarios to the architecture to understand the architectural approaches that have been employed. We document the architectural approaches using the template given in Figure 3.5, which is reproduced as Figure 5.9.

For example, we might elicit from an architect, in response to a utility tree scenario that required high availability from a system, the information shown in Figure 3.6, which is reproduced as Figure 5.10.

The first step is to refine the scenario by appealing to the attribute characterizations. What are the stimuli of interest? What are the responses of interest? What is the environment? Once this is established then the elicitation of the architectural approaches can proceed.

Analysis of Architectural Approach				
Scenario #: *Number*	**Scenario:** *Text of scenario from utility tree*			
Attribute(s)	*Quality attribute(s) with which this scenario is concerned*			
Environment	*Relevant assumptions about the environment in which the system resides, and the relevant conditions when the scenario is carried out*			
Stimulus	*A precise statement of the quality attribute stimulus (e.g., function invoked, failure, threat, modification . . .) embodied by the scenario*			
Response	*A precise statement of the quality attribute response (e.g., response time, measure of difficulty of modification)*			
Architectural Decisions	**Sensitivity**	**Tradeoff**	**Risk**	**Nonrisk**
Architectural decisions relevant to this scenario that affect quality attribute response	*Sensitivity Point #*	*Tradeoff Point #*	*Risk #*	*Nonrisk #*
. . .	. . .	. . .	. . .	. . .
. . .	. . .	. . .	. . .	. . .
Reasoning	*Qualitative and/or quantitative rationale for why the list of architectural decisions contribute to meeting each quality attribute requirement expressed by the scenario*			
Architecture Diagram	*Diagram or diagrams of architectural views annotated with architectural information to support the above reasoning, accompanied by explanatory text if desired*			

Figure 5.9   Template for Analysis of an Architectural Approach

To describe how the system's architecture will aid in responding to the stimuli of interest (in this case, a CPU failure) while ensuring an appropriate level of availability, the architect will reveal a set of architectural decisions that collectively allow him to reason about and address the stimuli of concern. These architectural decisions, the stimuli, and the desired responses should all be related to the quality attribute characterizations or lists of previously generated questions.

In the example given in Figure 5.10, the relationship to the attribute characterization is (hopefully) obvious. Even if the architect does not know to volunteer the appropriate information, the questioner/analysts can elicit the appropriate information by employing the relevant portions of the characterization.

For example, Figure 5.10 shows that there will be backup CPUs. The architect may have volunteered this information. But if not, the questioners

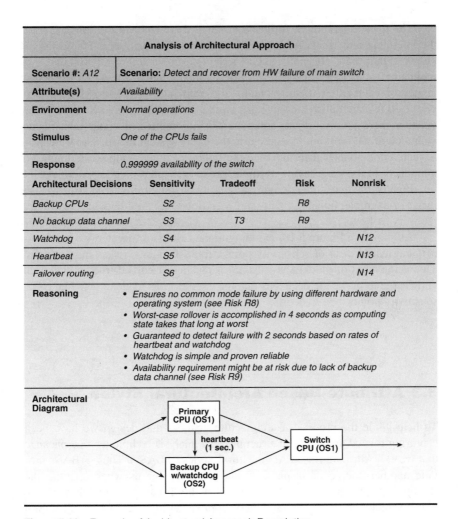

Analysis of Architectural Approach				
Scenario #: *A12*	**Scenario:** *Detect and recover from HW failure of main switch*			
Attribute(s)	*Availability*			
Environment	*Normal operations*			
Stimulus	*One of the CPUs fails*			
Response	*0.999999 availability of the switch*			
Architectural Decisions	**Sensitivity**	**Tradeoff**	**Risk**	**Nonrisk**
Backup CPUs	*S2*		*R8*	
No backup data channel	*S3*	*T3*	*R9*	
Watchdog	*S4*			*N12*
Heartbeat	*S5*			*N13*
Failover routing	*S6*			*N14*
Reasoning	• *Ensures no common mode failure by using different hardware and operating system (see Risk R8)* • *Worst-case rollover is accomplished in 4 seconds as computing state takes that long at worst* • *Guaranteed to detect failure with 2 seconds based on rates of heartbeat and watchdog* • *Watchdog is simple and proven reliable* • *Availability requirement might be at risk due to lack of backup data channel (see Risk R9)*			
Architectural Diagram				

Figure 5.10 Example of Architectural Approach Description

might have inquired about hardware redundancy, causing this information to be elicited. Similarly, the questioners, using the availability characterization, could elicit information about the second architectural decision: that there is no backup data channel. As far as fault detection goes, the architect might volunteer the information that he is using a watchdog/heartbeat scheme as part of his approach. This, once again, is found in the availability characterization. Finally, if the prime CPU fails, all communication to and from that CPU needs to be rerouted. In this case the architect might reveal another architectural decision stemming from the characterization, the use of failover routing.

The questioners might further use the attribute characterizations to probe the strengths and weaknesses of the architectural approaches. For example, knowing that there are multiple CPUs the questioner might ask whether this replication is exact or analytic (in other words, whether the CPUs are exact clones of each other or are actually different hardware and software programmed to accomplish the same or a similar task). The questions might probe whether there is any critical component or nonreplicated component in the architecture whose failure could cause the entire system to fail. The watchdog is such a component: if it fails then the failure of other components might go unnoticed. In this case having a simple, proven reliable watchdog is critical.

Finally, the questioners might ask about how the desired responses will be met. For example, how long will fault detection take? And how long will fault recovery (rollover) take?

As shown in Figure 5.10, based upon the results of this step we can identify and record a set of sensitivity points, tradeoff points, risks, and nonrisks. This is the heart of the ATAM—using (or reusing) tried-and-true architectural knowledge to probe the decisions that the architect has made to generate risks, sensitivity points, and tradeoffs.

5.3 Attribute-Based Architectural Styles

To help guide the process of architecture analysis and design we have been capturing related architectural structures and analysis techniques in a package that we call Attribute Based Architectural Styles (ABASs). These ABASs provide another source of inspiration and reference for us when creating the attribute-specific questions such as those listed in Figure 5.4. ABASs also provide a vehicle for further elaborating on approaches and recording architectural approaches such as the one illustrated in Figure 5.10.

An ABAS has four parts:

1. *Problem description:* what problem is being solved by this structure

2. *Stimuli/responses:* a characterization of the stimuli that this ABAS is designed to respond to and a description of the quality-attribute-specific measures of the response

3. *Architectural style:* the set of component and connector types, the topology, a description of the patterns of data and control interaction among the components (as in the standard definition of an architectural style), and any properties of the components or connectors that are germane to the quality attribute

4. *Analysis:* a quality-attribute-specific model that provides a method for reasoning about the behavior of component types that interact in the defined pattern

ABASs are simply a combination of a select few elements from the attribute characterization (the stimuli, responses, and architectural decisions) along with an analysis model. An ABAS packages this all together in a convenient, digestible form that makes it useful in an analysis. An extended example of an ABAS is given in Appendix A.

We believe that people will want to create their own ABASs for their own systems in their domain of expertise. If you are doing real-time embedded systems (with hard real-time constraints) then the ABASs that you will create will likely be different than those for a customer records database or a billing system (with soft timing constraints). The point is that ABASs should compile together into an engineering handbook of the important attribute-specific questions and typical answers that are found repeatedly for attributes that are important to you.

5.4 Summary

The power of the ATAM derives in part from the foundations provided by the technical concepts discussed here. These concepts work together synergistically.

The stimulus/response branches of the quality attribute characterizations provide a vocabulary for describing the problem the architecture is intended to solve. The elicitation of architectural structures results in pointed questions about how the proposed structures can actually solve the problems. These lead to the uncovering of risks, sensitivities, and tradeoffs.

In Step 2 of the ATAM the customer presents the business drivers for the problem being solved. The utility tree is used to translate the business context first into quality attribute drivers and then into concrete scenarios that represent each business driver. Each scenario is described in terms of a stimulus and the desired response. These scenarios are prioritized in terms of how important they are to the overall mission of the system and the perceived difficulty in realizing them in the system. The highest-priority scenarios are used in the analysis of the architecture.

In Step 3 the system architect presents the architecture to the evaluation team. The architect is encouraged to present the architecture in terms of the architectural approaches that are used to realize the most important quality attribute goals. The evaluation team also searches for architectural approaches as the architecture is presented. The approaches that address the highest-priority scenarios are the subject of analysis during the remainder of the evaluation.

Attribute-specific models (such as queuing models, modifiability models, and reliability models) as they apply to specific architectural styles can be codified in ABASs. ABASs help to facilitate the reuse of analysis associated with recurrent architectural approaches. These models plus the evaluators' experience provide attribute-specific questions that are employed to elicit the approaches used by the architect to achieve the quality attribute requirements.

5.5 For Further Reading

To read more about software architecture patterns see Buschmann et al. [Buschmann 96] and Schmidt et al. [Schmidt 00]. The seminal reference on architectural styles is Shaw and Garlan [Shaw 96]. For a more detailed treatment of ABASs refer to Klein and Kazman [Klein 99].

5.6 Discussion Questions

1. For each of the quality attributes covered in this chapter, try to derive a few more analysis questions beyond the ones presented.
2. Sketch quality attribute characterizations for two or three quality attributes other than the ones included in this chapter. You might begin with security, using the taxonomy given in Table 9.2 in Chapter 9.
3. Produce a set of analysis questions based on the characterizations you produced for the previous question.
4. For a system that you know, pick a scenario that you are familiar with and fill out the architectural approach template as demonstrated in Figure 5.10.
5. Using the ABAS shown in Appendix A as an example, record the information captured in the previous question in the form of an ABAS.

6

A Case Study in Applying the ATAM

In theory, there is no difference between theory and practice; In practice, there is.

— attributed to Chuck Reid

We hope by now you are comfortable with the ATAM method and its underlying concepts and have digested the first simple case study, the BCS. In this chapter we recount a more complete case study and take considerable pains to describe not only the *what* and *why* of each step but also our personal experiences with the steps. This case study took place in the middle of 2000, and the client was the Goddard Space Flight Center, part of the National Aeronautics and Space Administration (NASA), located in Greenbelt, Maryland.

We chose to describe this evaluation for several reasons. First, the members of the architecture and development team at NASA were interested in not only evaluating the system at hand but also learning enough about the ATAM to be able to apply it themselves on systems in the future. As a result, everyone was painstakingly thorough in applying each step, and everyone was very conscious of the ATAM process itself. This provided a great deal of detail for us to relate. Second, while every engagement using the ATAM is unique in some way, this one on the whole was as typical as any in terms of the architectural insights it uncovered. And third, all three authors of this book participated.

After reading this chapter, you should have a feeling for what an evaluation using the ATAM is like in practice. At each step along the way, we share with you what happened during this evaluation plus any other advice or experience we have about that step in general. We take you through each step of each phase of the ATAM. Our goal for this chapter is to allow you to vicariously experience an actual evaluation.

We recount each step as follows:

- **Step summary:** a short prose recap of the step, followed by a checklist of the input artifacts necessary for the step, the activities carried out in the step, and the outputs produced by the step

- **Step description:** a description of the step's activities that reinforces the description of the steps given in Chapter 3 but with a focus on finer-grained and more practical details

- **How it went:** what happened at the ATAM evaluation that is the subject of this case study

- **Speaking from experience:** typical experiences with this step, things that might go wrong in practice, or simple words of advice that we can share

6.1 Background

The Earth Observing System is a constellation of NASA satellites with names like Terra, Aqua, and Landsat as well as other kinds of land- and air-based sensors whose collective mission is to gather data about planet Earth to fuel the U.S. Global Change Research Program and other scientific communities worldwide.

Satellites are tireless workers, sending their data 24 hours a day, 7 days a week, 365 days a year, year after year. Did you ever wonder what happens to all that data?

In the case of the Earth Observing System, the system that handles the data is called ECS. ECS stands for EOSDIS Core System, where EOSDIS in turn stands for Earth Observing System Data Information System. ECS takes the data from various downlink stations around the world. The data must first be stored, but that's only part of the story. The data must be processed into higher-form information and made available in searchable form to scientists around the world. And it never stops. Handling this data is the mission of ECS.

The numbers are eye-popping. Hundreds of gigabytes of raw data per day flow into the system—data about vegetation, lightning, surface images, atmospheric soundings, trace gas quantities, atmospheric dynamics and chemistry, ice topography, sea surface winds, ocean color, volcanic activity, evaporation amounts, and altimetry of all sorts. The data is processed and analyzed and refined. Hundreds of gigabytes come in, but the processing produces thousands of gigabytes that get warehoused and made available to the scientific community—every day. The overall mission is to understand earth processes and potential global climate changes and to provide information for planning and adaptation.

The requirements for the ECS system are, roughly speaking, as follows:

- It must ingest, process, archive, and distribute data from 24 sensors on ten spacecraft, numbers destined to grow steadily over time.
- It must compute about 250 standard data products, which are predefined analyses that transform raw data into information packets about the physical world.
- It must archive the data and these data products in eight data centers (warehouses) across the United States.
- It must enable heterogeneous access and analysis operations at these data centers plus forty-some distributed scientific computing facilities.
- It must provide capacity for testing and incorporation of new processing algorithms and new data product definitions, and it must support data/information searches.
- It must do all of this while meeting the performance and reliability requirements to allow it to keep up with the never-ending flood of incoming data and never-ending stream of scientific analysis to be performed on it.

Before EOSDIS, satellite data was stored and formatted in ways specific to each satellite; accessing this data (let alone using it for analysis) was almost impossible for scientists not directly affiliated with that satellite's science project. An important feature of EOSDIS was to provide a common way to store (and hence, process) data and a public mechanism to introduce new data formats and processing algorithms, thus making the information widely available to the scientific community at large.

The first operational version of ECS was delivered in early 1999. Raytheon is the prime contractor. The system has been fielded incrementally, its growing capabilities coordinated with the launch of new spacecraft that will "feed" it.

In spring 2000, NASA wanted to know if the software architecture for this system would support the kinds of performance, scalability, modifiability, and operability that would be required to take the system into its mature years. The agency decided to use the ATAM to perform an evaluation of the software architecture for ECS.

6.2 Phase 0: Partnership and Preparation

Phase 0 establishes a formal agreement between the organization performing the ATAM and the client. How contact is made is beyond the scope of this summary, but many avenues are possible. If you are part of an evaluation unit within a larger organization, or if you are a consultant performing evaluations at large, somehow you and your clientele have to make contact with each other.

Phase 0 consists of the following steps:

1. Present the ATAM
2. Describe candidate system
3. Make a go/no-go decision
4. Negotiate the statement of work
5. Form the core evaluation team
6. Hold evaluation team kick-off meeting
7. Prepare for Phase 1
8. Review the architecture

In spring 1999, the project manager for ECS at NASA contacted our organization and inquired about our architecture evaluation capabilities. We pick up the story from there.

6.2.1   Phase 0, Step 1: Present the ATAM

Step Summary

The evaluation leader describes the evaluation method to the assembled participants, tries to set their expectations, and answers questions they may have.

Inputs

   [ ] Viewgraphs for a presentation about the ATAM. Figure 6.6 on page 151 gives an outline for such a presentation.

   [ ] A written description of the ATAM, to leave behind with the client for further reading.

   [ ] Published ATAM papers. (Optional—some clients may find the papers too technical or overwhelming.)

   [ ] ATAM effort data from previous exercises.

   [ ] Anecdotal benefit data. (Optional—not all anecdotes of savings will apply to every client. Use judgment about sharing past experience if the information might put off the client because it doesn't apply to his or her situation.)

Activities

   [ ] Evaluation organization representative makes sure the client understands the mechanics of the evaluation method to his or her satisfaction through one or more of the following activities:

   [ ] Making a presentation about the method.

   [ ] Giving the client a product/service description.

   [ ] Giving the client a copy of this book and pointing out those sections listed in the Reader's Guide as pertaining to evaluation clients.

   [ ] Referring the client to any of the published papers on the ATAM listed in the References section of this book. Mail them if requested.

[ ] Evaluation organization representative makes sure the client understands the costs and benefits of an architecture evaluation by providing the client with cost/benefit data.

[ ] Evaluation organization representative records questions asked about the method or the process for possible inclusion in a Frequently Asked Questions list. Duration and depth vary depending on the interest and background of the audience. This activity might take place any number of times with diverse audiences.

Output(s)

[ ] Names and addresses of contacts interested in pursuing the ATAM.

Step Description

This is usually the first time that a (prospective) client learns about what the ATAM is and what it can do for his or her organization. The object of the step is to explain the method clearly enough so that the client can decide whether or not to engage. The briefing that the evaluation team presents is the same one that is used in Phase 1 and Phase 2. However, in Phase 0, the client is also concerned about what an ATAM evaluation will cost in terms of time and other resources, so the standard ATAM briefing is augmented by cost data based on your own experience in conducting past evaluations using the ATAM. If you have no such data at this point, you can use the cost data in Chapter 2 as a starting point.

How It Went

Managers at NASA learned of the ATAM through public sources: our organization's Web site and published papers. They did enough homework to be convinced that architecture evaluation in general, and this technique in particular, would bring value to their organization. Two people from our organization went to visit NASA to make the presentation to the ECS project manager and two people on his technical staff. The part of the ATAM that produced a prioritized explicit articulation of the quality attributes resonated strongly with the project manager; he had been having thoughts about how to accomplish exactly that. He also saw the ATAM as a way to achieve consensus among a very disparate group of widely dispersed stakeholders: the consumers of the processed satellite data around the world, all of whom wanted the next increment of ECS to address their special needs.

Speaking from Experience

The presentation is informal, and typically only a few people are present: at a minimum, someone who can speak for the evaluation organization and someone who can speak for the client organization. Both need to be able to commit to the evaluation from their respective sides and to work out dates and logistics.

This presentation often results in interesting questions about the ATAM and its results because it is the point at which the client organization gains its first understanding of the method. We try to record questions asked during this presentation for inclusion in a Frequently Asked Questions list that we then turn around to give to our next potential client as part of ATAM read-ahead material.

At times the client organization sees this meeting as an opportunity for a "free lecture" on architecture and architecture analysis. We have had as many as 50 people attend the ATAM presentation. This is not a problem, as long as some "intimate" time with the clients is provided as well.

6.2.2   Phase 0, Step 2: Describe Candidate System

Step Summary

A spokesperson for the architecture to be evaluated describes the system to convey its essential functionality, the quality attributes, the status of the architecture, and the context.

Inputs
- [ ] Candidate system viewgraphs (desirable but optional).
- [ ] Other candidate system documents, especially architecture documents (desirable but optional).
- [ ] Client organization nondisclosure forms, to be left for signature by evaluation team members when assigned. (Optional—use if required by client.)

Activities
- [ ] Client representatives describe the candidate system with sufficient detail to convey the main architectural drivers (for example, business goals, requirements, constraints).
- [ ] Client and evaluation organization representatives agree on necessary architecture documentation.
- [ ] Work out issues of proprietary information. If necessary, have the client obtain nondisclosure forms for the evaluation team to sign.
- [ ] Evaluation organization representative records business goals, architectural constraints, and a list of architecture documentation to be delivered to the evaluation team.

Outputs
- [ ] List of business goals and architectural constraints.
- [ ] List of architecture documentation that will be delivered to the evaluation team.
- [ ] Client nondisclosure forms, to be signed by the evaluation team (optional—if required by client organization).

Step Description

A primary purpose of this step is to feed the go/no-go decision in the next step: Is there an architecture here that is far enough along to be evaluated? The client makes an overview presentation of some sort or perhaps just talks about the system informally.

The representative of the evaluation organization should listen for a few key things and ask about them if they are not forthcoming in the presentation.

- Listen for ways to define the scope of the system being evaluated. Does the evaluation include the software to generate or build the system? Does it include any software with which the primary system interacts?
- Listen for stakeholders or stakeholder roles to be mentioned.
- Listen for quality attributes of importance to be mentioned. This will give you hints about how to staff the evaluation team.
- Listen for any mention of commercial off-the-shelf software packages that have been chosen or mandated. These often have architectural and quality attribute impacts.
- Listen for the status of the architecture. Ideally, before this meeting, ask the client to bring a sample of the architecture documentation.

At the end of the client's presentation, summarize what you heard and see if he or she agrees. This information will be useful later.

How It Went

ECS turned out to be a case in which the architecture to be evaluated was already supporting a running, fielded system. We asked why the project manager wanted to evaluate an architecture already built. He told us he was concerned about the system's ability to handle much larger quantities of data, which it would have to do as more and more satellites joined the EOS fleet. If there was a flaw, he wanted to find it now rather than later. He also wanted exposure to the ATAM so that he could try to grow an architecture evaluation capability in his own organization. And last but hardly least, he viewed the consensus-building qualities of the ATAM, especially with regard to prioritizing stakeholder input, as an ideal means to achieve buy-in for the ECS project plan from a wide variety of ECS users—consumers of the data in the scientific community.

Speaking from Experience

Clients almost always have some sort of project briefing already packaged that they can present; the briefing was probably prepared for the project's sponsor somewhere along the way.

Unless your client is from an organization brimming over with architectural maturity, keep your expectations for the architecture documentation low. You want to establish what documentation exists and then decide if it is sufficient for proceeding with the evaluation.

Sometimes there is clearly an architecture, but documentation for it is poor or nonexistent. The ATAM can still proceed if the architect can speak authoritatively about the design decisions. An evaluation under these conditions is certainly likely—obligated, even—to report the lack of documentation as a serious risk, but as long as the client understands that the basis for the evaluation will be what the architect *says*, the exercise can continue. Better still, you can provide clients with documentation requirements and have them produce architectural representations that are suitable for analysis. We did this during the BCS case study, as we reported in Chapter 4: we provided a set of documentation requirements to the client, who responded with much improved architectural information and representations.

Frequently you will be asked to evaluate the architecture for a system that's already up and running. While this may seem akin to checking the barn door after the horse is on the track, it often makes sense. The system may be an early version with limited functionality, or the client may be concerned with its long-term viability or ability to grow, scale up, or accommodate change. In many ways using the ATAM to evaluate an already-running system is easier: the architect is unlikely to answer an analysis question by saying, "We haven't thought about that yet."

6.2.3   Phase 0, Step 3: Make a Go/No-Go Decision

Step Summary

Decide whether the state of the project warrants an ATAM evaluation

Inputs
  [ ] ATAM go/no-go decision criteria specific to your organization.
  [ ] Candidate system documents from Step 2.

Activities
  [ ] Apply go/no-go decision criteria.

Output
  [ ] If "no go," letter sent to client explaining the reasons for declining the work and suggesting remediation steps to enable future work.

Step Description

Apply your organization's criteria for continuing with the engagement or breaking it off. If there is not yet an architecture nor enough architectural decisions to be subjected to the scrutiny of an evaluation, then performing an evaluation will not be a good use of resources. If your decision is "no go," then explain to the client what is lacking and (depending on your relationship) help him or her address the project's shortcomings so that an evaluation will be fruitful.

How It Went

Not surprisingly, our decision was "go." The members of this client organization demonstrated architectural maturity through their clear understanding of the ATAM and why it would help them. Also, since an early version of the system was up and running, there was little doubt that they had an architecture to be evaluated.

Speaking from Experience

For some years now we've tried to codify our go/no-go criteria, and they always seem to elude us. You may be more structured than we are in this area, but in our organization we tend to judge each case on its own merits. Some customers are simply too important to our long-term interests to turn down. If their architecture is sorely lacking, then we often try to work with them to bring it to the state where it can be evaluated.

Use this step to set the client's expectations about what the ATAM will produce for the project. Even if there is no architecture in place, you may still wish to proceed with the joint understanding that the ATAM will produce a set of stakeholder-adopted scenarios that articulate the project's quality attribute priorities for the architecture. At that point, the clients may need to decide if they want to proceed under these conditions. They'll get better requirements, a set of stakeholders that have learned how to act in concert with each other, and a clear understanding of the architectural decisions that need to be made. Is that enough to warrant the investment? Perhaps. We don't think of this step as invoking a rigid set of criteria so much as achieving a mutual understanding and comfort level with what we expect the ATAM will produce in each case.

We have followed this advice and conducted evaluations when the architecture was substantially nonexistent or at least woefully underspecified. Even in these cases the ATAM was deemed beneficial by the participants. Scenarios always are useful, and many times new architectural insights emerge even for incipient architectures.

6.2.4   Phase 0, Step 4: Negotiate the Statement of Work

Step Summary

Agree on the contractual framework for the evaluation

Inputs
- [ ] ATAM documents used in Step 1, with emphasis on cost, effort, and benefit data.
- [ ] Candidate system documents from Step 2.
- [ ] Sample statement of work from a previous exercise, or using a template specific to your organization.

Activities

These activities might take place over a span of time involving multiple meetings.

[ ] Evaluation organization representatives negotiate a contract or statement of work with the client. Make sure that your statement of work resolves the following issues:

    [ ] Period of performance.

    [ ] Scope of work.

    [ ] Scope of system to be evaluated.

    [ ] Costs.

    [ ] Deliverables.

    [ ] Candidate schedule.

    [ ] Responsibility for providing resources such as supplies, facilities, food, presence of stakeholders, and presence of architect and other project representatives.

    [ ] The evaluation organization's availability (or nonavailability) for follow-up work.

    [ ] Outline, contents, and disposition of the final report.

    [ ] Client's agreement to participate in near-term and follow-up surveys.

[ ] Record questions asked about the method or the process for possible inclusion in a Frequently Asked Questions list.

Outputs

[ ] Statement of work as described above.

[ ] Agreed dates for Phase 1 and Phase 2 steps.

Step Description

A statement of work establishes a contract between the evaluation group and the client's organization. This contract will help set expectations on both sides about what will be produced and its disposition. Make sure the contract specifies:

- Period of performance

- Scope of work

- Scope of system to be evaluated (for example, does it include software to generate or build the system? Does it include any software with which the primary system interacts?)

- Costs

- Deliverables, to whom they will be delivered, and when

- Candidate schedule

- Responsibility for providing resources such as supplies, facilities, food, presence of stakeholders, and presence of architect and other project representatives

- The evaluation organization's availability (or nonavailability) for follow-up work
- Outline, contents, and disposition of the final report
- Client's agreement to participate in near-term and follow-up surveys

The near-term and follow-up surveys will help you improve your application of the method by gauging results and incorporating improvements.

How It Went

Our organization uses a fairly standard statement of work. Our business development people used it to establish a contract with NASA, and there were no complications.

Speaking from Experience

What you can expect depends on how your organization is related to the client's organization and what the working relationship is between the two. You might expect to have to negotiate about schedule, cost, and delivery. The client will need to understand about participating in short-term and long-term surveys, and you should expect to have to explain that.

This agreement and the process surrounding it are often political. At times we have found that getting buy-in from a key stakeholder might require special rules. For example, we might need to agree on rules regarding the disposition of reports, such as, "We will show the report to you and give you a chance to formally respond before we show it to your funding organization."

6.2.5   Phase 0, Step 5: Form the Core Evaluation Team

Step Summary

Choose the evaluation team members who will participate in Phase 1.

Inputs

[ ] Candidate evaluation schedule (from Step 4 and client's desire).

[ ] Potential team members' availability (from internal schedules).

[ ] Candidate quality attributes of interest (for example, performance, modifiability, security, dependability) from client's description of the system in Step 2.

[ ] Team role definitions, given in Table 3.3.

Activities

These activities might take place over a span of time, including negotiation for services of domain/attribute experts.

[ ] Evaluation organization management (or designee):

    [ ] Form the evaluation team. Aim for an overall team size of four to six members. Participants discuss scheduling options and assign roles. Assign as many of the roles as practical at this time. Questioners may

be assigned based on initial understanding of what the driving quality attributes will be.[1]

[ ] Ascertain team members' availability during the evaluation period so that the evaluation can be scheduled with the client.

[ ] Make travel arrangements as necessary.

[ ] If team members' schedules do not support the schedule previously proposed to client, produce a revised schedule.

Outputs

[ ] Revised schedule to be proposed to client, if applicable.

[ ] List of team role assignments.

Step Description

This step consists of finding individuals who will serve on the evaluation team, scheduling their time, and assigning them team roles (see Table 3.3).

The evaluation leader should normally be the most experienced member of the team, unless a new evaluation leader is being groomed. In any case, the evaluation leader will be the primary "face" that the evaluation team shows to the project members and the stakeholders assembled to help with the evaluation, so it is important that this person show confidence and possess first-class facilitation and communication skills.

The duties of the questioners will depend upon the specific quality attributes of interest for the system being evaluated. Sometimes questioners are added to the team only after Phase 1 in which those quality attributes are discovered. Other teams have access to "jack-of-all-trades" questioners knowledgeable in many attribute areas, so the evaluation's team kick-off meeting determines their line of inquiry but their participation is already settled.

Figure 6.1 shows a small but typical evaluation team and how roles may be assigned to individuals.

All members of the team should be well grounded in architectural concepts and be perceived as objective and impartial by the development team whose architecture is being reviewed and by the client. This means that members of the development project itself, or members of a project that competes in some way, should not be chosen. Having individuals on the team who are knowledgeable about the relevant domain is a distinct advantage.

Team members should expect to devote approximately one or two person-weeks each to the evaluation: a day or two studying read-ahead material about the architecture and/or helping to set up the exercise, about three days for the exercise itself, and up to another week to help go over the analysis and write the final report. Travel time, if any, to and from the evaluation site is additional.

---

1. More questioners may be assigned later (see Phase 2, Step 0: Prepare for Phase 2) based on their quality attribute expertise.

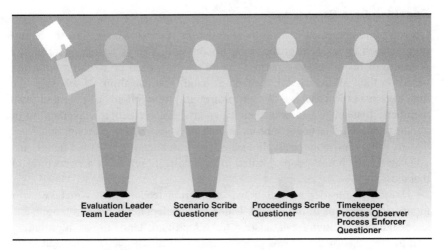

Evaluation Leader Scenario Scribe Proceedings Scribe Timekeeper
Team Leader   Questioner   Questioner   Process Observer
                                                      Process Enforcer
                                                      Questioner

Figure 6.1   One Way to Assign Evaluation Team Roles to a Small Group of Individuals

How It Went

For this evaluation, the team consisted of the three authors plus a fourth member who was chosen because he had broad experience in large-system architectures, real-time systems, and government procurements. We assigned team roles as shown in Table 6.1.

Normally a single person would be the process observer, and another will be the process enforcer. For this evaluation, which featured a heightened awareness of the process steps, we decided to share these duties among all of us.

Table 6.1   ECS Evaluation Team Roles

Team Member	Role
#1	Team leader Evaluation leader
#2	Scenario scribe Questioner
#3	Proceedings scribe Questioner
#4	Timekeeper Questioner
All	Process observer Process enforcer

Speaking from Experience

Do you remember the old *Mission: Impossible* television series? At the beginning of each episode, after receiving his mission, Phelps would go through a portfolio of his agents and choose the ones who would be working with him based on their skills and the mission at hand. You can think of this step like that, except in our case, we don't flip through glossy photos of potential team members. Instead, we inspect their calendars. Expect people's availability or commitment to other tasks to be an important factor in their participation.

At this point, you know about the target architecture in broad detail, and you can try to choose people skilled in the application area or architectures of that class.

Strongly consider assigning two evaluation leaders who will take turns facilitating the steps of the ATAM. Using two leaders helps prevent fatigue and keeps the proceedings fresh. Also, a fresh facilitator tends to pay more attention to the steps of the ATAM process, resulting in a higher-fidelity and more repeatable exercise.

Another point needs to be made regarding the formation of the team. There are times when a small team is possible and even desirable. For example, the project may be small and a big-budget evaluation is not warranted. In such a case it is perfectly reasonable to create a "mini-ATAM" team consisting of one to three people; each person wears multiple hats.

It is also acceptable to use people from the client's organization as members of the evaluation team. We know of several evaluations for which this worked particularly well. In one case the SEI leader of the evaluation decided that he wanted to engage the client organization a little more closely during the evaluation. He invited one of the architects to share the facilitation duties. This had a very positive energizing effect. The ECS case study is another successful example. In this case the goal of inviting NASA's participation was to start transitioning to NASA the capability of performing architecture evaluations. This also worked well for another organization whose members wanted to learn the ATAM.

6.2.6   Phase 0, Step 6: Hold Evaluation Team Kick-off Meeting

Step Summary

Assign roles and plan Phase 1.

Inputs

    [ ] List of team role assignments from Step 5.

    [ ] Sample scenarios from your own repository of scenarios from previous evaluations.

    [ ] Candidate quality attributes of interest (derived business goals and architectural drivers) recorded during Step 2.

[ ] Client's nondisclosure forms, if procured during Step 2.

[ ] System documents received from client during Step 2.

Activities

[ ] Evaluation team leader:

    [ ] Send a message to the evaluation team announcing the time and place for the kick-off meeting and asking them to read the scenarios in this book (or in your own repository of scenarios) and to be ready to suggest those that may be applicable to the architecture being evaluated.

    [ ] Distribute any system and/or architecture documents already received from client.

    [ ] Announce roles and make sure that each team member is comfortable with the responsibilities of the role(s) he or she was assigned.

    [ ] Assign responsibility for writing various sections of the final report (if required), and for producing the viewgraphs for presenting results. The expectation is that the presentation and the report will be produced as the evaluation progresses, not all at once at the end.

    [ ] Make plans with the team to meet and confer throughout the ATAM exercise (for example, hold evening caucuses over dinner) to gauge progress, air concerns, and assess how the evaluation is proceeding (optional but strongly recommended).

[ ] Team members:

    [ ] Select appropriate example scenarios using your organization's own repository as candidates. Scenario scribe records the list.

    [ ] Sign nondisclosure forms (if provided); team leader returns them to client.

Outputs

[ ] List of selected example scenarios.

[ ] Signed nondisclosure forms (if provided by client) returned to client.

[ ] Responsibilities for final report and results presentation assigned.

Step Description

At the kick-off meeting, team members receive their role assignments. They also receive their assignments for specific sections of the results presentation and final report. Any information gleaned from the previous steps about the architecture to be evaluated is shared. The schedule for the evaluation is finalized. Travel logistics, if any, are worked out. Nondisclosure agreements, if any, are signed and returned to the client.

Depending on your team's experience, you may want to

- Go over the responsibilities and expectations associated with each team role
- Discuss possible analysis questions, based on your preliminary understanding of the architecture and its goals

- Discuss letting a junior member of the team take on added responsibilities (such as making the ATAM presentation or carrying out the evaluation leader's role for a portion of the evaluation) as a way to gain experience

Besides assigning roles, responsibility for the final report and the results presentation of Step 9 in Phase 2 needs to be assigned. By assigning sections of the report and presentation, team members can be gathering the right information for those sections as the evaluation proceeds. Putting together the presentation and report then becomes a matter of assembly rather than creation, which dramatically increases the quality of the results and decreases the time it takes to produce them.

How It Went

We had set a date with the client for Phase 1 based on mutual availability. NASA had previously sent us some overview information about ECS and its architecture, and we went through that material as a group to start learning the relevant concepts and terminology. The meeting took about an hour and a half; one of the team members participated by telephone. We paid special attention to the data-intensive nature of ECS. This started us thinking about performance issues associated with high-workload systems.

Speaking from Experience

We often try to assign roles to team members based upon their expertise with specific subsystems or quality attributes. We look at the requirements that have been provided and find the key ones with respect to the quality attributes. We try to see if there are important quality attributes that are missing or underspecified, and we try to understand how the architecture (if it has been described) might satisfy, or fail to satisfy, the requirements.

6.2.7 Phase 0, Step 7: Prepare for Phase 1

Step Summary

The evaluation team leader communicates with the client to arrange the necessary logistics for the Phase 1 meeting.

Inputs
 [ ] Sample Phase 1 agenda (see Figure 6.4).
 [ ] Sample scenarios produced from Step 6.
 [ ] Supply list, such as the one in Figure 6.2.
 [ ] Template for presentation of architecture (see Figure 3.2).
 [ ] Template for presentation of business drivers (see Figure 3.1).

Activities
[ ] Evaluation team leader communicates with client about Phase 1 to:
    [ ] Outline the purpose of the meeting.
    [ ] Confirm the time and place.
    [ ] Include an agenda.
    [ ] Ask the client to arrange a presentation of a system overview and context presentation, including business goals and constraints of the system. (Send Template for Presentation of Business Drivers.)
    [ ] Ask the architect (or ask the client to ask the architect) to present the architecture. (Send Template for Presentation of Architecture.)
    [ ] Include a list of applicable scenarios that may help stimulate thinking.
    [ ] Optional: Ask the client to bring an organizational chart showing the development team structure and the client's relationship to it.
    [ ] Assure the presence of the architect and any other project representative(s) whose presence is appropriate.
[ ] Arrange for food and necessary supplies (overhead projector, flipchart, markers, whiteboard, and so on) at the place of the meeting.
[ ] Assure the presence of the core evaluation team.

Output
[ ] Communication to client.

Step Description

Many logistical details must be handled before an ATAM Phase 1 meeting can take place. The most important issue is agreeing on a date for Phase 1 and making sure that the right people from both sides will be present and prepared to carry out their roles. In addition to the evaluation team, Phase 1 should be attended by people who can speak for the system whose architecture is being evaluated. This means people who can name the quality attribute goals that are driving the architecture and can articulate whatever future visions exist for the system. This also means people who can speak authoritatively about the architecture and the ways in which the architecture achieves the quality-specific attributes demanded of it. In short, the architect should be present.

Secondary details include making sure that necessary supplies will be present (such as an overhead projector, whiteboards, and flipcharts), making lunch arrangements, and finalizing the agenda. Figure 6.2 shows a sample supply list; you can use something similar to check off the things you need.

If the evaluation team has not yet received architecture documentation for the project, ask for it as part of this step; the team will need to look it over before Phase 1 begins. It's a good idea to brief the architect on what is expected of his or her presentation and to go over the kind of information he or she will convey. A good checklist is given in Figure 6.3. It's also a good idea to hold a similar conversation with the person who will be presenting the business drivers.

Facilities and Food

- Meeting room large enough to hold _____ people, preferably arranged with conference-style (U-shaped) seating, reserved for the duration of the evaluation

- Security badges for participants

- Food for meals and snacks if there are no nearby dining facilities

- Writing supplies

- Large flipcharts (two or three) for recording the brainstormed scenarios, issues, risks, etc.

- Markers for writing on the flipcharts

- Whiteboard for drawing diagrams, recording scenarios, tallying votes, etc.

- Markers for writing on the whiteboard

- Adhesive tape for hanging flipcharts around the room

- Blank viewgraphs for making new slides as needed

- Markers for writing on the viewgraphs

- Three pads of self-adhesive note papers, 2" x 2" or larger

- Name badges or "name tents" for participants

Electrical/Electronic Needs

- Laptop computer for use by the proceedings scribe

- Computer video projector for computer-based presentations

- Overhead projector for showing background slides, agenda, adopted scenarios, etc.

- Electrical extension cord

Read-Ahead or Other Written Material

- Overview of system being evaluated, including its context and goals, delivered by the client to the evaluation team leader _____ weeks before the start of the evaluation exercise

- Architecture documentation for the system being evaluated, as agreed upon during Phase 0, delivered by the client to the evaluation team leader _____ weeks before the start of the evaluation exercise

- Evaluation method overview, distributed to participants _____ weeks before the start of the evaluation exercise (optional)

- Copies of participants' end-of-exercise survey to hand out at conclusion of exercise

- Electronic copy of viewgraph templates for presentation of results

Figure 6.2   Supply Checklist for an ATAM Exercise

1. What are the driving architectural constraints, and where are they documented? Are they requirements or goals? Are they measurably quantitative or qualitative? In particular, what are the system's real-time constraints?
2. What component types are defined? For each, what are its:
   - Characteristics
   - Methods
   - Data members
   - Limitations
   - Composition rules
3. What component instances are defined by the architecture?
4. How do components communicate and synchronize? In particular:
   - Mechanisms used
   - Restrictions on use
   - Integration into component type definitions
5. What are the system partitions?
   - Composition
   - Restrictions on use and visibility
   - Functional allocations
6. What are the styles or architectural approaches?
7. What constitutes the system infrastructure?
   - Supplied functionality
   - Resource management
   - Uniform APIs
   - Restrictions
8. What are the system interfaces?
   - Identification
   - Participants
   - Identification of coordination mechanisms used
   - Typing of interfaces
9. What is the process/thread model of the architecture?
10. What is the deployment model of the system?
11. What are the system states and modes?
    - Control
    - Responsibilities
    - State knowledge dispersal
12. What variability mechanisms and variation points are included in the architecture (variability in terms of implementation changes and not data or scenario changes)?
13. How far along is the development? Were the block delivery dates met? Did the blocks meet their functionality requirements?
14. What documentation tree and human help do new employees get?

Figure 6.3   Checklist of Questions the Architect Should Plan to Answer

An organizational chart is useful to reveal who works for whom, and what people's areas of responsibilities are. Sometimes, during an evaluation, there may be tension between staff and management, and this will help you manage that. If you think this is useful, ask your client for it during this step.

How It Went

We carried out this step through a combination of e-mail and telephone conversations. We established a mutually agreeable date via e-mail. The team leader then telephoned the NASA project leader, and the two of them went over the agenda for Phase 1. They chatted about who would be present and what kind of presentations would be appropriate for communicating the business drivers (Phase 1, Step 2) and the architecture (Phase 1, Step 3). The team leader followed up by sending the NASA project leader templates for the presentations, a list of necessary supplies, and a written copy of the agenda (such as the one in Figure 6.4, which is based on the ATAM agenda given in Chapter 3).

Speaking from Experience

Speaking to the architect and the business drivers presenter in this step is the single most effective thing you can do to prevent unpleasant surprises during their presentations in Phase 1. Often, project representatives use presentations

Time	Activity
08:30–10:00	Introductions; Step 1: Present the ATAM
10:00–10:45	Step 2: Present Business Drivers
10:45–11:00	Break
11:00–12:00	Step 3: Present Architecture
12:00–12:30	Step 4: Identify Architectural Approaches
12:30–1:45	Lunch
1:45–2:45	Step 5: Generate Quality Attribute Utility Tree
2:45–3:45	Step 6: Analyze Architectural Approaches
3:45–4:00	Break
4:00–4:30	Step 6: Analyze Architectural Approaches
4:30–5:00	Action Items and Preparation for Phase 2

Figure 6.4 Sample Agenda for ATAM Phase 1

they have on hand rather than presentations that really convey the information desired for the ATAM. The more of their presentations you can see beforehand, the more of a chance you'll have to offer suggestions or midcourse corrections, and Phase 1 will go much smoother. One of the most frustrating experiences we've had as ATAM evaluation leaders is listening to a presentation that is not conveying the information the evaluation team needs. The result is an all-around bad day: the already-tight agenda is blown while the team digs for the right information, the project representatives feel awkward because they've misconnected, and the team leader feels guilty because he or she failed to communicate the team's needs clearly.

6.2.8 Phase 0, Step 8: Review the Architecture

Step Summary
The evaluation team walks through the architecture documentation.

Input
[ ] Architecture documentation identified in Step 2.

Activities
[ ] Evaluation leader facilitates a meeting with the evaluation team in which the architecture documentation is examined and team members attempt to explain it to each other and identify questions or areas of incompleteness.
[ ] Proceedings scribe captures a list of questions to present to architect either during or before Phase 1.

Output
[ ] List of questions for architect.

Step Description
During this step, the evaluation team meets to go through the architecture documentation provided by the client. In theory, this step could be combined with the evaluation team kick-off meeting; in practice, however, the architecture documentation may not have been transmitted by the time the kick-off meeting takes place.

For this meeting, all team members are expected to have read the documentation beforehand to become familiar with its organization and content. In addition, the team leader appoints one or more members of the team to lead a discussion about the architecture. The discussion leaders' task is to try to *explain* the architecture to the other members of the team, based on the information in the documentation. The other team members see if they agree with the explanation, and the whole team catalogs questions that arise during the meeting. These questions, if pertinent to the achievement of important quality attributes, are posed to the architect during the presentation of the architecture during Phase 1.

How It Went

One week before Phase 1 commenced, the evaluation team met for two hours to discuss the documentation. One team member participated by telephone. The team leader had appointed a discussion leader who led us through the documentation until we all had a good understanding of the role each document played in conveying the overall architectural picture. Each of us posed one or two functional scenarios—satellites sending down data, for instance, or a scientist making a query of the data warehouse—and we walked through the architecture until we were satisfied that we knew (or at least *believed* that we knew) how the scenarios would be handled by the architecture.

Speaking from Experience

As noted above, you could combine this meeting with the evaluation team kick-off meeting. However, people in our organization tend to prefer a couple of shorter meetings to one longer meeting; they are also easier to schedule. But there are other reasons to make this a separate, later meeting. First, documentation tends to arrive when it arrives. It might arrive very early, when the client first explains the system. It might arrive some time after that. But it is most likely to arrive very late, just before Phase 1 begins. More often than not, the architect is still working on it. Second, reviewing the documentation just before Phase 1 makes the architecture and its associated issues fresh in the evaluation team members' minds, which is just what you want. Early ATAM exercises did not include this activity as an explicit preparation step; rather, we left it up to each team member to look at the documentation on his or her own. The difference this step makes is noticeable. The team arrives at the client's site well-versed in the architecture and its documentation, with a *shared* understanding of what its status is. The result is a much more effective and cohesive evaluation team.

6.3 Phase 1: Initial Evaluation

Phase 1 of an evaluation using the ATAM is when the evaluation team is formally introduced to the architecture for the first time. Phase 1 comprises the *presentation* activities (Steps 1–3) and the *investigation and analysis* activities (Steps 4–6). Finally, by the end of Phase 1 a list of action items should be crafted that, upon completion, will lay the groundwork for Phase 2 and bring the evaluation to a successful conclusion.

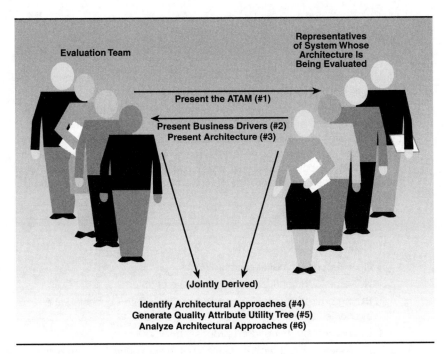

Figure 6.5   ATAM Phase 1 Information Exchange. (Numbers in parentheses refer to Phase 1 steps.)

The steps of Phase 1 are

1. Present the ATAM
2. Present business drivers
3. Present architecture
4. Identify architectural approaches
5. Generate quality attribute utility tree
6. Analyze architectural approaches

Figure 6.5 shows the flow of information in Phase 1.

In mid-April 2000, all four evaluation team members for the case study met with the core architecture and development team in the contractor's headquarters in Landover, Maryland. This was Phase 1 of the ATAM for ECS.

6.3.1   Phase 1, Step 1: Present the ATAM

Step Summary

The evaluation leader describes the evaluation method to the assembled participants, tries to set their expectations, and answers questions they may have.

Input

   [ ] ATAM presentation viewgraphs.

Activities

The evaluation leader may designate another qualified member of the team to conduct the activities of this step.

   [ ] Evaluation leader presents the ATAM, describing the techniques that will be used for elicitation and analysis and the outputs from the evaluation. The team entertains and answers questions, making sure all of the stakeholders have a clear understanding of the method and its goals. This can eliminate or avoid hostility among, for example, the project representatives who may view the evaluation as an intrusion. The object is discovery and communication, not criticism.

   [ ] Evaluation leader emphasizes the importance of the rules of engagement:

      [ ] No side conversations.

      [ ] No hidden agendas.

      [ ] No wandering in/out of proceedings.

      [ ] No value judgments about contributions of others.

      [ ] During brainstorming, all scenarios are fair game—choosing and refining come later.

      [ ] During brainstorming, don't propose answers.

   [ ] Evaluation leader asks the participants what their expectations are of the ATAM. Scenario scribe records them where all can see. Leader identifies those expectations that are *unlikely* to be met by the ATAM (perhaps because of the limitations of the method, the quality of prework, and so on) to avoid disappointment and misunderstanding later.

   [ ] Evaluation leader clarifies the team members' roles and the roles of other participants.

Output

   [ ] None.

Step Description

Step 1 kicks off the meeting, and hence there are some meeting kick-off details that need to be handled here.

- Have the client open the meeting, since he or she is the one at whose behest the stakeholders have assembled. The client should say a few words about the purpose of the meeting, ideally stressing the importance of the architecture evaluation. Then he or she introduces the evaluation leader.

- The evaluation leader should welcome all the participants and have them introduce themselves and their role with respect to the system being evaluated.

- Either the evaluation team can introduce themselves or the evaluation leader can introduce them one by one and explain the assignment each team member has. This helps the participants understand why the evaluation team consists of four or five people—they can see that each member has a job to do.

- The evaluation leader presents the agenda for the meeting. Ideally the agenda should stay posted where everyone can see it throughout the meeting, or it can be distributed as a handout. (A typical agenda for Phase 1 is shown in Figure 6.4.)

- The evaluation leader explains the "rules of engagement" for the meeting. This makes it clear what behavior is expected of the participants: no side conversations, no coming and going, no hidden agendas, no individual dominates the discussion, participation by everyone, and respect for everyone's opinions. Announcing the rules up front will make enforcing them, if necessary, easier.

The evaluation leader then gives a standard one-hour presentation about the ATAM, laying out its steps and what it produces. An outline of the presentation we use is given in Figure 6.6.

How It Went

The project manager, who was sponsoring the evaluation, kicked off the meeting by stating the purpose and goals of the exercise and introducing the participants. Our evaluation leader then introduced the team members and stated the

Presentation	Explanation
Architectural analysis and the ATAM	Tells why architectural analysis is valuable and introduces the ATAM. Introduces concepts of risks, sensitivity points, and tradeoff points. Makes clear that purpose is not detailed analysis but finding trends and correlating architectural decisions to relevant impacts they have. Summarizes benefits of an ATAM evaluation.
Steps of the ATAM	Introduces the nine steps of Phase 1 and Phase 2 of the ATAM. Explains what information is sought in the business drivers and architecture presentations. Discusses architectural approaches. Shows small example of a utility tree. Introduces concept of scenarios, gives examples, and shows the stimulus–environment–response form. Shows examples of quality attribute questions used during analysis steps. Gives examples of risks, nonrisks, sensitivity points, and tradeoff points. Explains how the nine steps are distributed over two phases.
Example	A small ATAM exercise is exemplified. For each step, results are shown based on the BCS example given in Chapter 4.
Conclusions	Short summary and wrap-up. Reminder of the ATAM outputs.

Figure 6.6 Outline of Standard ATAM Presentation

team roles each one would be carrying out. He then gave the standard ATAM presentation. He emphasized the point that the purpose of the ATAM is to assess the consequences of architectural decisions in light of quality attribute requirements derived from business goals. He stressed that we were not attempting to precisely predict quality attribute behavior but rather were interested in identifying the key architectural decisions that affected the most important quality attribute requirements. As such our goal was to elicit and record risks, sensitivity points, and tradeoff points. We would also capture nonrisks as they emerged during the exercise.

Questions from the audience centered around details of Step 5's utility tree. It turned out that this group had already done a great deal of thinking about iterative refinement of quality attribute goals and was anxious to codify those goals with the utility tree.

Speaking from Experience

In general, you can expect a few questions during the presentation, but most will come at the end. Some questions are about particular steps of the method, but most questions center on the results that the exercise will produce. You may be asked about the distribution of the final report; if so, you can relate the terms agreed to under the statement of work negotiated in Phase 0, or you can simply defer to the client and let him or her answer the question. Sometimes people ask about the agenda or about the difference between Steps 6 and 8 (the two analysis steps).

The evaluation leader normally makes the ATAM presentation, but that's not necessary. Having a junior team member lead this step provides excellent training.

It's a good idea to emphasize two aspects during this step. First, always make sure to express appreciation for the presence of the participants—especially the architect. The people you want to attend an evaluation are almost always the busiest, and they're taking time out from their normal routine to participate. Second, it is worth taking great pains to avoid saying anything that would introduce an "us versus them" flavor. There is no "them"—it's all "us." Everyone works as a single team to apply the method to the architecture.

6.3.2   Phase 1, Step 2: Present Business Drivers

Step Summary

A project spokesperson (ideally the project manager or system customer) describes what business goals are motivating the development effort and hence what will be the primary architectural drivers (for example, high availability, quick time to market, or high security).

Inputs
  [ ] System overview presentation documents, if available from client.

Activities
  [ ] Client or project manager presents the system's overview, including scope, business goals, constraints, and quality attributes of interest.
  [ ] During the presentation, all evaluation team members will
    [ ] Look for ways to define the scope of the system being evaluated. Is software to generate or build the system included? What about software with which the primary system interacts?
    [ ] Listen for stakeholder roles to be mentioned.
    [ ] Listen for quality attributes of importance to be mentioned.
    [ ] Identify business goals and constraints.
  [ ] After the presentation, evaluation leader recaps the list of business drivers. If desired, leader polls participants to ask for their lists of stakeholder roles, quality attributes, goals, and constraints. Proceedings scribe records the lists. Scenario scribe records the list of business drivers publicly.

Outputs
  [ ] List of business goals.
  [ ] List of quality attributes of interest.
  [ ] Preliminary list of stakeholder roles that need to be represented during Phase 2.
  [ ] Definition of scope of system. (Optional—this may not emerge until after the architecture is presented.)

Step Description

We want the architecture evaluation to focus on those aspects of the architecture that are important for achieving the business objectives of the system. So the ATAM includes a step that makes those objectives explicit. Here, a representative of the project makes a presentation, about an hour in length, that includes

- A description of the business environment, history, market differentiators, driving requirements, stakeholders, current need, and how the proposed system will meet those needs/requirements
- A description of business constraints (for example, time to market, customer demands, standards, cost, and so on)
- A description of the technical constraints (for example, COTS products that must be used, interoperation with other systems, required hardware or software platform, reuse of legacy code, and so on)
- Quality attribute requirements and from what business needs they are derived

During the presentation, evaluation team members listen for and list key information, including business goals, quality attributes, stakeholder roles, and any delimiting of the system's scope. At the end of the presentation, the evaluation leader summarizes the key business drivers. The proceedings scribe captures the summary for inclusion in the results presentation and the final report.

How It Went

The project manager described NASA's business objectives for ECS. The ECS processes, archives, and distributes earth science data from and about 15 scientific data collection instruments on seven major satellites. Examples of types of data are ocean color, sulfur dioxide from volcanoes, air temperature, moisture, sea surface winds, ice topography, and so on. The goal of the system is to make these data widely available, worldwide, 24 hours per day, in various forms in support of interdisciplinary earth science. There is a diverse user community with various interests in subsets of the collected data and their scientific processing.

The system is distributed at four data centers across the United States:

1. Earth Resources Observation System Data Center, Sioux Falls, SD
2. Goddard Space Flight Center, Greenbelt, MD
3. Langley Research Center, Hampton, VA
4. National Snow and Ice Data Center, Boulder, CO

Authority for various aspects of the system is decentralized. Data centers maintain control of their local facilities and interface with data users. Scientific teams maintain control over their science software and data products. The ECS project management team is responsible for maintaining and planning the evolution of the system. The intended operational life of the system is roughly from 1999 to 2013.

The size of the problem is unprecedented for NASA. The system is large, comprising about 1.2 million lines of custom code. It employs about 50 COTS products integrated with the custom code. The same version of the software runs on each of the distributed sites, deployed on about 20 Unix servers from multiple vendors at each site.

ECS manages large geospatial databases. It archives large amounts of data, adding about 1.5 terabytes per day. It distributes about 2 terabytes of data daily in several different formats. The system also executes complex science algorithms provided by the science community and interfaces to about 34 external systems. Figure 6.7 illustrates the system context for ECS in a viewgraph presented by the project manager. ECS is the portion of the system inside the bold rectangle.

The ECS team had done its homework about the ATAM and surprised us (pleasantly) by including an early version of a utility tree in their business drivers presentation. They had worked this out among themselves in advance of our Phase 1 visit. They felt this was the best way to explain the quality attributes of interest. There was an emphasis on maintainability and operability

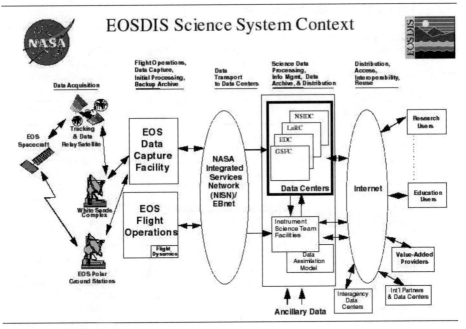

Figure 6.7   ECS in Context

concerns. The other quality attributes of concern were reliability, scalability, and performance. A subset of their preliminary utility tree is shown in Table 6.2.[2]

In Step 5, the scenarios are refined to be more specific (and hence, more analyzable) than some of these.

Quality attributes are shown on the left, and corresponding scenarios (with IDs for easy reference) are shown on the right.

At the end of the client's presentation, we captured the following essential business drivers for ECS.

- Primary business goals:
  - Support for interdisciplinary earth science
  - Concurrent ingest, production, and distribution of high data volumes
  - One-stop shopping (location transparency of system components and data)

---

2. Recall that in a utility tree, the first level is simply "Utility," the second level names a broad quality attribute, the third level is a refinement of the general quality, and the fourth level is a scenario expressing the third-level refinement. Table 6.2 shows the second and fourth levels, which the client labeled "Quality Attribute Goals" and "Attribute-Specific Requirements," respectively.

Table 6.2   ECS Quality Attributes of Interest

Quality Attribute Goals	ID	Attribute-Specific Requirements
Maintainability	M1	Changes to one subsystem require no changes to other subsystems.
	M2	Independently roll back subsystem deployments.
	M3	Reduce regression testing from 5 days to 1 day.
	M4	Reduce time to upgrade operating system, database, and archival management of COTS products by 50 percent or within 6 months of release, whichever is sooner.
Operability	O10	System should be able to reprioritize 1,000 orders in 20 minutes by user class, data types, media type, destination, or user.
	O14	System should be able to service 1,000 concurrent requests through V0 gateway or MTM gateway without operations intervention.
Reliability	R1	No system resources held by data inputs or outputs that are failed or suspended for more than 10 minutes.
	R2	Data errors with one part of request (input/output) should not prevent fulfillment of other parts.
	R6	No requests should be lost as a result of system overloads or failures.
	R8	Search, browse, and order submission are down for no more than 1 hour per week due to either failure or backup.
Scalability	S2	System can support 50 sites.
	S3	System can support ingest from 100 data sources.
	S4	System can support electronic distribution to 2,000 sites.
Performance	P1	Fivefold improvement for search response times for Landsat L-7 searches.

- Secondary business goals:
  - Support for externally developed science algorithms/applications
  - Science data reprocessing (that is, lineage, version management, processing, and reprocessing, including evolution of algorithms used)
- Other business goals:
  - All data holdings available all the time to all

- Assurance of data integrity for archive
- Automated operations to minimize operational costs
- Management of geospatial data

The proceedings scribe stored this list for later incorporation into the presentation of results.

Speaking from Experience

A project organization as well prepared for an ATAM evaluation as NASA is, in our experience, the exception rather than the rule. Not only had the NASA participants studied the method from the open literature before our arrival, but they also had proceeded to begin ATAM activities—drafting a utility tree and using it in their business drivers presentation—before the ATAM exercise even began. More often is the case where the project organization prepares a rudimentary presentation culled from existing viewgraphs for, say, their project sponsor. You should take steps to make sure that the business drivers presentation covers the information relevant to the evaluation. Talking to the presenter beforehand (during Step 7 of Phase 0) will help with this, but the evaluation leader should also be prepared to politely intervene during the presentation itself if the topic is wandering off course.

One thing to keep in mind as the business drivers are being presented is the importance of creating a distillation that can be used throughout the remainder of the evaluation. If the presenter has not done so, the evaluation team should elicit in bullet form five to ten key business drivers and their associated quality attribute. It is the ability of the system to serve these drivers that ultimately determines its success or failure. These drivers usually express important market differentiators and cost constraints that have strong implications for system quality attributes. One of the key aspects of the evaluation involves establishing the link between the risk themes that emerge during the evaluation and these business drivers. Keeping this in mind during the evaluation helps to focus the evaluation.

6.3.3 Phase 1, Step 3: Present the Architecture

Step Summary

The architect describes the architecture, focusing on how it addresses the business drivers.

Inputs

[ ] Description of important attribute-specific requirements from Phase 0, Step 2, and Phase 1, Step 2.

[ ] All available documentation for architecture being evaluated.

[ ] Description of any attribute-specific architectural approaches from Phase 0, Step 2.

[ ] Sample quality attribute characterizations, such as those shown in Chapter 5.

Activities

[ ] Architect describes technical constraints, other systems with which the system must interact, and attribute-specific architectural approaches.

[ ] Proceedings scribe records highlights of architect's explanations.

[ ] All evaluation team members note architectural approaches used/mentioned, potential risks in light of drivers, and additional stakeholder roles mentioned.

Outputs

[ ] Summary of architecture presentation, recorded by proceedings scribe.

[ ] Architecture presentation materials.

Step Description

In this step, the architect spends anywhere from one to three hours presenting the software architecture that is to be evaluated. As a result of the setup step for this phase, he or she will have received a suggested presentation template like the one shown in Figure 3.2. We ask the architect to cover the following information:

- The driving architectural requirements, the measurable quantities associated with these requirements, and any existing standards, models, and approaches for meeting these

- Major functions, key system abstractions, and domain elements along with their dependencies and data flow

- The subsystems, layers, and modules that describe the system's decomposition of functionality, along with the objects, procedures, and functions that populate these and the relations among them (for example, procedure call, method invocation, callback, containment)

- Processes, threads along with the synchronization, data flow, and events that connect them

- Hardware involved, including CPUs, storage, external devices, or sensors along with the networks and communication devices that connect them

- Architectural approaches, styles, patterns, or mechanisms employed, including what quality attributes they address and a description of how the approaches address those attributes

- Use of COTS products and how they are chosen and integrated

- A trace of one to three of the most important use case scenarios including, if possible, the run-time resources consumed for each scenario

- A trace of one to three of the most important change scenarios describing, if possible, the change impact (estimated size and difficulty of the change) in terms of the changed components, connectors, or interfaces

- Architectural issues and risks with respect to meeting the driving architectural requirements

During the presentation, the evaluation team members listen for architectural approaches; these will be catalogued in the next step. They also listen for quality attribute requirements that have not been previously captured.

How It Went

The project manager and one of the architects took turns presenting various aspects of the architecture for this large, complex data acquisition and management system. Figure 6.8 shows a viewgraph that NASA presented to give an overview of ECS.

The key subsystems of ECS are data management, data server, data ingestion, data processing and planning, management interoperability, and user interface. A portion of the system is concerned with the automatic "pushing" of raw data or synthesized data into the system. Another portion of the system is concerned with manual and automatic "pulling" of selected data products to the user community.

Data Management and Data Server Subsystems   Managing data, at the heart of the system, is accomplished through two subsystems: the data management and data server subsystems. The data server subsystem is primarily responsible for data storage and retrieval, whereas the data management subsystem is

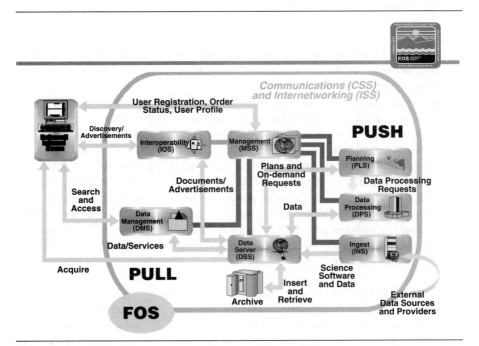

Figure 6.8   View of ECS Components, as Provided by the Client

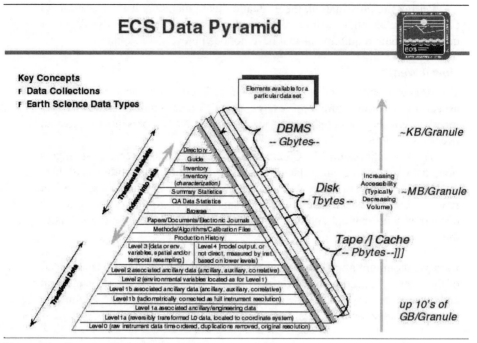

Figure 6.9   Common Metamodel for ECS Data

responsible for searching through the data. Data products are described by metadata (the model for which is shown in Figure 6.9) to enable browsing and searching through terabytes of data.

The metamodel defines all stored data types, their attributes, and their relationships. Each pyramid is known as an *earth science data type*. Raw sensor data is at the bottom of the pyramid. The next level is data synthesized from the raw data using science algorithms. Relevant metadata is stored further up the pyramid. Some attributes are defined across all data types; other attributes are specific to a data type. Storage of the product data associated with a data type can be configured on a type-by-type basis. Portions of a data collection may be allocated across multiple storage units (for example, silos) to improve performance—allocations may be changed over time to support new access patterns. Data collections may be replicated to protect against data loss. Support exists for on-line query of data.

Data Ingestion Subsystem   The data ingestion subsystem is the entry point for instrument data. It supports concurrent ingestion from multiple data sources; accommodates diverse interface requirements; allows tailoring of data checking, conversion, and preprocessing; and performs data source authentication, data transmission checking, and metadata validation.

Data Processing and Planning Subsystems   While the data ingestion subsystem is responsible for acquiring raw data, the data processing and planning subsystems are concerned with producing higher-level data products. Data processing supports the integration and execution of software algorithms developed by teams of earth scientists. The raw data collected by the ingestion subsystem is transformed and coalesced into higher-level data products using various earth science algorithms and then ultimately used by the earth science communities. Planning supports the automated scheduling of algorithm executions based on either data arrival or user requests such as:

- Routine production requests (always generate a product when input data arrives)
- On-demand requests (generate a product only when requested)
- Product requests tied to future events (a data acquisition request, for example)

Multiple algorithms may be chained together. Production rules determine which data are used for input. The data products managed by ECS include some generated by ECS using earth science software and products produced by other computation/science centers that are redistributed and reprocessed into higher-level products by ECS.

Management and Interoperability Subsystems   The management subsystem supports manual and automatic ordering and delivery of data. Interoperability subscription mechanisms support automatic delivery of data when it becomes available, and notification mechanisms support notification based on ingestion of data of interest. Different media delivery options and data compression options are supported.

User Interface Subsystem   ECS supports a Web-based interface that permits searches against metadata attributes and provides integrated, on-line access to browse data prior to ordering full data products.

Other Subsystems   The flight operations segment (FOS) is outside the scope of ECS. ECS is supported by a communications infrastructure that is simply pictured as a ring around the ECS subsystems in Figure 6.8.

Other Views   Deployment views were also presented but not heavily used during the evaluation. In fact, ECS comes with volumes of documentation, and we could have easily spent a month or more listening to presentations about the design and operation of the system. The point of the first four steps of Phase 1 is to acquire a broad overview of the architecture so that the evaluators can begin to formulate probing questions.

Speaking from Experience

At this point in an evaluation more detail is not necessarily better. Preparing one hour of the right high-level depiction of the architecture is a useful exercise in its own right and provides better information to the evaluation team than many hours of details. We have found it useful to review the architecture ahead of time. In fact, at this point in time the evaluation team should have already had an opportunity to see and react to at least some of the architecture documentation. Sending questions in advance to the architect can serve as a guide for what to present during this step. Let the utility tree direct you later to places where more detail is necessary, and let the subsequent analysis drive the need for detail.

Still, you can expect a flood of information to be poured on you at this point. The architects are in their glory and will talk for 20 hours if you let them. Often the information they provide is vague (and hence unanalyzable). Architecture teams often have canned presentations. Try to discourage architects from rattling through these. Keep the end goal in mind—to elicit enough architecture information to understand the architecture approaches that address the high-priority items from the utility tree.

We recommend here, just as we did for the business drivers presentation, that the evaluation team be watchful for and urge the architect to present key architectural approaches. One of the main goals of this presentation is to end up with a distillation of the approaches the architect has used to address what he or she considers to be the important quality attribute goals the architecture needs to satisfy. These will formally be listed in the next step of the ATAM, but being watchful for them here is important.

6.3.4   Phase 1, Step 4: Identify Architectural Approaches

Step Summary

Architectural approaches are identified by the architect but are not analyzed.

Inputs

- [ ] Description of important attribute-specific requirements from Phase 0, Step 2, and Phase 1, Step 2.
- [ ] Architecture presentation materials from Step 3.
- [ ] Description of any attribute-specific architectural approaches from Phase 0, Step 2.
- [ ] Architectural approaches identified by team members during presentation of the architecture.
- [ ] Sample quality attribute characterizations, such as those shown in Chapter 5.

Activities

- [ ] Evaluation team identifies approaches inherent in the architecture as presented. Options:
    - [ ] Evaluation leader asks architect to quickly identify the major approaches he or she thinks were used.

  [ ] Evaluation leader polls team to gather the approaches identified by each member.
  [ ] Evaluation leader asks architect to validate the list gathered.
  [ ] Scenario scribe records the list of approaches for all to see.

Outputs
  [ ] List of approaches recorded by scenario and proceedings scribes.

Step Description

The main purpose of looking for approaches during the architecture presentation is to start formulating questions and drawing preliminary conclusions about how the architecture is realizing key quality attribute goals.

During this step, the evaluation leader asks the architect to recount the dominant architectural approaches used in the system, and the scenario scribe captures the list for all the participants to see. Evaluation team members augment the list with any other approaches they heard during the previous step or noted during their review of the architecture documentation in Step 8 of Phase 0.

How It Went

Several architectural approaches were identified during the ECS architecture presentation.

- The client-server approach is used heavily since this is a data-centric system.
- Distributed data repositories are used to accommodate the distribution of the user community, to enhance performance and for reliability.
- Distributed objects with location transparency are used to achieve modifiability in a distributed setting.
- A three-tiered layered approach separates the rules for automatic higher-level data generation and data subscription from data management and storage.
- Metadata can be thought of as an approach that supports usability, the ability to give meaning to terabytes of data.

Each approach suggests some issues to think about.

- Client-server approach: possibility of contention for databases and throughput issues
- Distributed data repository: issues of database consistency and possible modifiability concerns
- Distributed objects: a plus for modifiability but with potential performance consequences
- Three-tiered layers: again, a plus for modifiability but with potential performance consequences

- Metadata: sounds splendid for usability (but, to foreshadow a bit, could cause some modifiability problems)

Speaking from Experience

This is one of the most straightforward steps of the ATAM. We seldom devote more than 30 minutes to it. It is much more a matter of compiling than creating. The evaluation team already has a set of approaches in mind from working with the architect to craft the architecture presentation and from reviewing the architecture documentation in Step 8 of Phase 0. The architect, ideally, already explicitly named the approaches during the Step 3 presentation.

On the other hand, we have seen cases in which this step seems very mysterious, especially when the architect has not even thought of his or her architecture in terms of architectural approaches. Moreover, many stakeholders in the audience might not be familiar with what an architectural approach is, let alone know about specific ones. However, as the evaluation team extracts examples of approaches from the architecture, other people will begin to understand the essence of what is being captured. They will begin to see that an architectural approach is a collection of architectural decisions, which work in concert to contribute to the achievement of a quality attribute goal. They will also begin to understand the kinds of architectural decisions that the ATAM processes in its analysis mill. Participants who wondered how any method could claim to evaluate something as amorphous and monolithic as an architecture now begin to see that architectures emerge from many discrete decisions, and those can be analyzed and scrutinized.

Notice the pattern for Steps 2 through 4: present, distill, present, distill. In Step 2 business drivers are presented and then at the end of the presentation they are distilled into a list. In Step 3 the architecture is presented and then in Step 4 the architecture is distilled into a list of architectural approaches. These distillations should be in everyone's mind for the duration of the evaluation, and should be posted where everyone can see them. They serve to frame the whole evaluation. The rest of the evaluation determines whether the business drivers are supported by the architectural approaches.

6.3.5 Phase 1, Step 5: Generate Quality Attribute Utility Tree

Step Summary

The quality factors that comprise system "utility" (performance, availability, security, modifiability, and so on) are elicited, specified down to the level of scenarios, annotated with stimuli and responses, and prioritized.

Inputs

    [ ] Business drivers and quality attributes from Step 2.
    [ ] List of architectural approaches recorded during Step 4.

[ ] Template for the utility tree for the proceedings scribe to use when capturing the utility tree. The template can be a table such as Table 6.2 on page 156 with the entries blanked out.

Activities

[ ] Evaluation leader facilitates the identification, prioritization, and refinement (to scenarios) of the most important quality attributes. Address the following steps
   [ ] Assign "Utility" as root.
   [ ] Assign quality attributes identified as important to this system as children of root.
   [ ] Facilitate identification of third-level nodes as refinements of second-level nodes, for example, "latency" might be a refinement of "performance" or "resistance to spoofing" might be a refinement of "security." Use sample quality attribute characterizations to stimulate discussion.
   [ ] Facilitate identification of quality attribute scenarios as fourth-level nodes.
   [ ] Ask development organization participants to assign importance to the scenarios, using H/M/L scale.
   [ ] For those scenarios rated "H," ask the architect to rate them in terms of how difficult he or she believes they will be to achieve. Use H/M/L scale.
[ ] Questioners make sure that important quality attributes are represented in the tree or point out differences between what has been generated and what was presented as drivers or what appeared in requirements specification. Questioners also listen for additional stakeholder roles mentioned.
[ ] Scenario scribe records the utility tree publicly.
[ ] Proceedings scribe records the utility tree in the electronic record.

Output

[ ] Utility tree of specific quality attributes requirements prioritized by importance and difficulty.

Step Description

This step involves facilitated, directed brainstorming aimed at filling the leaves and internal nodes of a blank utility tree. The intermediate and final results should be made public for all participants to see with flipcharts, viewgraph slides, or a projected PC display.

The root (Level 1) of the tree is "Utility." Level 2 consists of broad quality attributes such as "performance." Begin filling in the second level by listing the quality attributes that were named in the Step 2 presentation of business drivers. Ask the participants for other quality attributes at this level. Evaluation team members (especially questioners, who are assigned to "oversee" certain quality attributes) are free to make suggestions, but all candidates should receive group consensus before being added to the tree.

After the group agrees that the quality attribute list at the second level is fairly complete, move to the third level and begin filling in quality attribute refinements. For each Level 2 quality attribute, ask what it means in more concrete terms or how it is measured. These will lead to the Level 3 quality attribute refinements.

Finally, proceed to Level 4, and solicit quality attribute scenarios that capture in analyzable detail what each quality attribute means. Aim for two or three scenarios for each quality attribute refinement on Level 3.

How It Went

For ECS, we had the prototype utility tree from Step 2 for a starting point, an unusual but happy circumstance that gave us a head start.

Working at the Top   As the result of a previous independent (but ATAM-influenced) effort at articulating their goals for the architecture, the client team had a set of fifty-some "study goals" for the ECS architecture. These goals were each mapped to one or more "high-level goals" (to use the client's term):

- Operability (O)
- Maintainability (M)
- Scalability (Sc)
- Performance (P)
- Flexibility/extensibility (F)
- Reliability/availability (Ra)
- Security (S)
- Usability (U)

These became second-level quality attributes in the ECS utility tree. Quality attribute refinements on Level 3 quickly followed from these.

Crafting Scenarios   To fill out the fourth level of the utility tree, we focused on refining the quality attribute refinements into analyzable quality attribute scenarios. For example:

- **Quality attribute refinement (Level 3):** Changes to one subsystem require no changes to other subsystems.
- **Quality attribute scenario (Level 4):** Deploy the next version (5B) of the science data server with an update to the earth science data types and latitude/longitude box support into the current (5A) baseline in less than eight hours with no impact on other subsystems or search, browse, and order availability.

The Level 3 quality attribute refinement describes the maintainability measure as the degree to which changes in one subsystem propagate to other subsystems. The quality attribute scenario refines this by specifying the subsystem, specifying a specific change, and specifying a bound on how long this change should take.

Another example, this one for reliability/availability:

- **Quality attribute refinement (Level 3):** Search, browse, and order submission downtime.
- **Quality attribute scenario (Level 4):** Search, browse, and order submission are down for no more than one hour per week due to either failure or backup.

The attribute-specific requirement describes the reliability measure as the amount of downtime for a specific system capability. The quality attribute scenario refines this by adding causes for downtime and a bound on the amount of downtime.

Finally, one more example, this time for performance:

- **Quality attribute refinement (Level 3):** Fivefold improvement for search response times for Landsat L-7 searches.
- **Quality attribute scenario (Level 4):** A Landsat L-7 search with 100 hits received under normal operations takes 30 seconds or less.

The attribute-specific requirement describes the performance measure of response time for searching for Landsat data. The quality attribute scenario refines this by specifying the size of the search in terms of the number of data base hits and an upper bound on the response time.

The NASA participants were quite conscientious at trying to pose scenarios in good stimulus–environment–response form, often reminding each other (before we had a chance to) to try to phrase the scenarios using the preferred structure.

Prioritizing Utility Tree Scenarios   The ECS team was methodical in interpreting the difficulty; difficulty was defined in terms of an estimate of how long it would take to create a new architectural design and/or implementation to realize the scenario and the level of expertise needed to create the design. The scale they used for both difficulty and importance was numeric: 10 was low, 20 was medium, and 30 was high. They preferred a numeric scale because they could sum the two factors to produce an overall measure of importance. Table 6.3 contains a subset of the ECS utility tree (shown in the tabular template used by the evaluation team's proceedings scribe to capture it); the final priority associated with a scenario was calculated by summing the difficulty and importance.

Speaking from Experience

Quality Attribute Names   Quality attribute names that appear at the second level of the utility tree (such as performance, reliability, operability, and so on) have different meanings to different communities. Sometimes they have special meaning within organizations. Sometimes they have only very broad,

Table 6.3   Subset of the ECS Utility Tree with Priorities[a]

Level 2: Quality Attribute	Level 3: Quality Attribute Refinement	Level 4: Quality Attribute Scenario	Importance	Difficulty	Sum
Maintainability	M1: Changes to one subsystem require no changes to other subsystems.	M1.1: Deploy 5B version of the science data server with an update to the earth science data types and latitude/longitude box support into 5A baseline in less than 8 hours with no impact on other subsystems or search, browse, and order availability.	30	30	60
	M2: Independently roll back subsystem deployments.	M2.1: Perform rollback of the science data server from M1.	20	20	40
	M3: Reduce regression testing from 5 days to 1 day.	M3.1: Regression test the science data server deployment from M1 in 1 day.	20	10	30
	M4: Reduce time to upgrade operating system, database, and archival management COTS by 50 percent or within 6 months of release, whichever is sooner.	M4.1: Upgrade from IRIX 6.2 to IRIX 6.5 and replace some hardware in 1 day.	30	30	60
		M4.2: Upgrade Sybase in 1 Day	30	20	50
		M4.3: Upgrade DCE in 1 Day	30	30	60
Operability	O10: System should be able to reprioritize 1,000 orders in 20 minutes by user class, data types, media type, destination, or user.	O10.1: Backlog management—after 24 hours of downtime, operations reprioritizes backlogged workload in 30 minutes to ensure tasks are worked off in priority order and that normal operations continue to be supported with no degraded throughput following resumption of normal operations.	30	20	50

(continued)

Table 6.3 Subset of the ECS Utility Tree with Priorities[a] (*continued*)

Level 2: Quality Attribute	Level 3: Quality Attribute Refinement	Level 4: Quality Attribute Scenario	Importance	Difficulty	Sum
Operability (*continued*)	O14: System should be able to service 1,000 concurrent requests through V0 Gateway or MTMGW without operations intervention.	O14.1: MODAPS down for 24 hours, recovers and requests 2 days of data; work off in priority order.	20	20	40
		O14.2: Receive 100 concurrent search requests, don't reject high-priority requests, and work-off without overloading system as capacity permits.	20	20	40
Reliability/ Availability	Ra1: No system resources should be held by data inputs or outputs that are failed or suspended for more than 10 minutes.	Ra1.1: L-7 fixed scene orders for electronic FTP push to a site whose FTP server is down, system suspends within 10 minutes of first failed request, and all resources are available while requests are suspended. Distribution to others not impacted.	30	10	40
	Ra2: Data errors with one part of request (input/output) should not prevent fulfillment of other parts.	Ra2.1: Order for 100 granules, 3 on off-line tape/drive, system suspends these requests in 10 minutes of first failure and operator is able to resume remainder.	30	10	40
	Ra6: No requests should be lost as a result of system overloads or failures.	Ra6.1: DDIST must be cold-started due to hardware problem, pending orders identified and re-started in 5 minutes.	10	10	20
	Ra8: Search, browse and order submission downtime	Ra8.1: Search, browse and order submission are down for no more than 1 hour per week due to either failure or backup.	30	20	50

(*continued*)

Table 6.3 Subset of the ECS Utility Tree with Priorities[a] (*continued*)

Level 2: Quality Attribute	Level 3: Quality Attribute Refinement	Level 4: Quality Attribute Scenario	Importance	Difficulty	Sum
Scalability	Sc2: System can support 50 sites.	Sc2.1: Cross-site order tracking across 50 sites, status in 2 minutes for a 5-site order.	20	30	50
		Sc2.2: Cross-site user registration in 24 hours across 50 sites.	20	30	50
	Sc3: System can support ingest from 100 data sources.	Sc3.1: Receive ingest requests from 100 sites; work off in priority order and manage throughput to requirements.	20	20	40
	Sc4: System can support electronic distribution to 2,000 sites.	Sc4.1: Subscription fires for 2,000 users to send 1 GB of data to each; system works in priority order.	20	10	30
	Sc5: System able to scale to 10x requirements for ingest, distribution and processing without software changes.	Sc5.1: 10,000 data processing requests (DPRs) per day; an additional 6,000 DPRs will be planned and executed each day as part of normal operations with no additional staff or hardware.	20	30	50
Performance	P1: Fivefold improvement for search response times for Landsat L-7 searches.	P1.1: L-7 search with 100 hits under normal operations, result in 30 seconds.	30	20	50

a. Level 1 ("Utility") has been omitted to conserve space.

imprecise meaning. And yet one of the important goals of the ATAM is to elicit the precise quality attribute goals for the system being evaluated.

For the ECS system, operability was important. Operability is concerned with the level of operator intervention necessary to use the system. The stimulus for operability is a request for operator intervention. The response is the amount of time it takes for an operator to carry out the request. Operability directly impacts the number of operators needed to run the system.

Calibratability was an important attribute for another architecture evaluation. Calibratability is similar to operability. It is a measure of the amount of time it takes a calibration engineer to calibrate the physical models that are an integral part of the system.

Even an attribute as common as performance has different meanings for different people. To some people performance connotes functionality, to others availability, and to others it has to do with timing-related behavior.

The ATAM handles this ambiguity just fine since it has a built-in disambiguation mechanism. We let clients use whatever terms they want for the second level of the utility tree; the evaluation team requires clarity beginning at the third level of the utility tree. If the name of the quality attribute is ambiguous, its quality attribute refinement at Level 3 of the utility tree imbues it with meaning. This allows organizations to use familiar terminology while allowing the ATAM evaluation to proceed by creating unambiguous scenarios reflecting the organization's quality attribute requirements.

Missing Leaves   It is often the case that people refine quality attributes on the second level into quality attribute refinements on the third level but then fail to provide any scenarios to instantiate the qualities any further. The result is a utility tree with a filled-out internal structure but some missing scenario leaves. That's OK. If nobody can think of a scenario, then it probably means that the quality attribute (or at least the third-level refinement of it) is not particularly critical to the system.

Well-Formed Scenarios   Don't expect participants to propose scenarios in perfect stimulus–environment–response form. You should encourage people to think in those terms, but it is not necessary at this point to enforce well-formedness rules. That can come later, when you pick the ones for analysis. Remind people of the goal, though—it will help clarify their thinking. The ECS group, in fact, found the structured form of scenarios (stimulus–environment–response) helpful because it caused them to ask the right questions to produce clear, well-defined scenarios.

Scenarios versus Requirements   You might expect a discussion about the relationship of scenarios to detailed requirements specifications. While it doesn't make sense to spend time crafting scenarios that duplicate functional requirements, we don't want to leave requirements-based scenarios out of the analysis mix, either. A good compromise is to try to identify certain key functional requirements that are indicative of the main work of the system, especially under environmental circumstances that were at the edge of the envelope of one or more system quality attributes.

Rank Assignment   Some groups are not content to assign "H," "M," or "L" (or, as in the case of ECS, values of 10, 20, or 30) to scenarios without coming to a precise agreement beforehand as to what those terms mean. In most evaluations using the ATAM, we have simply let the stakeholders assign intuitive and informal meanings to the terms, but occasionally a group is determined to do better than that.

Here's one way. Ask the group to rate the scenario in terms of how important it is to the system's overall acceptability. Assuming all the scenarios are on the table, ask them to pretend that they aren't allowed to have them all. Which ones would they be the least willing to give up? That is, which ones would (if removed) leave an unacceptable product? Those are the "H" ones. For ranking in terms of difficulty, you can try to use a measure of time it would take to carry out the scenario.

- "H" could mean the scenario would require two or more person-years to implement, would require the services of a senior engineer, and had an unclear or unknown solution.
- "M" could mean a scenario with a known solution requiring two or more person-years to carry out by senior technical staff.
- "L" could refer to everything else.

We have observed, however, that even after a group exhaustively defines the terms, scenarios tend to be rated by simply comparing them to previously rated scenarios: "Do you think scenario 52 is as hard as scenario 38? No? Well, that makes it an 'M', then."

When assigning difficulty, try not to be too formal about projecting effort—we're after coarse-grained divisions here, not detailed analysis.

Finally, some people wonder why prioritization is done by consensus in Step 5 but by a detailed and carefully controlled voting procedure in Step 7. The primary reason is because this combination takes less time and it works. It's easier to form a consensus among the small group attending Phase 1, whereas a consensus informally wrung from a large group would be much less reliable. Nevertheless, if your group decides every scenario in the utility tree warrants a rating of (H,H), you may want to use a voting scheme similar to the one in Step 7. Let the architect and any designers present vote on the difficulty rating, but let everyone from the project team vote on the importance rating.

6.3.6   Phase 1, Step 6: Analyze the Architectural Approaches

Step Summary

Based on the high-priority factors identified in Step 5, the architectural approaches that address those factors are elicited and analyzed (for example, an architectural approach aimed at meeting performance goals will be subjected to a performance analysis). During this step architectural risks, nonrisks, sensitivity points, and tradeoff points are identified.

Inputs

[ ] Utility tree from Step 5.

[ ] List of architectural approaches from Step 4.

[ ] Analysis of architectural approach template (see Figure 3.5).

[ ] Sample quality attribute characterizations such as those shown in Chapter 5.

Activities

[ ] Architect identifies components, connectors, configuration, and constraints relevant to the highest-priority utility tree scenario nodes.

[ ] Evaluation team generates style-specific and quality-attribute-specific questions as starting points for discussion. Use the architectural mechanisms in the sample quality attribute characterizations as a guide.

[ ] Proceedings scribe records discussion and records risks, nonrisks, sensitivity points, and tradeoff points.

[ ] Scenario scribe records risks, nonrisks, sensitivities, tradeoffs, and open issues as they arise, as identified by evaluation leader.

Outputs

[ ] Analysis of architectural approach templates, filled out for analyzed scenario.

[ ] List of sensitivity points, tradeoff points, risks, and nonrisks.

Step Description

Analysis in this step does not entail detailed simulation or precise mathematical modeling. It is more of a qualitative analysis, perhaps similar to detective work in that we are looking for architectural clues that might reveal suspects. Precise analysis is impractical to carry out in real time in front of a large group. Moreover, it is not cost effective; it would take more time than it is worth to apply detailed analysis to many scenarios. On the other hand, our investigation is informed by knowledge of the mechanisms that are commonly used to realize quality attribute requirements.

To carry out this step, let the template for analysis of architectural approaches (see Figure 3.5) be your guide. Begin by making sure the scenario's stimulus, environment, and response are clearly stated; if not, take the time to put it in proper form. Then, with the architect's help, identify the architectural approaches that are relevant to carrying out this scenario. Using the style-based analysis questions, begin probing for known risks with the approach. Try to see how the approaches affect each quality attribute of interest, including those beyond the one with which the scenario is associated. Judge the answers you receive as problematic or not with respect to the quality attribute goals.

When a risk, sensitivity, tradeoff, or nonrisk is identified, make sure the scenario scribe captures it publicly.

At the conclusion of each scenario's analysis, each member of the team tries to formulate (in his or her mind) a set of risk themes based on the total set of risks identified so far. As more risks are uncovered, the team gathers evidence for or against the risk themes hypothesized. These risk themes play an important role in the presentation of results and the final report.

How It Went

In this section, we recount the analysis of three high-priority scenarios. These scenarios are M1.1, RA8.1, and P1.1, maintainability, reliability/availability, and performance scenarios, respectively. We discuss the analysis for scenario M1.1 in great detail and then offer a more cursory discussion for scenarios RA8.1 and P1.1.

For each scenario the stimulus, response, and attribute of concern are highlighted. The key architectural decisions impacting the scenario are then elicited and each is indicated as being a risk, nonrisk, sensitivity point, and/or tradeoff point. For each scenario that we analyzed we filled out an analysis template; our proceedings scribe kept a record by using a corresponding template in his laptop computer.

Analyzing Scenario M1.1   One of the highest-priority scenarios in the utility tree was maintainability scenario M1.1. Table 6.4 shows the results of its analysis in the tabular form captured by the proceedings scribe. The scenario was decomposed into its stimulus and response to ensure that each had been captured with sufficient precision. We then asked the ECS architect (and anyone else who could contribute) to enumerate the architectural decisions relevant to achieving this specific maintainability requirement. For each scenario a sequence of steps emerged. These steps provided grist for our group discussion, which led to the architectural decisions and associated risks, nonrisks, sensitivity points, and tradeoffs listed in Table 6.4.

We asked the architect to walk us through the scenario. He responded by giving the steps for realizing the scenario as follows:

1. Shut down the system in preparation for updating the science data server.
2. Perform a science data server database backup and check.
3. Install the new science data server code and GUI code.
4. Apply the changes to the configuration parameters that are related to the new capabilities.
5. Apply the science data server database patch.
6. With operations still down, perform a database check.
7. Reinitiate operations.

Enumerating steps is a useful way to consider a scenario, but this is not the end goal; the goal is to determine the impact the set of architectural decisions has on realizing the scenario.

The architect made the point that the upgrade was carefully controlled to keep the science data server interfaces, client library, and DLLs (Dynamic Link

Library) unchanged. This resulted in the recording of architectural decision AD1, which is about preserving the backward compatibility of the interface.

Table 6.4   Analyzing Scenario M1.1

Scenario #: M1.1	Scenario: (M1.1) Deploy 5B version of the science data server with an update to the earth science data types and latitude/longitude box support into 5A baseline in less than 8 hours with no impact on other subsystems or search, browse, and order availability.			
Attribute(s)	Maintainability			
Environment	During routine maintenance			
Stimulus	Deploy 5B version of the science data server with an update to the earth science data types and latitude/longitude box support into 5A baseline.			
Response	Less than 8 hours with no impact on other subsystems or search, browse, and order availability.			
Architectural Decisions	**Risk**	**Sensitivity**	**Tradeoff**	**Nonrisk**
AD 1 Backward compatibility of interface	R1			
AD 2 Static linkage of client stubs in servers (static binding of libraries)	R2			
AD 3 Single copy of key operational databases	R3	S1	T1, T2	
AD 4 Information about data types distributed throughout system	R4, R5, R6	S2		
AD 5 Name independence of subsystems			T3	
AD 6 Distributed objects with stable, simple API				NR1
AD 7 Uncontrolled dependencies among source files	R7			
Reasoning	For the qualitative reasoning and architecture diagram associated with these architectural decisions, see the discussion related to this table.			
Architecture diagram	None			

This was the mechanism chosen to prevent the propagation of this change beyond the science data server. However, further discussion of this mechanism revealed a risk. Backward compatibility only ensured backward syntactic compatibility, but there are cases in which the same interface can have different meanings (for example, a change in measurement units for some type of data). ECS has the capability of denoting such semantic variations in an interface, but this mechanism was bypassed. This discovery was recorded as risk R1:

> R1. ECS is not using the infrastructure capability to "sign" an interface, thus ensuring only syntactic but not semantic compatibility. Consequence: interface may be syntactically compatible but semantically incompatible and system won't catch this. Could result in incorrect results or failure.

It was noted during the discussion of the above risk that if interfaces are required to change, then a new version of the entire system would have to be deployed. This is due to architectural decision AD2 about the static linkage of client stubs in servers. This concern was recorded as risk R2:

> R2. Static linkage of client stubs requires that a new version of the system be deployed when an interface changes. Consequence: unintended changes may be included with the interface changes.

Another point made during the discussion of the scenario was the lack of a secondary set of databases that could remain operational while the primary databases were being upgraded. This was noted as architectural decision AD3. The consequence of this decision is risk R3:

> R3. Single version of databases means that changes affecting the databases require significant testing. Consequence: changes require lots of testing and downtime.

This architectural decision was also denoted as sensitivity point S1:

> S1. Increasing the amount of downtime associated with a software upgrade increases the risk of the upgrade because rollback is difficult.

Two tradeoff points were also associated with this decision:

> T1. Availability may be negatively affected by having a single set of databases, but the single set is easier to maintain.

> T2. While implementing with a single database might be less expensive (cost is an attribute as well), maintainability suffers since there might be a reluctance to upgrade—having database replicas reduces time and risk of software upgrades, hence you are more willing to do them.

Figure 6.10 highlights architectural decision AD4, which holds that information about data types is distributed throughout the system. This resulted in several risks:

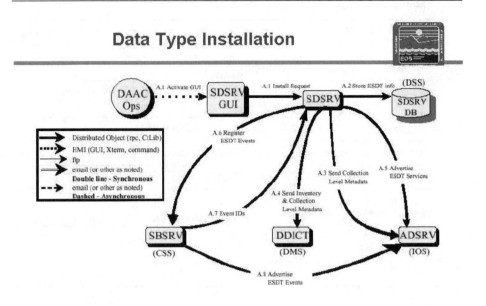

Figure 6.10   Data Type Installation

R4. Data type information is distributed throughout the system. Consequence: a change to a data type may "ripple" throughout the system.

R5. This decision makes it difficult to change data types. Consequence: increased modification costs and reluctance to make enhancements.

R6. All instances of data types may not be changed correctly. Consequence: database inconsistencies may result.

Architectural decision AD5 is one of the approaches that we identified in Step 4 of the method. A name server is used to provide location independence. This is a typical modifiability mechanism, namely a form of indirection. However, it is also very typical for indirection to have performance consequences and hence the tradeoff T3:

T3. Going through the name server enhances modifiability but imposes a performance cost.

Analyzing Scenario RA8.1   The ECS evaluation continued with scenario RA8.1, a reliability/availability scenario. Table 6.5 represents a portion of the architectural approach analysis table for this scenario; like Table 6.4, it reflects what was captured by our proceedings scribe.

Table 6.5 Analyzing Scenario RA8.1

Scenario #: RA8.1	Scenario (RA8.1): Search, browse, and order submission is down no more than 1 hour/week.			
Attribute	Availability			
Stimulus	Database goes down (for backup, therapeutic reboot, upgrade, fault).			
Response	Less than 1 hour of downtime/week.			
Architectural Decisions	**Risk**	**Sensitivity**	**Tradeoff**	**Nonrisk**
AD 8 Single on-line copy of Database	R8, R10	S3	T1, T4	
AD 9 Backup copy of Database on tape (not disk)	R9	S4		
AD 10 Database is not partitioned: single monolithic Database	R11	S5		
...	...	...	...	

There are two aspects of this scenario: routine database maintenance and recovery of a corrupted database. We focus on backup as the stimulus of interest for understanding this scenario. Again members of the ECS team enumerated a set of steps that elaborate the scenario.

1. Backing up is initiated by an operator. It entails running scripts that dump log files and/or the database, obtain index statistics, reorganize indices, and recompile stored procedures.

2. While the database backup is in progress, database searches experience increased response time.

3. If there is sufficient disk space to hold the backup, the database check is done against the backup, and upon completion of the check the database backup image is archived to tape.

4. If there is not sufficient disk space to hold the backup, the clients of the database are stopped, the science data server is taken down, the check is performed against the database itself, and then all system components are warm-started.

Once again these initial observations served as the starting point to identify key architectural decisions related to reliability, which in turn led to the identification of risks, nonrisks, sensitivity points and tradeoff points. But before we look at a couple of the architectural decisions let's step back for a second. The previous scenario was a maintainability scenario. The general concern of the scenario was localization of the effects of change to ensure that a change in one place did not propagate throughout the system. Therefore the architectural decisions that were highlighted revolved around mechanisms for preventing the propagation of change or finding places in which propagation was likely.

The current scenario is a reliability scenario. Reliability is concerned with the amount of time the system is available to perform the service for which it is intended. Therefore, the architectural decisions that are highlighted revolve around mechanisms that ensure the availability of services or decisions that cause services to be unavailable.

The focus of this scenario is on the effects on availability of backing up. Architectural decision AD8 highlights the fact that there is only a single on-line copy of the database. A risk results from this:

> R8. There is only a single copy of the database on-line. Consequence: all activity on the database is halted for database consistency check and upgrade.

The fact that all database-related activity is halted when the database is checked for consistency has a clear impact on achieving availability goals. Likewise, architectural decision AD9, backing up to tape rather than disk, is the reason for the consequence in the above risk. That is, since the consistency checking cannot take place on tape, it must take place on disk, and this requires a quiescent database. We continued in the same vein, eliciting architectural decisions and determining whether they were risks, sensitivity points, and/or tradeoff points.

Analyzing Scenario P1.1   This scenario is a performance scenario. The ECS architect walked us through a simple performance analysis for this scenario. Table 6.6 has an extra column indicating the architect's estimates of the execution times associated with each architectural decision. (For this scenario the scenario steps simply became the architectural decisions.)

This simple analysis (that is, adding up the execution times associated with the architectural decisions) shows very clearly that the desired response time will be missed by a significant margin. Furthermore, it highlights potential bottlenecks in the metadata database and in the use of the object description language library. As in the other cases related risks were discovered.

Analyzing other scenarios   This process continues until (1) time runs out, (2) the high-priority scenarios have all been analyzed, or (3) the client wishes to stop. The client may want to stop because of (1) or (2), or because he or she feels that the project organization can proceed to analyze the other high-priority scenarios on its own. In the case of ECS, the ECS project team tackled twenty additional scenarios without our assistance. This was extraordinary. In most cases, we aim for detailed analysis of just five to ten scenarios, and (even though we always emphasize that the project team is perfectly capable of continuing analysis on their own) the ATAM almost always stops when the evaluation team leaves.

Table 6.6   Analyzing Scenario P1.1

Scenario # P1.1	Scenario (P1.1): L-7 search with 100 hits under normal operations, result in 30 seconds				
Attribute	Performance				
Stimulus	Landsat L-7 search with 100 hits under normal operations				
Response	Search completed in 30 seconds or less				

Architectural Decisions	Execution Time	Risk	Sensitivity	Tradeoff	Nonrisk
AD 11 EDG as primary client	100 sec	R17	S8	T5, T8	
AD 12 Reused object description language library	65 sec	R18, R19	S9		
AD 13 Database not optimized for queries	12.5 sec	R20			
AD 14 Multiple data structure types used for query results	90 sec	R21	S10		
AD 15 Full materialization of metadata	30 sec	R22	S11	T6	
AD 16 All query results returned to gateway at one time	15 sec	R23, R24	S12, S13		
AD 17 Shared/multipurpose metadata database	100 sec	R25	S14	T7	

Significant findings emerged from just the three scenarios we recounted above.

- Maintainability is affected by the distribution of data type information throughout the system.
- Availability is impacted by having only a single copy of databases.
- Performance is impacted by the need to convert between various data types and the slowness of the object description language library.

These three findings formed the basis for some preliminary risk themes. As we analyzed other scenarios, these risk themes were refined to reflect commonalities among the risks that the scenarios as a whole revealed. Later, when we crafted the presentation of results in Step 9, the risk themes were mapped back to the business drivers that they could adversely affect, bringing closure to the method's findings by making clear the impact of not addressing the risks.

Speaking from Experience

One of the main benefits of identifying architectural approaches in Step 4 is that there are attribute-specific questions associated with each approach. A first attempt at codifying approaches and associated questions is the ABAS work that we referred to in Chapter 5. You should create your own bank of architecture approaches and attribute-specific questions so that future evaluations using the ATAM can capitalize on this storehouse of design evaluation information.

You might be wondering how to find these architectural decisions, risks, sensitivity points, and tradeoff points. We would like to think that it is totally a by-product of executing the method. In actuality we know this is not the case. There is a certain amount of informed inquiry that relies on the experience of the evaluators. However, we feel confident that the ATAM will navigate you to the neighborhood of interesting and important architectural decisions.

One of the nice features about the ATAM is that it is "self-scaling." The utility tree tells you what to focus on, and the architectural approaches tell you where to focus. The scenario analysis performed in Step 6 is very constrained and compartmentalized. You can perform two days of analysis or two months of analysis, depending on how many scenarios you study and the level of detail at which you study them. However, in all cases it is possible to perform high-level analysis on the top five to ten scenarios and reveal important risks, sensitivity points, and tradeoff points.

It was a bit surprising to us to see how sensitive this analysis can be to social issues in addition to technical issues. At one evaluation, it looked like the success of the evaluation was in serious jeopardy at one point. The analysis of one scenario was taking particularly long and the evaluation participants were getting tired and frustrated. It appeared that the evaluation team was starting to lose control. Fortunately we were saved by the bell—the lunch bell—which gave us time to ponder the situation. We determined that three factors contributed to this state of affairs. (1) The scenario that we were analyzing actually had two scenarios embedded in it and the analysis was unwittingly oscillating between the two implicit alternatives. (2) Lunchtime was approaching and the participants needed a break. (3) The company was a foreign company. To optimize their discussions, the participants politely asked if they could discuss this scenario in their native language. Of course, we said, fine. This was a mistake. We no longer could guide the discussion and it proceeded down several blind avenues.

After lunch we refined the scenario and requested that the discussion take place in English. The scenario analysis proceeded smoothly and everyone returned to feeling positive about the evaluation.

The moral of this story is that even for the most technical aspects of the ATAM, social issues are just as influential as technical issues on the success of the evaluation.

Leading an Evaluation

We have participated in many evaluations of software and system architectures in many different application domains over the last ten years. In reporting on these methods, we have almost always concentrated on the technical aspects. But as we were developing and refining these methods we were exposed to a wide variety of systems, along with their organizations, organizational goals, management styles, and individual personalities. These experiences have convinced us of the need to explicitly manage the *nontechnical* aspects of running a technical review. There are aspects of the management, psychology, and sociology of performing architecture evaluations that need to be given some thought. Getting these factors wrong can doom the best technical effort.

This observation is not particularly an artifact of software development; it holds true of any complex engineering effort.

> *When Brunel and Robert Stephenson were building railways in the 1830s and 1840s, they were expected to involve themselves with raising capital, appearing before Parliamentary Committees, conciliating influential people who might oppose the necessary bill in Parliament, negotiating with landlords over whose land the tracks were to be laid, managing huge gangs of labourers, and dealing with subcontractors. Railways engineers had to be expert in finance, in politics, in real estate, in labour management, and in procurement. Why should we be surprised if software engineers may need to draw on expertise in mathematics, financial analysis, business, production quality control, sociology, and law, as well as in each application area they deal with? [Freedman 90]*

To lead an architecture evaluation you must be aware of all the issues, technical and nontechnical, that may arise. Therefore when you embark upon an architecture review you need to get buy-in at both managerial and technical levels. You need to get buy-in at the managerial level because stakeholders must be gathered together in sufficient numbers for the review to proceed. You need buy-in from the architect and key developers because these are the roles most able to speak to the design and potential changes to the design. Without buy-in from both managerial and technical participants, the process will not work.

Without understanding the "people" issues involved, a review may be chaotic and unsuccessful. For example, although the process depends on the presence of stakeholders, having too many participants causes problems in crowd control. In one of our reviews we had about forty stakeholders in the room, despite our pleas to keep the stakeholder group small and focused. This system was a large government acquisition with many participating government agencies and many contractors developing different parts of the hardware and software. Everyone wanted to establish a presence to ensure that their interests were properly represented and to impress their client. The result, however, was an overloaded review that was difficult to steer and focus.

Furthermore, it is important when setting the context for a review that you align the evaluees' expectations and goals with what the method can and cannot do. For example, in an ATAM evaluation we scrutinize the architecture's ability to achieve its quality goals. We don't do the organization's architectural design for them (although we can enumerate design possibilities and limitations). And we don't evaluate the project's functional completeness, domain modeling, or interface specifications (although we do offer these services as part of a larger engagement). Any review technique has limited aims and scope. Because of this, it is critical to set customers' expectations in advance so that they are not surprised or angry by what actually transpires.

In a SAAM exercise we led, one stakeholder complained, after it was finished, that we did not cover "domain scoping," or whether the component interfaces were adequately defined. This was completely true; that aspect is simply outside the scope of our standard SAAM exercise. Thus we apparently did not make it sufficiently clear at the start of the SAAM exercise just what we could and could not do within that structure.

The review leader is responsible not only for controlling the unruly participants but also for bringing out the shy persons. Their ideas may be equally important, but their shyness may prevent them from being heard.

As a leader you may have to decide what to do when the rules of the game are violated (for example, when people have side conversations, try to steal the agenda, or resist providing information). You may need to control the pace, sometimes forcing people to stay on topic so that the review time is efficiently used.

This sidebar cannot begin to list all of the possible situations in which you might find yourself. So what can you do? Be aware that problems *will* arise. The stakeholders won't follow the steps as you had intended. Information may not be provided, or it may be provided in an unsuitable form. Stay calm. Stay in control. Always keep the end in mind and return to the agenda. You do not need to slavishly follow the agenda (you might, at times, choose to allow discussion on an interesting side issue for a few minutes because it builds the confidence of the stakeholders to work together as a group), but neither should it be hijacked by the will of a single person. Keep in mind that the process has been proven to work, and it will be most beneficial to the majority if it is followed.

—RK

6.4 Hiatus between Phase 1 and Phase 2

In the period of time between Phase 1 and Phase 2 we worked with the client team to refine the presentations of both the business drivers and the architecture. In that way, the information would be much more crisp when the full community of stakeholders met in Phase 2. This is very much a standard part of Phase 1: obtaining information and then working with the architect to refine the presentation for Phase 2.

But the primary activity carried out during the hiatus is a continuation of Step 6. By continuing analysis during the break between Phase 1 and Phase 2, the hiatus provides a safety valve in case the agenda of Phase 1 did not allow enough time to explore scenarios in depth. The hiatus can allow the evaluation team to engage the architect in a more leisurely manner, through whatever means is convenient. A rule of thumb we use is that if our goal is to analyze ten scenarios in total, then we would like seven of them analyzed by the time Phase 2 begins. We use the hiatus to meet that goal.

6.5 Phase 2: Complete Evaluation

On a Monday in early May, we convened for Phase 2.

Phase 2 begins with the step

0. Prepare for Phase 2

This step occurs during the hiatus between the Phase 1 meeting and the meeting in which the other steps of Phase 2 are carried out.

After the preparation step, the team briefly repeats Steps 1–6 of Phase 1 in the presence of the larger set of stakeholders. Recall from Chapter 3 that the Phase 2 steps consist of validating the information we learned in Phase 1. The elicitation and analysis steps (architectural approaches, utility tree) are recapped and summarized for the larger audience, as opposed to being performed from scratch. These steps are not redefined in this section; refer to the Phase 1 section instead. When the summary of Phase 1 is complete, Phase 2 is supplemented by the following steps:

7. Brainstorm and prioritize scenarios

8. Analyze the architectural approaches

9. Present the results

6.5.1 Phase 2, Step 0: Prepare for Phase 2

Step Summary

Handle logistics for the Phase 2 meeting. Augment the evaluation team with additional questioners if necessary.

Inputs
- [ ] All outputs generated during Phase 1.
- [ ] Team role definitions (see Table 3.3).

Activities
- [ ] Team leader addresses these points:
    - [ ] Augment the evaluation team, if necessary, by adding questioners expert in quality attribute areas identified during Step 2 and Step 5 during Phase 1. Add team members to fill open roles, if any.
    - [ ] Ascertain team members' availability during the evaluation period so that Phase 2 can be scheduled with the client.
    - [ ] Make travel arrangements as necessary.
- [ ] Evaluation leader communicates these points to the client:
    - [ ] Reiterate the scope of the system being (and not being) evaluated.
    - [ ] Send copy of utility tree generated in Phase 1.
    - [ ] Make sure client invites to Phase 2 the stakeholders who will represent the stakeholder roles identified in Phase 1 and vouches for their attendance. Aim for roughly 10–12.
    - [ ] Have client send stakeholders read-ahead material for Phase 2: business drivers presentation, architecture presentation, and scenarios from the utility tree from Phase 1 (optional).
    - [ ] Send the client any read-ahead material you agreed to provide about the evaluation method.
    - [ ] Ask for architecture documentation that was needed but missing during Phase 1.
    - [ ] Send an agenda for Phase 2.
    - [ ] Make sure person hosting Phase 2 has responsibility for arranging for site facilities, meals, and supplies.
    - [ ] Have team members who are assigned to produce presentation of results (see Phase 0, Step 6: Hold Evaluation Team Kick-off Meeting) draft the sections on business drivers, architecture, utility tree, and architecture analysis using results of Phase 1 (optional but recommended).
    - [ ] Have team members who are assigned to write final report draft the sections on business drivers, architecture, utility tree, and architecture analysis using results of Phase 1 (optional but recommended).
- [ ] All agree on dates, time, and venue for Phase 2. Plan for the activities to take place on consecutive days if possible.

Outputs
- [ ] Action item list and assignments, including
    - [ ] Evaluation leader—summary of Phase 1.
    - [ ] Client—list of stakeholders who will participate in the next phase.
    - [ ] Architect—missing architecture documentation, if any.

[ ] All—dates, times, venue for next step(s).
[ ] Host of Phase 2— Arrange site facilities, meals, and supplies for next step(s).
[ ] Updated list of team role assignments.
[ ] First draft of business drivers, architecture, utility tree, and analysis portions of results presentation and final report (optional).

Step Description

This step is the analog to the last step of Phase 0, which laid the logistical groundwork for Phase 1. This step makes sure that Phase 2 will go smoothly by putting the wheels in motion to guarantee the attendance of the right people and the presence of the right supplies and other preparatory materials.

Knowing that the presentation of results in Step 9 has to be drafted in very short order, you can use this step to get a head start on that task. At this point, you have the business drivers, architecture presentation, architectural approaches, utility tree, analysis of several scenarios, and a list of preliminary results: risks, nonrisks, sensitivity points, and tradeoff points. While the steps in Phase 2 can (and usually do) temper or modify the results obtained so far, it will more than pay off to prepare the presentation ahead of time using Phase 1 outputs. It will be much easier to modify the presentation when preparing for Step 9 than it would be to build it from scratch.

Finally, you'll want to send an agenda to the people attending, such as the one in Figure 3.9. The time allotted to Steps 1–6 is for presenting and letting the participants react to the results of Phase 1.

How It Went

We confirmed the time and place for Phase 2 with the client via e-mail and telephone. We also confirmed the attendance of the stakeholder contingent. For Phase 2, stakeholders for the ECS evaluation included:

- The ECS software architect
- The ECS system architect
- An ECS designer knowledgeable about the COTS components used
- Representatives of the ECS operator community
- A representative from another government agency
- Several NASA representatives

We chose not to augment our evaluation team with any additional members. Finally, we spent some time drafting sections of the results presentation for Step 9, producing about 15 viewgraphs summarizing the results from Phase 1.

Speaking from Experience

The quality of an architecture evaluation is a direct function of the quality of the stakeholders who have assembled to help evaluate it. Sometimes the client is reluctant to involve certain stakeholders, for whatever reason. You must impress upon the client that if key stakeholders are not present, then the ATAM will not be able to evaluate the architecture from those key points of view. The results may look satisfactory, but in fact they will have an unseen hole in them. The reason the evaluation team listens for stakeholder roles throughout the client's overview presentation and the project's business drivers presentation is to help the client bring stakeholders to the table whom he or she might otherwise forget (or wish to forget).

6.5.2   Phase 2, Steps 1–6

In Phase 2, Steps 1–6 are summarized for the Phase 2 participants. They are allowed to ask questions, point out and help correct any mistakes or misunderstandings, and offer any suggestions for improvement. However, unless some catastrophic misunderstanding evidences itself during the summaries, wholesale overhaul of the Phase 1 outputs is discouraged.

The outputs of Phase 1 should be made available to the Phase 2 participants in summary form. Printed handouts are a good idea, or summarizing flipcharts hung in plain view also work. The idea is to instill in the participants' minds the principal outputs of Phase 1 so that they need not spend their energies on issues already surfaced and resolved.

During the ECS evaluation, we printed a summary of the business drivers, a list of the architectural approaches, and the utility tree on handouts for the participants. We put the current list of risks, nonrisks, sensitivity points, and tradeoff points on flipcharts hung along one side wall of the conference room. The stakeholders had a number of questions about the precise meaning of some of the scenarios in the utility tree and a few questions about the precise meaning of some of the risks we had recorded. We sensed a fair amount of interest in the business drivers presentation, which is not unusual: this is where the stakeholders see how (or if) their particular interests have made it into the consciousness of the system builders.

6.5.3   Phase 2, Step 7: Brainstorm and Prioritize Scenarios

Step Summary

A larger set of scenarios is elicited from the entire group of stakeholders. This set of scenarios is prioritized via a voting process involving the entire stakeholder group.

Input
[ ] Scenarios from the leaves of the utility tree developed during Step 5.

Activities
[ ] Evaluation leader facilitates brainstorming activity.
>   [ ] Use the scenarios at the leaves of the utility tree to help facilitate this step by providing stakeholders with examples of relevant scenarios. Tell stakeholders that the leaves of the utility tree that were not analyzed are valid candidates for inclusion in this step.
>   [ ] Put up the list of stakeholders to stimulate scenario brainstorming.
>   [ ] Ask each stakeholder to contribute a scenario in a round-robin fashion.
>   [ ] Tell participants not to be constrained by the utility tree structure, attributes in the utility tree, or scenarios at the leaves of the utility tree.
>   [ ] Encourage participants to submit exploratory scenarios as well as use cases and growth scenarios.
>   [ ] Open the floor for spontaneous contributions from any stakeholder. Don't let one or two people dominate. Don't let people propose solutions to the scenarios. Don't let people disparage or dismiss a particular scenario. Aim for around 30–60 scenarios.
>   [ ] Questioners are responsible for brainstorming scenarios that address their assigned quality attributes. Make sure there are scenarios that represent each stakeholder.
>   [ ] Scenario scribe records each scenario for all to see, being careful to use the exact wording proposed or adopted by consensus.
[ ] Evaluation leader facilitates prioritizing of scenarios.
>   [ ] Allow 5 minutes for the consideration of voting.
>   [ ] Allow people to walk around the posted flipcharts and propose consolidation (a person places an adhesive note next to a scenario with the number of another scenario that he or she believes is similar).
>   [ ] After everyone sits down, the group adopts or rejects each consolidation proposal.
>   [ ] Write the scenario numbers on the whiteboard (leaving the posted scenarios up where people can see them).
>   [ ] Assign *n* votes to each participating member of the audience (including evaluation team members other than the team leader), where *n* is 30 percent of the number of scenarios. Each person may assign their *n* votes however they please: all for one scenario, one each to *n* scenarios, or any combination.
>   [ ] Go around the room and have each person publicly assign *one half* of their votes. Then go around the room in the opposite direction and have each person publicly assign the other half of their votes. (This prevents anyone from having undue influence on the voting merely by accident of their seating location.)
>   [ ] Tally votes in front of the users.

[ ] Use any naturally occurring break in the tallies to separate the high-priority scenarios from the lower ones. Only the high-priority ones are considered in future evaluation steps.

[ ] Allow anyone in the group to make impassioned pleas to include a scenario that would otherwise be excluded.

[ ] Exercise discretion to add scenarios that have not been voted "above the line," such as exploratory scenarios.

[ ] After prioritization, facilitate assignment of each high-priority scenario to a place in the utility tree. A scenario will already be present, will constitute a new leaf, or will constitute a new branch. If a whole new branch, have scribe record a possible risk that the relevant quality attribute was not considered by the architect.

[ ] Questioners make sure that scenarios represent the desired mix of quality attributes and/or stakeholder roles.

Outputs

[ ] List of high-priority scenarios.

[ ] List of remaining scenarios.

[ ] Augmented utility tree.

[ ] List of risks, if any, arising from mismatch between high-priority scenarios and utility tree.

Step Description

Utility trees provide a top-down mechanism for generating scenarios from business drivers and quality attributes. Scenario brainstorming, on the other hand, represents a bottom-up approach that lets stakeholders voice concerns connected to their roles outside the confines of any compartmentalized quality attributes. The two approaches in concert make it extremely likely that the relevant quality attribute requirements will be expressed to the evaluation team as a basis for analysis.

The scenario elicitation process allows stakeholders to contribute scenarios that reflect their concerns and understanding of how the architecture will accommodate their needs. Scenarios are collected by a round-robin brainstorming activity. In addition to proposing new scenarios, stakeholders can, if they wish, choose unanalyzed scenarios from the utility tree to put into the brainstorm pool. This can happen if a stakeholder feels that such a scenario is due more attention than it received during Phase 1. In fact, this step is the stakeholders' primary opportunity to recast the coverage and priority of quality attributes as embodied by the utility tree.

A particular scenario may, in fact, have implications for many stakeholders: for a modification, one stakeholder may be concerned with the difficulty of a change and its performance impact, while another may be interested in how the change will affect the integrability of the architecture.

Scenario Brainstorming   The evaluation leader asks the stakeholders to propose scenarios. A good facilitation technique, to make sure everyone participates, is to go around the table (or the room) asking each stakeholder in turn to submit a scenario. After a round or two like this, the evaluation leader can then open up the floor to submissions from anyone in any order.

Members of the evaluation team should feel free to submit scenarios. In fact, this is part of their role duties, especially the questioners. The evaluation team by now should have some insights into the architectural strengths and weaknesses and the quality attribute requirements that are important to the stakeholder community. Posing scenarios to the stakeholders may be a way to jog their thinking, and it poses no harm: if the stakeholders do not think the scenario is relevant or important, the upcoming prioritization process will eliminate it.

The scenario scribe plays his or her most important role during scenario brainstorming. The scribe should write down each scenario as expressed by the person who proposed it or as expressed (after clarification and restatement) by the evaluation leader. The scenario scribe should not paraphrase or add anything to the scenario; this is an instance where creativity is not part of the job description. It is important to capture the scenario that the stakeholder(s) proposed, possibly after public clarification by the evaluation leader. The scenario scribe should not be afraid to hold up the proceedings until the wording has been captured exactly.

It is up to the evaluation leader whether the team members propose scenarios along with everyone else or wait until the dam-burst of stakeholder-posed scenarios has subsided. The former enforces the unity of the gathered participants; the latter defers to shy stakeholders who might appreciate being given priority consideration.

The evaluation leader lets the process continue until he or she feels the time has come to call a halt. This may be due to time constraints, but eventually the "momentum" of the crowd will begin to wane. When people have to think very hard in order to propose a scenario, then the scenario will probably be one of the more esoteric ones not likely to be adopted as a high priority anyway; thus, it's a good time to call a halt and move on.

At this point, the stakeholders have produced several dozen scenarios, all of which may potentially be "run" against the architecture. These scenarios are written on flipchart papers and hung on the walls around the exercise room as shown in Figure 6.11. However, the brainstormed scenarios will have the following undesirable properties:

- Many overlap, probing roughly the same issues.
- Some address issues that are unlikely to arise in the system's lifetime.
- Some address issues that are of low priority to the development effort.

Also the list probably contains too many scenarios for evaluation in the time allotted. Hence, the list must be winnowed down. We do this in two steps:

Figure 6.11   How the Room Might Look After Scenario Brainstorming

merging and voting. Participants first will merge almost-alike scenarios and then vote on the ones to adopt for the forthcoming analysis step.

Merging   The motivation for merging scenarios, which should be made clear to the participants, is to make participants' votes go further. If people are concerned about an issue raised by two scenarios, they may split their votes among them, effectively eliminating both of them, whereas if the scenarios were merged the resulting single scenario would receive the sum of the votes and have a better chance of inclusion in the subsequent analysis.

To start the merging process, announce that the stakeholders have about 15 minutes to familiarize themselves with the scenarios. They should get up and walk around the room, browsing the flipchart pages. Their goal is to find pairs of scenarios that essentially address the same issue and hence can be merged.

After the time is up, have the participants sit down again, and then ask for proposals to merge pairs of scenarios. The evaluation leader should ask the group for a consensus opinion about each proposal. Barring objection, the proposal is accepted. Members of the evaluation team should also interject objections, if they feel that the two scenarios might actually reveal different aspects of the architecture. If a merger is accepted, then the scenario scribe should cross out one scenario, or modify the wording of one so that it reflects both of the original concerns. Merge conservatively: if anyone objects to a merger proposal, it's usually dropped. The process is rather like the climactic question at a wedding: "If anyone here knows any reason why these two should not be married. . . ."

A variation on this procedure is to have the participants make their proposals while they are walking around and browsing the scenarios. If they see a scenario that they think should be merged with another, have them write the second scenario's number on an adhesive note and post it next to the first scenario. That way, everyone can see all of the proposals as they are being made. The evaluation leader then asks for consensus about each proposal as explained above.

Voting After merging is complete, take the number of remaining scenarios and multiply it by 30 percent. Round that number up to the nearest even integer. This is the number of votes that each participant can cast for scenarios. For example, if there are 55 scenarios after merging, each participant receives 18 votes ($0.30 \times 55 = 16.5$, rounded up to 18).

Write the number of each remaining scenario on the whiteboard, a flipchart, or a blank viewgraph everyone can see. Go around the room and ask each participant to cast half of his or her votes. People can distribute their votes among the scenarios however they like: one vote for each of several scenarios, or all votes for a single scenario, or something in between. When everyone in the room has voted, repeat the process in the opposite direction, having each participant cast the second half of his or her votes. Everyone except the evaluation leader (including other members of the evaluation team) gets to vote.

During the voting process, record the votes on a flipchart or blank viewgraph. This can be done very informally; Figure 6.12 shows an example from a recent evaluation.

When voting is concluded, the highest-rated scenarios are the ones that will be used for the upcoming analysis step. The combined goal for Phase 1 and Phase 2 is to evaluate roughly 12–15 scenarios. For longer evaluations, choose a correspondingly higher number. There will almost always be a natural break point in the vote totals; choose the scenarios above the break.

At this point, we open the floor for what we call the "impassioned plea" round. Participants are allowed to make a compelling argument to add a scenario that was not included as a result of voting. The evaluation leader should be especially sympathetic to suggestions from the client, the architect, or the customer.

The proceedings scribe should record the selected scenarios. If possible, a handout that lists these scenarios should be made for the participants as soon as practical.

Although the voting process we have described may sound somewhat arcane, there are several reasons why we prefer it.

- Voting in two rounds means that people who vote last will not have undue influence on the outcome. Since the voting is public, if everyone cast all their votes at once, people at the end could largely determine which scenarios are included by (1) not wasting their votes on scenarios that already have a high score and (2) clustering their votes on otherwise-unpopular scenarios.
- Public voting contributes to the group dynamic.

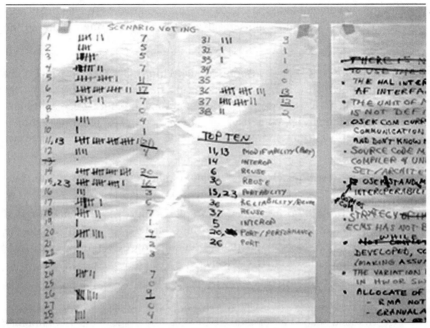

Figure 6.12 Recording Scenario Vote Totals

- It's fun. Participants almost always enjoy this step of the ATAM the most. They enjoy watching dark-horse scenarios emerge triumphant.

Here are some other voting schemes that we have either tried or heard suggested, and why we do not prefer them.

- Secret ballot. Under this scheme, the group is a collection of individuals and there is no sense of group identity.
- One-pass public voting, where everyone casts all their votes at once. As we said, this allows people at the end to influence the outcome. It's also necessary under this scheme to make sure the customer of the system votes last, so that other stakeholders don't vote for scenarios just to play to the customer's desires.
- Nonvoting consensus. The group chats for a while and announces a verdict (or the evaluation leader facilitates a consensus verdict). This is an unreliable way to extract the sense of a large group because it favors the loud and boisterous participants and puts the shy and quiet ones in the worst position possible.
- Show of hands. For each scenario, have the group vote by a show of hands whether that scenario is "high," "medium," or "low" in importance, and then proceed to analyze all of the scenarios that received a "high." This

scheme is vulnerable to the case where the group votes to give every scenario a "high" rating. It is useful to have a strict ordering among all the scenarios.

Reconciling the High-Priority Scenarios with the Utility Tree   At this point in the evaluation, pause and compare the results of scenario prioritization with the results of the utility tree exercise from Step 5 and look for agreement or disagreement. Using group consensus, try to place each high-priority brainstormed scenario into an appropriate leaf node in the utility tree. There are three possibilities:

1. The scenario will match and essentially duplicate an already-existing leaf node.

2. The scenario will go into a new leaf node of an existing branch (or, if it addresses more than one quality attribute, it will be replicated into the leaves of several branches, perhaps after some rewording to make its relevance to each quality attribute clear).

3. The scenario will fit in no branch of the tree because it expresses a quality attribute not previously considered.

The first and second cases indicate that the larger stakeholder community was thinking along the same lines as the architect. The third case, however, suggests that the architect may have failed to consider an important quality attribute, and subsequent probing here may produce a risk to document.

This step of reconciliation between the utility tree and the high-priority brainstormed scenarios keeps the utility tree as the authoritative repository of all the detailed high-priority quality attribute requirements from all sources.

How It Went

Usually scenario brainstorming yields 30–50 scenarios. For the ECS evaluation, the utility tree exercise yielded roughly 60 scenarios, but more significantly, the utility tree scenarios already reflected the views of many system stakeholders. While new stakeholders were present for scenario brainstorming, we found that they basically agreed with the findings up to that point in the evaluation. They offered the new scenarios listed in Table 6.7.

Since the utility tree was fairly comprehensive, the brainstorming activity resulted in only 13 new scenarios. Forty votes were allocated to the 13 scenarios as show in Table 6.7. The top 3 of these scenarios were incorporated into the utility tree. The final utility tree had 50 scenarios.

Speaking from Experience

Most participants say that this is their favorite step of any ATAM exercise. Evaluation leaders like it because they don't have to be thinking hard about the architecture, as some of the other steps require. Here, we rely on the stakeholders

Table 6.7 New ECS Scenarios Collected in Phase 2

Number	Scenario Description	Votes
1	System is able to transition all data (5PB) in archive within 1 year.	4
2	Create a plan for 4,000 data processing requests (DPRs) in 1 hour.	2
3	System can support 3x number of DPRs supported today with only hardware capacity increase.	1
4	In advance of a planned outage operator has to be able to determine time to quiesce system in 2 minutes (under any operating conditions).	0
5	Operator should be able to quiesce the system within 15 minutes (under any operating conditions).	7
6	Order for 2,000 L7 scenes is processed with 25% fewer resources than 2,000 individual orders and no impact to other concurrent orders. Bulk order processed within 1 week.	4
7	System processes orders so that tape hits are maximized.	1
8	A data center becomes operational with new distribution media DVD support in 6 months after support requested.	2
9	System is able to run an end-to-end test of new hardware installation after PCA (Physical Configuration Audit) in 1 day after software installation.	3
10	Add 1,000 new PSAs (Product Specific Attribute) with no impact to search, order, or backup times after 3.5M granules with these PSAs have been inserted.	8
11	In the event of a penetration attack (unauthorized access to science data server) operator is notified within 1 hour.	1
12	Notify operator of penetration attack attempts within 15 minutes.	0
13	Create a report for the execution of the results of a specific run of a scientific algorithm.	7

to do what comes naturally for them: express their concerns. The evaluation leader still has to coach the stakeholders to produce well-formed scenarios, but that's a fairly easy task. (The evaluation teams' questioners, on the other hand, have to be on their toes during this step, proposing scenarios if they feel the quality attribute they've been assigned is not getting sufficient coverage.) This step makes the stakeholder group come together in a cooperative spirit, and the combined input drives the evaluation from this point forward. Finally, voting and seeing which scenarios come out on top is just plain fun. There's an element of suspense to it, like watching a horse race.

This step is another excellent place for the evaluation leader to stand aside and let a junior member of the team take over to gain experience.

Often the scenarios contributed by the evaluation team end up being adopted, so team members shouldn't feel shy about contributing. Why is that? We're objective. We're focused on scenarios that are going to reveal problems. Also, when the emperor is wearing no clothes (the design is flawed), we're the ones who aren't afraid to point it out by proposing the scenarios that will do just that. We also have a sense by now of where the problems are.

6.5.4   Phase 2, Step 8: Analyze Architectural Approaches

Step Summary

This step reiterates the activities of Step 6 using the highly ranked scenarios from Step 7. Those scenarios are considered to be test cases for the analysis performed so far. The analysis may uncover additional architectural approaches, risks, sensitivity points, and tradeoff points which are then documented.

Input
    [ ] List of high-priority scenarios from Step 7.

Activities
This step continues the analysis using the scenarios Step 7 as input. In addition to the activities listed for Phase 1, Step 6, the following activities take place.

    [ ] Timekeeper divides available time by the number of scenarios to come up with a time budget for the analysis of each. This is a target time only; it is reasonable that the highest-priority scenarios receive more time and attention. Also, the earlier scenarios tend to take more time to explore.

    [ ] Questioners note for each scenario places where architect failed to invoke a style or structure earlier revealed as an approach to achieving the quality attribute addressed by the scenario.

Outputs
    [ ] List of architectural components involved in or affected by each scenario and the (potential) effects on system attribute-specific requirements.

    [ ] List of scenarios annotated with their (potential) sensitivity points, issues, and attribute-specific tradeoffs. Issues include decisions not yet made.

    [ ] List of risks (sensitivity points associated with important functions).

    [ ] Summary of architect's explanation of each scenario's mapping, as recorded by proceedings scribe.

Step Description

The analysis performed in this step is exactly the same kind of analysis performed in Step 6 but applied to any new scenarios that resulted from brainstorming.

How It Went

In this section, we recount the analysis of scenario 13 (O15.1), an operability scenario. ("O15.1" is a designator as to where this scenario was placed in the utility tree.) Scenario 13 is one of the scenarios that resulted from scenario brainstorming in the previous step. It is not the highest priority scenario, however, the client chose to analyze this scenario since the group had not yet analyzed an operability scenario.

We asked the architect to walk us through the scenario. He responded by giving the steps for realizing the scenario as follows:

1. Operator creates a table of expected executions by looking at the planning and subscription database, and ingest schedules with historic rates including scanning and generated logs for failures.

2. Operator writes an SQL query against the parameter identification database to determine which algorithm executed last. This involves writing SQL queries to determine which algorithms started but did not complete. It also involves writing an SQL query against the data distribution database to get algorithm data (but operator can't get granule time ranges that are not classified by users).

3. Operator scans application logs to find failures (using the data distribution database) by writing SQL queries against the science data server database and the ingest database for algorithm data and scans application logs for failures.

As a consequence of analyzing this scenario we generated additional risks and sensitivity points, but no new tradeoff points or nonrisks (Table 6.8).

The new risks that were elicited appear below.

R26. The lack of system-wide request tracking leads to a very labor intensive manual process for finding the status of any functional thread. Consequence: status requests require considerable operator intervention.

R27. Inconsistent format and reporting makes it difficult to correlate information across subsystem logs. Consequence: inability to create a system-wide picture of resource requirements for executing scientific algorithms will eventually lead to performance degradation.

R28. Product distribution information is unavailable at the granule level. Consequence: results in the inability to create accurate forecasts of system usage.

Table 6.8   Analyzing Scenario 13 (O15.1)

Scenario #: 13 (O15.1)	Scenario 13 (O15.1): Create a report for the execution of the results of a specific run of a scientific algorithm.
Attribute	Operability
Environment	During routine operation
Stimulus	Request to make a report documenting the results of the execution of a specific scientific algorithm.
Response	Operator must create report within 2 hours of request.

Architectural Decisions	Risk	Sensitivity	Tradeoff	Nonrisk
Distributed logs	R26, R27	S15, S16, S17		
No granule-level order tracking	R28	S17, S18		
Error and requests in logs are not cross-correlated	R27, R28	S16, S17		
Subsystems don't make available performance throughput information; no integrated throughput information kept	R27, R28, R29	S19, S20		
No system-wide request tracking	R26	S16, S17		
Error information for some subsystems (for example, science data server and subscription management) not in database	R27	S15, S17		
No automated roll up of the throughput data	R27, R28, R29			
Subsystems do not retain historical data on throughput that could be used for generating expectations	R30	S17, S20, S21		

Reasoning	The scenario walk-through follows this table. The walk-through reveals many reasons why it is very cumbersome for an operator to fulfill this scenario.
Architecture diagram	None

R29. Lack of system throughput information results in an inability to derive system performance information, especially in real time. Consequence: operators cannot tune system performance in real time.

R30. The lack of historical throughput data makes it very labor intensive to calculate expected performance. Consequence: performance predictions are rarely made and often inaccurate.

The new sensitivity points that were elicited are:

S15. Performance is sensitive to the level of detail captured in logs and to whether logs are stored in files or databases.

S16. Performance is sensitive to the degree to which the various logs are integrated and coordinated.

S17. The level of operator intervention, skill, and effort is directly correlated to the logging approach.

S18. Since products are ordered at the granule level, the ability to track user satisfaction is sensitive to the level of order tracking.

S19. The ability of the operators to manage system load in real time is sensitive to the availability of system throughput data.

S20. System performance is sensitive to the availability of throughput data (since such data is required by the operators to tune the system).

S21. Performance is sensitive to tracking the throughput associated with various types of scientific calculations.

Speaking from Experience

In another ATAM-based evaluation all of the high-priority scenarios turned out to be performance scenarios. However, when it came to choosing a scenario to analyze, almost all of the stakeholders wanted to look at lower priority reliability scenarios. They were already aware of the system performance blemishes; even though the scenarios were very important and very dificult to deal with, this was not new news. In such a case, use your judgment about how to proceed so that you bring the most value to your client.

6.5.5 Phase 2, Step 9: Present Results

Step Summary

Based on the information collected in the ATAM (approaches, scenarios, attribute-specific questions, the utility tree, risks, nonrisks, sensitivity points, tradeoff points), the ATAM team presents the findings to the assembled stakeholders.

Inputs

[ ] Participants' end-of-exercise survey as shown in Figure 10.1.

[ ] List of issues, sensitivity points, and tradeoff points from previous steps.

[ ] Template for presentation of results (Figure 6.13).

Activities
   [ ] Data gatherer hands out the end-of-exercise survey.
   [ ] Evaluation leader announces a break, during which time:
      [ ] Evaluation team meets to prepare presentation of results.
      [ ] Participants fill out surveys.
   [ ] After break, evaluation leader summarizes findings based on publicly recorded lists of risks, sensitivity points, tradeoff points, and other issues. If a final report is part of the statement of work, the evaluation leader announces when it will be submitted.
   [ ] Team leader thanks participants for their help and announces the schedule for delivery of the final report.
      [ ] Team leader makes sure evaluation sponsor receives electronic or printed copy of presentation viewgraphs before evaluation team leaves.
   [ ] Data gatherer collects participants' end-of-exercise surveys. These are turned over to the team leader.

Outputs
   [ ] ATAM participants' survey, filled out by all non-evaluation-team participants.
   [ ] ATAM results presentation, in electronic or printed form.

Step Description

In this step, the evaluation team summarizes the findings of the ATAM exercise. After Step 8 is concluded, the evaluation leader announces a break of about 45 minutes to an hour. During this break, the evaluation team meets to prepare the viewgraphs for the final presentation. Figure 6.13 shows the outline of the presentation that we use. The first slide recaps the steps of the method. Subsequent slides summarize the findings.

The presentation, with questions, typically takes between one and two hours.

How It Went

We made a one-hour presentation that summarized the ATAM exercise, the business drivers, the architectural approaches, the utility tree, and the analysis we performed (during Phase 1, the hiatus, and Phase 2). We recapped the risks, nonrisks, sensitivity points, and tradeoff points we discovered. Finally, we presented the five risk themes that we saw running through the individual risks we captured:

1. There was no consistent strategy for controlling and referencing data types and interfaces.
2. There was a single on-line copy of the database, and this resulted in performance and availability compromises.
3. The COTS database imposed performance restrictions.

Outline of Results Presentation	Explanation
ATAM Steps	A viewgraph listing the nine steps of Phase 1 and Phase 2
Business Drivers	A summary of the business drivers given in Step 2 of Phase 1
Architectural approaches	A summary of the architectural approaches indentified in Step 4 of Phase 1
Utility tree	The utility tree built in Step 5 of Phase 1
Scenarios	A summary of the scenarios brainstormed and prioritized during Step 7 of Phase 2
Scenario discussions	A summary of the analysis performed in Step 6 of Phase 1 and Step 8 of Phase 2 (typically 1–2 viewgraphs per scenario subjected to analysis, presented using the Analysis of an Architectural Approach template)
Risks, nonrisks, sensitivity points, tradeoff points	A compilation of the risks, nonrisks, sensitivity points, and tradeoff points found during the exercise
Other issues	A compilation of any other issues uncovered during the evaluation, each listed along with a short explanation of its cause and impact (typically 1 issue per viewgraph)
Summary	Summary in terms of the risk themes identified by the evaluation team after examining the risks as a group; explanation of how each risk theme, if not addressed, will threaten achievement of specific business drivers

Figure 6.13 Outline of Results Presentation

4. The object description language library was slow and could not be (easily) multi-threaded.
5. The system had little support for quiescing.

Then, for each risk theme, we identified the business driver or drivers to which it posed a threat. For example, the risk themes 2, 3, and 4 affected the achievement of one of the primary business drivers: concurrent ingest, production, and distribution of high data volumes.

Speaking from Experience

The fact that the evaluation team can prepare a comprehensive one-hour summary of an in-depth architecture evaluation during a 45-minute break is a testament to the rigor of the ATAM steps. It is also one of the aspects of the ATAM that makes it popular with clients: results are available immediately at the end of the exercise; no waiting is necessary.

This step is the best illustration of the maxim that preparation pays off. Look at how much up-front preparation has come home to roost:

- When the evaluation team was formed in Phase 0, segments of the presentation were assigned to individual team members.
- As much of the presentation as possible was drafted in Step 0 of Phase 2.
- The business drivers and architectural approaches were summarized and captured publicly.
- The analysis of each scenario was carried out publicly, and the results were recorded in a template.
- The risks, nonrisks, sensitivity points, and tradeoff points were publicly recorded and displayed throughout the exercise.

The fact that almost all of the information was publicly recorded before the results presentation yields two happy circumstances. First, the proceedings scribe can easily turn the electronic record into viewgraphs with a few deft cut-and-paste operations. Second, the information in the summary comes as a surprise to no one. We have never experienced an evaluation using the ATAM where someone was upset at the results, because the results (by the time of the presentation) are not new. The reiteration of previously derived results also reinforces the repeatable, methodical nature of the method, to the pleasure of the participants.

Finally, mapping the risk themes to the business drivers they affect produces two positive effects. First, it gives the impression of closing the circle. Although the business drivers help us to establish context for the evaluation in general and begin to nail down the utility tree in particular, participants sometimes cannot remember exactly why they were so important. Mapping the risks back to the business drivers instills the drivers with an importance they might not otherwise have. Second, it puts the ATAM results in terms that are unmistakably significant to the client because they are couched in terms that he or she is used to discussing.

6.6 Phase 3: Follow-Up

The steps of the follow-up phase are:

1. Produce the final report
2. Hold the postmortem meeting
3. Build the portfolio and update artifact repositories

6.6.1   Phase 3, Step 1: Produce the Final Report

Step Summary

Inputs

[ ] Template for final report (see Figure 6.14).

[ ] Outputs from Phase 1 and Phase 2.

Activities

Using a template for the final report:

[ ] Write what you did: method summary, who was present, scenarios recorded.

[ ] Write what you saw: architecture summary, analysis summary, results of applying scenarios.

[ ] Write what you concluded: draw analytical conclusions, identify risks, make recommendations.

[ ] Have entire team review report.

[ ] Send report to client for review, to correct factual mistakes.

[ ] Revise report based on client's feedback.

[ ] Transmit final report.

Output

[ ] Final report.

Step Description

After Phase 2 is over and the evaluation team has recovered from the intensity of the exercise, the team leader convenes a meeting (or sends e-mail) to remind the team members of their individual responsibilities in producing the final written report for the client. An outline of the final report template that we use is given in Figure 6.14.

We strive to produce the final report, have all team members review it, and transmit it to the client within ten working days of the end of Phase 2.

How It Went

The final report for the NASA ECS ATAM exercise was 48 pages in length and followed the template shown in Figure 6.14.

Speaking from Experience

Once again, preparation pays off. Sections 1, 2, and 3 of our final report template are fairly pro forma and do not change from exercise to exercise. Section 4, a brief narrative about the particular evaluation, contains blanks for the time and place of the exercise, the name and nature of the system whose architecture was evaluated, and the names and contact information of all the participants. Sections 5–10 are narrative forms of the information from the presentation of results produced at the end of Phase 2, and the production of these sections is

Executive Summary	
Section 1	Introduction
Section 2	Evaluating a Software Architecture
Section 3	ATAM Overview
Section 4	The ATAM for (name of system)
Section 5	Summary of Business Drivers
Section 6	Summary of Architecture Presentation
Section 7	Quality Attribute Utility Tree
Section 8	Scenario Generation, Consolidation, and Prioritization
Section 9	Analysis of Architectural Approaches
Section 10	Risks, Sensitivities, Tradeoffs, Nonrisks, and Other Issues
Section 11	Conclusions

Figure 6.14   Sample Outline for an ATAM Final Report

straightforward. Section 11 summarizes the risk themes and relates them to the business drivers they impact.

6.6.2   Phase 3, Step 2: Hold the Postmortem Meeting

Step Summary

Hold a meeting to gather surveys and data, look for improvements to be made to the method or its artifacts, and assess the overall quality of the exercise.

Inputs
[ ] Evaluation team post-exercise improvement survey.
[ ] Evaluation team post-exercise effort survey.
[ ] Participants' end-of-exercise survey (see Figure 10.1).
[ ] Sample agenda for postmortem meeting (see Figure 6.15).
[ ] Process observer's report.

Activities
[ ] Team members:
    [ ] Fill out evaluation team post-exercise improvement survey.
    [ ] Fill out evaluation team post-exercise effort survey.
[ ] Team leader:
    [ ] Collect process observer's report.

[ ] Collect non-evaluation-team participants' effort data. Most will have submitted this via the participants' end-of-exercise survey. Contact the client to receive effort data for anyone who participated but did not fill out that form.

[ ] Collect evaluation team post-exercise improvement surveys.

[ ] Collect evaluation team post-exercise effort surveys.

[ ] Schedule and hold a postmortem meeting with the evaluation group to discuss the lessons learned from the exercise and record ideas for improvement. Bring the surveys for circulation, or distribute them prior to the meeting.

[ ] Summarize changes necessary to reflect improvements.

[ ] Update the ATAM process model.

Outputs

[ ] Completed surveys and cost data.

[ ] Improvement ideas.

[ ] Updated ATAM process model.

Step Description

The ATAM prescribes the use of three after-action surveys (plus another that will be discussed in the next step):

- Participants' end-of-exercise survey (handed out at the end of Phase 2)
- Evaluation team post-exercise improvement survey
- Evaluation team post-exercise effort survey

The first three gauge the effort and impressions of all the participants, whether a member of the evaluation team or a representative of the client or project organization.

In addition, the process observer should submit his or her written notes, which should contain areas where the process deviated from what is prescribed.

The purpose of all of this data and information is to help the ATAM process become more effective and more repeatable. A deviation from the prescribed process can be handled in one of three ways:

1. Recognize that the circumstances were unique and the deviation was warranted.

2. Recognize that the deviation was undesirable and take steps to avoid it in the future.

3. Recognize that the deviation represented a situation likely to occur again, and change the ATAM steps to accommodate it.

A sample agenda for the postmortem meeting is given in Figure 6.15.

Duration	Activity
30 minutes	Evaluation team members' quick impressions of process, and estimation of value for client
30 minutes	Review of • Process observer's report • Evaluation team post-exercise improvement survey • Participants' end-of-exercise survey
15 minutes	Summary of total effort required for the exercise, using • Evaluation team post-exercise effort survey • Effort data from the participants' end-of-exercise survey
30 minutes	Discussion of specific suggested changes to ATAM process and materials; assignment of action items

Figure 6.15   Sample Agenda for ATAM Postmortem Meeting

How It Went

We held a postmortem meeting three days after we transmitted the final report to the client. The ECS evaluation required 128 person-hours on the part of the evaluation team and 154 person-hours on the part of the project organization.

For this evaluation, all members of the evaluation team served as process observers. We found no major deviations but spent our time discussing which steps we thought the client found most valuable and why.

Participants reported highest satisfaction with the utility tree part of the exercise. They felt that overall the exercise was a valuable use of their time; in fact, many expressed pleasure at having the quality attribute goals explicitly articulated and prioritized.

Some of the participants would have liked more read-ahead material about the method.

Speaking from Experience

The postmortem meeting is a hard meeting to hold because everyone is tired and the final report is finished. But it's the best way we know to bring home the lessons of each ATAM experience to our architecture evaluation group as a whole. Our entire group attends each postmortem meeting, not just the evaluation team that was involved. Attending a postmortem is an excellent way for junior members of the group, or people being trained for ATAM-based evaluations, to hear real war stories and begin to gain a sense for what an actual evaluation is like.

Resist the temptation to change the ATAM after every experience using it. We will be the first to admit that there is a big difference between writing and speaking about the method and actually carrying it out—you will find places to tailor and improve the method as you gain experience with it. However, when something does not work out as planned, the cure more often lies in more experience rather than reflexively making changes that may never converge.

6.6.3   Phase 3, Step 3: Build Portfolio and Update Artifact Repositories

Step Summary

Build up the portfolio of artifacts generated during the ATAM exercise. Record survey and effort data. Update the list of scenarios and analysis questions.

Inputs

    [ ] Utility tree, scenarios, and analysis questions used during the evaluation.

    [ ] Survey and cost outputs from the postmortem meeting.

    [ ] Presentation of results from Step 9 of Phase 2.

    [ ] Final report.

    [ ] Process observer's report.

    [ ] Survey of client long-term benefit.

Activities

There may be a designated role in the evaluation organization to build the exercise portfolio and update the artifact repositories. Otherwise, the responsibility falls to the team leader.

    [ ] Team leader establishes the evaluation portfolio for the evaluation just completed, including

        [ ] Participant evaluations

        [ ] Team evaluations

        [ ] Process observer's report

        [ ] Copy of presentation of results

        [ ] Copy of final report

        [ ] Long-term benefits survey

    [ ] Team leader adds scenarios to the scenario repository.

    [ ] Six months after evaluation, team leader sends to client a survey of long-term benefits.

Outputs

    [ ] Updated repositories.

    [ ] ATAM end-of-exercise portfolio.

Step Description

You should maintain repositories of the artifacts you used or produced during each previous evaluation. These will serve you during future evaluations.

In addition to recording the cost and benefit information, store the scenarios that you produced. If future systems that you evaluate are similar in nature, then you will probably find that the scenarios that express the architecture's requirements will converge into a uniform set. This gives you a powerful opportunity to streamline the evaluation method: you can dispense with the scenario brainstorming and prioritization steps of the ATAM altogether and simply use the standard scenario set for your domain. The scenarios have in some sense graduated to become a checklist, and checklists are extremely useful because each architect in the developing organization can keep a copy of the checklist in his or her desk drawer and make sure the architecture passes with respect to it. Then an evaluation becomes more of a confirmation exercise than an investigatory one. Stakeholders' involvement becomes minimal—as long as you have confidence in the applicability and completeness of the checklist with respect to the new system under evaluation—thus reducing the expense of the evaluation still further.

Besides the scenarios, add the analysis questions and the participants' comments to a repository as well. Future evaluation leaders can read through these and gain valuable insights into the details and idiosyncrasies of past evaluations. These exercise summaries provide excellent training material for new evaluation leaders.

Finally, keep a copy of the final report, sanitized if necessary to avoid identifying the system or spreading any incriminating remarks. Future evaluation teams will appreciate having a template to use for the reports they produce.

How It Went

Six months after the ATAM exercise, we sent the ECS program manager our standard long-term improvement survey, which asks what the long-term effects of the ATAM exercise were.[3] Here's what he had to say.

Before the ATAM:

- *Justifications for key architectural decisions were not well documented; knowledge limited to a few system architects.*

- *Little analysis on risks, sensitivities, and tradeoffs associated with architectural decisions, especially for ongoing maintenance changes.*

- *Stakeholders other than development staff viewed all requested changes as largely independent and equally plausible.*

As a result of our first ATAM experience:

- *Operations, customer, architect, and development stakeholders reached a common understanding of how the system addresses the 45 quality attribute requirements addressed by this review.*

---

3. A sample of such a survey is given in Chapter 10.

- *Stakeholder team identified and documented ~50 key architectural decisions and more than 100 associated risks, sensitivities, and tradeoffs.*
- *Based on these results and the prioritized quality attribute requirements, the stakeholder team was able to identify and compare the technical merits of more than 60 proposed architectural changes.*

We anticipate greater stakeholder satisfaction given buy-in to tradeoffs.

Speaking from Experience

In our organization, the task of building the exercise portfolio falls to a conscientious support person who is responsible for obtaining the artifacts from the team leader and for reminding the team leader when it is time to issue the long-term improvement survey.

6.7 For Further Reading

To learn more about the Earth Observing System, visit NASA's Web site at http://eospso.gsfc.nasa.gov/. Terra is the name of one of the major satellites in the EOS fleet, and http://terra.nasa.gov contains excellent information about and images from that satellite.

6.8 Discussion Questions

1. Try building a utility tree for a system that you are familiar with. Are any of the attributes discussed in this chapter relevant to your system? Do the attributes have the same meaning for your system as they do for the ECS system? How do you know whether they do or not?

2. Choose a couple of the quality attributes from the utility tree you created for the previous question. What are the architectural approaches used in your system to achieve those quality attribute requirements?

3. Pretend that you are leading the evaluation that we discussed in this chapter and are responsible for constructing the final presentation. In particular, you are thinking about the last few slides that show how the risk themes impact the business drivers. What would you say on these final slides of the presentation?

4. The NASA client for the ECS evaluation is planning to incorporate the ATAM as part of his office's software maintenance and evolution process. How would you incorporate the ATAM into your organization's development and maintenance process?

5. One of the benefits the client perceived from this ATAM exercise was the chance to achieve consensus among the stakeholders about which system enhancements to tackle first. Suppose that was your only goal. Propose a new method, called Stakeholder Consensus Realization Analysis Method (SCRAM), and define its steps, phases, participants, and artifacts produced.

7

Using the SAAM to Evaluate an Example Architecture

with Stephan Kurpjuweit

Do not believe in anything simply because you have heard it. Do not believe in anything simply because it is spoken and rumored by many. Do not believe in anything simply because it is found written in your religious books. Do not believe in anything merely on the authority of your teachers and elders. . . . But after observation and analysis, when you find that anything agrees with reason and is conducive to the good and benefit of one and all, then accept it and live up to it.

—The Buddha
Kalama Sutra

The Software Architecture Analysis Method (SAAM) was, as far as we know, the first documented, widely promulgated architecture analysis method. Its premises are straightforward. First of all, development of the SAAM was motivated by the observation that practitioners regularly made claims about their software architectures ("This system is more robust than its predecessor," "Using CORBA will make our system easy to modify and upgrade," "The Model-View-Controller paradigm ensures the maintainability of this architecture," and so on) that were effectively untestable. So the creators of the SAAM set out to operationalize the testing of such claims by replacing claims of quality attributes (words like *maintainability, modifiability, robustness, flexibility,* and so forth) with scenarios that operationalize those claims.

The SAAM was originally created to analyze an architecture for modifiability in its various forms and names, that is, the operation of a human attempting to modify a body of software. But in reality, the SAAM has proven useful for quickly assessing many quality attributes (such as modifiability, portability, extensibility, integrability), as well as functional coverage. The SAAM can also be used for heuristic evaluation of other system qualities such as performance or reliability, but this aspect of the SAAM has largely been superseded by the ATAM and will not be explored further in this chapter.

7.1 Overview of the SAAM

The SAAM is a simple method, easy to learn and easy to carry out with relatively small amounts of training and preparation. It is a good place to start if you have never done an architecture evaluation before, particularly if you care about modifiability and functionality. You can cover considerably more ground (albeit in less detail) in a SAAM-based evaluation than in an ATAM-based evaluation.

The SAAM asks the system's various stakeholders to enumerate a set of scenarios that represent the known or likely changes that the system will undergo in the future. These scenarios are scrutinized, prioritized, and mapped onto a representation of the architecture. The activity of mapping indicates problem areas: areas where the architecture is overly complex (if many distinctly different scenarios affect the same component or components) or where key design details are not encapsulated but rather are distributed throughout the architecture (if a scenario causes changes to large numbers of components). Mapping can also indicate areas where the architectural documentation is not presented at the correct level of detail. Frequently a system's architecture is documented imperfectly or not at all, and this poses a risk for the project. The act of performing a SAAM-based evaluation forces the architect to document the architecture in sufficient detail to support the analysis.

In addition to these technical benefits, a SAAM-based evaluation also produces many important social benefits. The SAAM causes a wide group of stakeholders to come together, often for the first time, and discuss the architecture. The architecture is a communication vehicle for them—a shared language—that allows them to discuss their concerns in a mutually comprehensible language. The set of stakeholders who might participate in a SAAM-based evaluation are the same as those for an ATAM evaluation, as described in Chapter 3.

A SAAM-based analysis requires a number of inputs and produces a number of outputs. These are detailed next.

7.1.1 Inputs to a SAAM Evaluation

For a SAAM evaluation to proceed, some form of description of the architecture is required. In the beginning of a SAAM analysis, the group uses whatever description of the architecture is available, and the evaluation proceeds based on this description. If other views or finer-grained representations of the architecture are needed, the SAAM process makes their need clear as it progresses.

It is necessary to enumerate a number of scenarios as inputs to the SAAM exercise for understanding and evaluating the software architecture. As previously stated, quality attributes are too complex and amorphous to be evaluated on a simple scale, in spite of the persistence of the software engineering community in treating them that way. A system's accommodation of these qualities can be understood only *within a context*. This notion of context-based evaluation of qualities has led us to adopt scenarios as the descriptive means of specifying and evaluating qualities. A scenario, as explained in Chapter 3, is a short statement describing an interaction of one of the stakeholders with the system.

7.1.2 Outputs from a SAAM Evaluation

The process of performing a SAAM-based analysis has benefits in addition to the obvious one of evaluating an architecture or comparing competing architectures. For example, the SAAM steps help stakeholders gain a more in-depth understanding of an architecture. The process of performing a SAAM-based evaluation has, in practice, resulted in better-documented software architectures, often because it forces the architect to create architectural documentation where none existed before. The process—like any formal technical review—also enhances communication among the participating stakeholders.

The main tangible outputs of the SAAM are

- A mapping onto the architectures of scenarios that represent possible future changes to the system, indicating areas of high potential future complexity, plus estimates of the anticipated amount of work associated with each of those changes
- An understanding of the functionality of the system, or even a comparison of multiple architectures with respect to the amount of functionality that each supports without modification

Performing a SAAM-based evaluation forces the key system stakeholders to determine a relative ranking among the various potential change pressures that the system faces. This judgment is used in the evaluation for prioritizing and weighting the various scenarios, but it also implicitly creates a roadmap for future development. The prioritization of the scenarios derives from the business goals that the scenarios support, so the process of prioritizing one leads to a prioritization of the other. This is another useful side effect of a SAAM evaluation.

If a single architecture is being evaluated, the SAAM indicates places where that architecture fails to meet its modifiability requirements and in some cases shows obvious alternative designs that would work better. The SAAM can also produce a relative ranking if two or more candidate architectures are being compared to see which one satisfies its quality requirements more fully with less modification and with less resulting future complexity.

7.2 Steps of a SAAM Evaluation

Figure 7.1 illustrates the steps in a SAAM evaluation. These steps are typically preceded by a brief system overview, including a presentation of the business goals for the architecture.

7.2.1 Step 1: Develop Scenarios

Scenarios, as discussed earlier in the book, should illustrate the kinds of activities that the system must support. They should also illustrate the kinds of changes that the client anticipates will be made to the system. In developing these scenarios, it is crucial to capture all of the major uses of a system, users of a system, anticipated changes to the system, and qualities that a system must satisfy now and in the foreseeable future. Thus scenarios represent tasks relevant to different roles, such as end user, customer, marketing specialist, system administrator, maintainer, and developer.

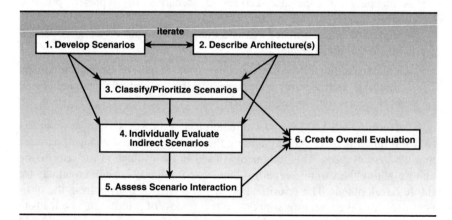

Figure 7.1 Activities and Dependencies in a SAAM Analysis

Their Own Worst Critics

The system under evaluation was an airborne command and control platform, and we were in the morning of the first day. The architect hadn't said much during the exercise so far, but his expression showed that he was deep in thought about what was happening. "At least he's engaged," I thought. "I just hope he's not feeling like his intellectual creation is about to be dismantled by the group." Up to this point, he had been friendly but not terribly outgoing. It's something we always worry about—how can we make sure that the architect doesn't feel threatened and as a result become indifferent or even uncooperative?

We were in the scenario brainstorming session, in which the architect usually discovers what diabolical ideas the stakeholders have in mind for meddling with his or her architecture. About a dozen scenarios had been suggested by the group when the architect's expression cleared somewhat, and he put up his hand. I wondered what was coming.

"What about a scenario where we make the system entirely operable using remote controllers?" he asked. "I know the customer would really like that because that would let the platform fly longer missions. And I think it would really stress the architecture."

Inside, I was smiling and shaking my head in delighted disbelief, but I hoped it didn't show. It had happened again: the most challenging scenario, one that very well could reduce the architecture to a puddle of well-intentioned but inadequate boxes and lines, had been proposed by the architect himself.

It turns out that the architect is often the source of the most challenging scenarios for his or her own architecture. It doesn't always happen, but it's not unusual. Of course, it's just what you want—what better source for proposing scenarios that reveal the edge of the architectural envelope? The architect knows best where the stress points are.

What is it about architects and the evaluation process that makes them so eager to help poke at their own creations? First, architects love the process of creation; it's why they're architects. But more than that, *good* architects strive to create designs that are as capable and robust and elegant as possible—in short, designs in which they can take pride. Project exigencies, however, always intrude; the creation is born of a little more expediency and a little less conceptual elegance than the architect dreamed of imparting. The architect may yearn for what might have been, so some architects view the evaluation process as a way to put in a plug for more time and resources to set right those nagging blemishes on his creation. Or at the very least, the architect can demonstrate that he or she knows where the creation has fallen short of perfection. "Let me show you what I *would* have done, if only I could have," seems to be the message.

Second, architects tend to enjoy an intellectual challenge. They often enjoy listening to hard scenarios and figuring out how they would address them. To architects, architecture is problem solving; so what if the problem was posed by themselves?

I think the format of the evaluation also helps. When a particularly good or challenging scenario is suggested, the group may very well "ooh" and "aah" with approval, so there is some reinforcement for proposing hard cases. The group dynamic of jointly striving to achieve a goal—in this case, a high-quality exercising of the architecture—also kicks in, and architects will catch the spirit of the moment.

Whatever the reason, it's a wonderful phenomenon. When you see it, it's a good sign that the architect has come to regard the evaluation (and your presence) as a help and not a bother. You should, of course, do whatever you can to cultivate that feeling: be understanding, don't be critical, listen carefully, and respect the design. And when it happens, you should feel good that you've gotten the evaluation off to an excellent start. Your most important ally is on board.

—PCC

The scenario elicitation process is a brainstorming exercise. It allows stakeholders to contribute scenarios, in a criticism-free environment, that reflect their concerns and understanding of how the architecture will accommodate their needs. A single scenario may have implications for many stakeholders: for a modification, one stakeholder may be concerned with the difficulty of a change and its performance impact, while another may be interested in how the change will affect the integrability of the architecture. As scenarios are generated in an evaluation, a scribe records them for all to see.

Scenarios are often elicited and collected in two or more iterations. The process of scenario development and architectural description are related and iterative. As more architectural information is collected and shared, more scenarios are typically surfaced by the stakeholders.

7.2.2   Step 2: Describe the Architecture(s)

The candidate architecture or architectures should be described in an architectural notation that is well understood by the parties involved in the analysis. These architectural descriptions must indicate the system's computation and data components as well as all relevant connections. Accompanying this static representation of the architecture is a description of how the system behaves over time or a more dynamic representation. This can take the form of a natural-language specification of the overall behavior or some other more formal specification.

The development of scenarios and the description of the architecture usually drive each other. On one hand, the presence of an architectural description forces the stakeholders to think about scenarios that address specific character-istics of the architecture under consideration. On the other hand, scenarios reflect requirements for the architecture and hence must be realized in the architectural description. Consequently, the development of scenarios and the description of the architecture are usually done in an interleaved way or in several iterations, until both activities come up with satisfying results (as shown in Figure 7.1).

7.2.3 Step 3: Classify and Prioritize the Scenarios

A scenario in the SAAM is a brief description of some anticipated or desired use of a system. The architecture may directly support that scenario, meaning that anticipated use requires no modification to the architecture for the scenario to be performed. This would usually be determined by demonstrating how the existing architecture would behave in performing the scenario (rather like a sim-ulation of the architecture). In the SAAM these are classified as *direct scenarios*. Direct scenarios are those that are satisfied by the architecture through the exe-cution of the system. Direct scenarios that correspond to requirements previ-ously addressed in the design process will not surprise the stakeholders but will increase their understanding of the architecture and allow systematic investiga-tion of other architectural qualities such as performance and reliability.

If a scenario is not directly supported, there must be some change to the architecture that we can represent. This could be a change to how one or more components perform an assigned activity, the addition of a component to per-form some activity, the addition of a relation between existing components, the removal of a component or relation, a change to an interface, or a combination of these. These are classified as *indirect scenarios*. An indirect scenario is one that requires a modification to the architecture to be satisfied; indirect scenarios are central to the measurement of the degree to which an architecture can accommodate evolutionary changes that are important to the stakeholders. The cumulative impact of indirect scenarios on an architecture measure its suitabil-ity for ongoing use throughout the lifetime of a family of related systems. Direct scenarios are similar to *use cases* (in, for example, UML notation) and indirect scenarios are sometimes known as *change cases*.

Prioritization of the scenarios allows the most important scenarios to be addressed within the limited amount of time available for the evaluation. Here, *important* is defined entirely by the stakeholders and their concerns. They express their interests and concerns by voting. They are each given a fixed number of votes to allocate to the scenario list. We typically use 30 percent of the total number of scenarios as the number of votes to give each stakeholder, and they can allocate these votes in any way they see fit, assigning single or multiple votes to any scenario.

Typically a SAAM-based evaluation focuses on quality attributes such as modifiability, so classification is done before prioritization. Stakeholder groups are usually most interested in understanding the effects of the indirect scenarios when they are mapped onto the architecture. This is done next.

7.2.4   Step 4: Individually Evaluate Indirect Scenarios

Once a set of scenarios has been chosen for consideration, these scenarios are mapped onto the architectural description. In the case of a direct scenario, the architect demonstrates how the scenario would be executed by the architecture. In the case of an indirect scenario, the architect describes how the architecture would need to be changed to accommodate the scenario—this is the typical case with the SAAM.

This exercise also gives reviewers and stakeholders some insight into the structure of the architecture and the dynamic interaction of its components. Stakeholder discussion is important to elaborate the intended meaning of a scenario description and to discuss how the mapping is or is not suitable from their perspective. The mapping process also illustrates weaknesses in the architecture and its documentation.

For each indirect scenario, the changes to the architecture that are necessary for it to support the scenario must be listed and the cost of performing the change must be estimated. A modification to the architecture means that either a new component or connection is introduced or an existing component or connection requires a change in its specification. By the end of this stage, there should be a summary table that lists all scenarios (direct and indirect). For each indirect scenario, the set of changes required should be described and recorded by the scribe. This description should include an estimate of the effort to fully complete each change, including debugging and testing time.

An example from a SAAM evaluation of an experimental tool is given in Table 7.1.

7.2.5   Step 5: Assess Scenario Interactions

When two or more indirect scenarios require changes to a single component of an architecture, they are said to *interact* in that component. Scenario interaction is important to highlight for two reasons. First, it exposes the allocation of functionality to the product's design. The interaction of semantically unrelated scenarios explicitly shows which architecture components are computing semantically unrelated functions. Areas of high scenario interaction reveal potentially poor separation of concerns in a component. Thus, areas of scenario interaction indicate where the designer should focus subsequent attention. The amount of scenario interaction is related to metrics such as structural complexity, coupling, and cohesion. Therefore, it is likely to be strongly correlated with the number of defects in the final product.

A second reason to examine scenario interaction is that it can reveal that the architecture is not documented to the right level of structural decomposition.

Table 7.1 Examples of SAAM Scenario Evaluations

Scenario Number	Scenario Description	Direct/ Indirect	Required Changes	Number of Changed/ Added Components	Effort for Changes (estimate)
7	Change the underlying LAN for communication to a WAN	Indirect	Abstraction, interface to data repository	1	1 person-month
8	Change relationships between data items (e.g., add the ability to associate lists of scenarios with stakeholders)	Indirect	The agent for scenarios and stakeholders	2	2 person-days
13	Change the data structure of an entity (e.g., store a data item with each scenario)	Indirect	The agent for the affected entity	1	1 person-day

This will be the case if scenarios interact within a component but that component can actually be decomposed into smaller sub-components that do not exhibit the scenario interaction. If this is the case then Step 2, describing the architecture(s), will need to be revisited.

7.2.6 Step 6: Create the Overall Evaluation

Finally, a weight may be assigned to each scenario in terms of its relative importance to the success of the system. This weighting usually ties back to the business goals that each scenario is supporting.

The weighting can be used to determine an overall ranking if multiple architectures are being compared or if different architectural alternatives are being proposed for a single architecture. The purpose of assigning weights is to resolve the situation in which the first candidate architecture scores well on approximately half of the scenarios and the second candidate architecture scores better on the other half. Assigning weights is a subjective process involving all of the stakeholders, but it should be done in a structured fashion whereby the weights and their rationale are publicly discussed and debated.

Table 7.2   Example of an Evaluation Summary Table

	Scenario 1	Scenario 2	Scenario 3	Scenario 4	Contention
Shared memory	0	0	–	–	–
Abstract data types	0	0	+	+	+

For example, scenarios might be weighted by their anticipated cost, risk, time to market, or some other agreed-upon criterion.

Also, if multiple architectures are being compared, the number of direct scenarios supported by each one affects the evaluation, since direct scenarios indicate that a user task is supported without requiring modification of the system.

A tabular summary is often useful when comparing alternative architectural candidates because it provides an easy way to determine which architecture better supports a collection of scenarios. For example, Table 7.2 compares two architectural approaches to a simple problem of creating a Key Word in Context (KWIC) system. One of these approaches uses shared memory and one uses abstract data types. These approaches are compared with respect to four indirect scenarios, and also with respect to the amount of scenario interaction discovered. A + means that this architecture is better (i.e. affects fewer components), a – means that this architecture is worse, and a *0* means that there is no significant difference, as determined by the architects. Other ranking systems (such as high/medium/low or a 10 point scale) are also commonly used.

Assigning weights to the scenarios and a numeric value to the – and + rankings will result in an overall score for each architecture.

7.3 A Sample SAAM Agenda

The preceding steps are only the templates for structuring the technical portion of a SAAM evaluation. Partnership and preparation activities, like those in Phase 0 of the ATAM, are also required. The meetings have to be planned, the team assembled, rooms booked, stakeholders invited, supplies gathered, schedules meshed, and so forth. Because those activities, while necessary, are not much different for the SAAM than those for the ATAM, their explanations will not be repeated here.

The team roles defined for the ATAM in Table 3.3 also apply to the SAAM. However, SAAM teams are usually smaller than ATAM teams. The process enforcer and process observer are working with a lighter-weight process, so they have less to do. The scribes are not striving to capture information comprehensive enough to produce a near-real-time summary at the end of the exercise. And since the quality attributes of concern to the SAAM are more restricted than those of the ATAM, fewer questioners are needed. A typical evaluation team for a SAAM exercise is three or four people.

We find that SAAM meetings of two consecutive days work well, but certainly other arrangements (shorter, longer and more detailed, or small meetings spread out over many days) are also possible. Table 7.3 presents a typical SAAM agenda.

Table 7.3   Sample Agenda for a SAAM Exercise

Time	Agenda item
Day 1	
8:15–8:45	Introductions, statement of evaluation goals, overview of evaluation method, ground rules
8:45–9:00	Overview of system being evaluated, including goals for the architecture.
9:00–10:00	Develop scenarios (Step 1)
10:00–10:30	Break
10:30–12:00	Develop scenarios (Step 1)
12:00–1:00	Lunch
1:00–2:30	Describe the architecture(s) (Step 2)
2:30–3:00	Break
3:00–3:30	Develop scenarios (Step 1)
3:30–5:00	Classify and prioritize scenarios (Step 3)
Day 2	
8:15–10:00	Individually evaluate indirect scenarios (Step 4)
10:00–10:30	Break
10:30–12:00	Individually evaluate indirect scenarios (Step 4)
12:00–1:00	Lunch
1:00–2:30	Assess scenario interactions (Step 5)
2:30–3:30	Create the overall evaluation (Step 6)
3:30–4:00	Break
4:00–5:00	Wrapup, summarization, reports

7.4 A SAAM Case Study

To illustrate how architecture evaluations with the SAAM work in practice, we describe the application of the SAAM to a software system that was created within the Software Engineering Institute.

7.4.1 ATAT System Overview

The system, called ATAT (Architecture Tradeoff Analysis Tool), was created as an experimental tool for aiding with architecture evaluations and for managing and analyzing architecture specifications. The tool was heavily influenced by our experience in performing architecture design and analysis with large software development organizations. Since architecture analysis and design methods involve the manipulation of large amounts of information, the linkage of information from many sources, and the analysis of such information, tool support for these methods is welcome. A tool could help to formalize the methods in practice and to build a knowledge base of reusable architectural assets and analyses, hence making software architecture development more disciplined.

The tool was aimed at providing four major categories of support, as follows:

1. *Representation support:* Both architectural elements (components and relations/connectors) and nonarchitectural elements (for example, requirements, scenarios, use cases, stakeholders) must be treated as first-class entities. The tool must be able to maintain arbitrary associations between these elements and organize them into appropriate data structures (lists, trees, graphs, and arbitrary groups). The tool must facilitate style-based documentation of architectures by defining, instantiating, and combining architectural approaches. The tool must be able to represent architectures in multiple views and hierarchically decompose architectural elements.

2. *Process support:* The tool must be able to enact processes, provide process guidance to the user, and ensure that the user is aware of the current process state. Since architectural analysis and design is a team effort, the tool must provide groupware support to facilitate and guide interactions among team members (such as brainstorming and prioritizing scenarios). Different organizations apply different architectural analysis and design methods and these methods evolve over time, so the tool must be able to facilitate customized processes.

3. *Analysis support:* The tool must support the definition and application of analysis models. Analysis models explicitly link architectural decisions to quality attributes of the system and guide the user to collect the right information, manage this information, and interpret and document the analysis results. The tool must support quantitative and qualitative analysis models. Wherever possible, analyses should be automated.

4. *Usability:* Usability is a driving quality requirement for the tool. The tool is intended to be used in environments where people interact and exchange ideas quickly and spontaneously (for example, in ATAM meetings). To be useful in these environments, the tool must allow people who are not trained to use the tool to quickly sketch and communicate their ideas (for example, architectural structures, scenarios, quality attribute requirements, and so on).

We were concerned about the system architecture's ability to support the wide variety of uses and changes that we could foresee with respect to these four categories of support. To address this concern we scheduled an architectural evaluation, using the SAAM, for the ATAT system. We chose to perform a SAAM evaluation because our single overriding concern for this system was its modifiability. The SAAM process we went through is described next.

Be aware that in this process we used the SAAM to compare two competing architectures for a portion of the ATAT tool.

7.4.2 Step 1: Develop Scenarios, First Iteration

Scenarios for the ATAT tool were collected in two iterations. The brainstorming was performed in a round-robin fashion in which no criticism and little or no clarification was provided. The raw scenarios that resulted from the first iteration are shown in Table 7.4. Since the architecture of the system had not yet been presented to the stakeholders, these scenarios were solely based on the requirements for the tool and on some general knowledge about the application domain.

Table 7.4 Raw Scenarios Collected from the Stakeholders (First Iteration)

Scenario Number	Scenario Description
1	Modify the system to be able to dynamically add a computer to the suite without affecting the operation of the other users.
2	Modify the tool so that it shows the following behavior: user performs an operation that results in a constraint violation. The tool performs the operation and informs the user about the constraint violation.
3	Double the number of concurrent users.
4	Double the number of networked computers on which the tool is run as a distributed system.
5	Modify the tool to be able to dynamically interpret process descriptions.
6	Change the process to be supported (e.g., change from vanilla ATAM to a customized version of ATAM).

(continued)

Table 7.4   Raw Scenarios Collected from the Stakeholders (First Iteration)
(*continued*)

Scenario Number	Scenario Description
7	Change the underlying LAN for communication to a WAN.
8	Change the relationships between data items to be maintained (e.g., add the ability to associate scenarios with stakeholders).
9	Use data encryption/decryption on all communications.
10	Exchange data with a variety of architectural design environments.
11	Add new data items to be maintained.
12	Integrate with the Dali toolkit.
13	Change the data structure of an entity (e.g., store a date with each scenario).
14	Change the constraints on relationships and organizational structure of entities (e.g., don't allow each scenario group to have both scenarios and subgroups as members but only one type of member).
15	All task-level operations can be undone except when the user is warned otherwise.
16	Add a new data item/data structure to the architectural description.
17	Support ATAM-based evaluations for product line architectures. In particular, support the notion of variation points in scenarios, constraints, and analyses.

7.4.3   Step 2: Describe the Architecture(s), First Iteration

The overall ATAT architecture was first described by the architect using four views: a functional view, a concurrency view, a physical view, and a code (class) view. The functional and code views are presented below. The other views, while important for the overall architectural design, were not directly relevant to the SAAM evaluation.

The functional view of the ATAT architecture, presented in Figure 7.2, shows a number of editors. These editors are controlled by a process support component (which can start and stop them in appropriate states) and share data via a central data repository. The central data repository in turn makes use of a constraint checker to ensure the validity and consistency of the data entered.

Each editor operates independently and is organized around collecting and manipulating a specific artifact of architectural documentation. Recognizing that this collection of editors would share a significant portion of their functionality, the architecture was designed to support a family of such editors by

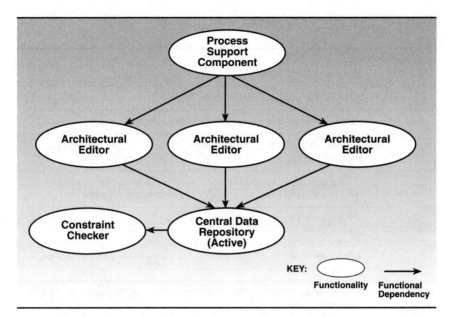

Figure 7.2   Functional View of the ATAT Architecture

providing a component that is a generic editor. This single editor could provide each instance of editor functionality shown in Figure 7.2. (This generic editor is the portion of the ATAT tool for which there were two competing architectures.)

7.4.4   Step 1: Develop Scenarios, Second Iteration

Inspired by the architectural description above and the presentation and explanation of the tool's functional architecture by the software architect, a second round of scenario brainstorming was held. The result of this activity was the 24 new scenarios listed in Table 7.5.

Table 7.5   Raw Scenarios Collected from the Stakeholders (Second Iteration)

Scenario Number	Scenario Description
18	Export the object model to other tools via Microsoft COM.
19	Change the user interface to a Web-based GUI.
20	Change the GUI toolset used to build the tool.
21	Change the underlying database from a flat file to SQL.

(continued)

Table 7.5   Raw Scenarios Collected from the Stakeholders (Second Iteration) (*continued*)

Scenario Number	Scenario Description
22	Change the communication infrastructure.
23	Change the level of granularity of data exchange.
24	Make constraint checking operate in an incremental rather than a batch fashion.
25	To support the possibility to work off-line and to recover from network and machine failures, add the possibility to reconcile data.
26	Change the GUI to reflect user feedback.
27	Create a stakeholder editor using the existing implementation of the utility tree editor as a basis. Both editors use a tree view, a list view, and a detailed view.
28	Create an editor for architectural descriptions using the existing implementation of the utility tree editor as a basis. Instead of a tree view the new editor uses a graph view to display arbitrary graphs.
29	Change the interface to the central data repository.
30	The relationships between data items have been changed in one editor (e.g., the ability to associate scenarios with stakeholders has been added to the stakeholder editor). Update all other editors so that they also reflect the changed relationships between data items.
31	Migrate to a new Acme[a] concept for representing graphs. A new version of the Acme language offers concepts that can be used to represent graphs and allows an easier way to check topological constraints.
32	Migrate to a new Acme concept for representing links (e.g., from UID-based links to Acme mappings).
33	Migrate to a new Acme concept for representing groups.
34	Change the implementation of the list view in the utility tree editor so that it shows the following behavior: In the tree view a quality attribute is selected, and the list view lists all categories that refine this quality attribute. Then the user selects a category in the tree view; the list view displays all scenarios that refine the current category. List view has to change the displayed columns.
35	Change the communication mechanism between editors and the central data repository.
36	Migrate from the central data repository to a distributed data repository.
37	Change mechanism/protocol to ensure data consistency (e.g., change from locking to a dOPT concurrency control scheme).

(*continued*)

Table 7.5 Raw Scenarios Collected from the Stakeholders (Second Iteration) (*continued*)

Scenario Number	Scenario Description
38	Add a new editor to display a new view of an existing data item.
39	Change the number of editors installed on one computer.
40	Change the underlying data representation language from Acme to another representation language.
41	The user creates a new editor reusing all common facilities.

a. Acme is the underlying data representation language.

7.4.5 Step 2: Describe the Architecture(s), Second Iteration

At this point, the architect proposed two candidate architectures for the generic editor (note that each editor instance is shown as a separate box in Figure 7.2).

One candidate architecture for the generic editor was based on the Model-View-Controller (MVC) pattern; the other candidate architecture was based on the Presentation-Abstraction-Control (PAC) pattern. One goal of the architectural evaluation was to decide which candidate architecture should be used for the implementation of the product line of editors. The SAAM was our means to base this decision on a rationale rather than relying on our intuition and taste.

Figure 7.3 shows the code view of the first candidate architecture that was based on the MVC architectural pattern. The MVC pattern decouples the user interface of an application from the rest of the application. The view component implements the user interface. The model component encapsulates the data model and provides operations to access and manipulate this data model. The controller component handles inputs from the user interface and requests the appropriate services from the view component or the model component. Whenever a data item is changed in the model component, the view component is updated via a change propagation mechanism.

ATAT's user interface provides three views of the data model: a tree view, a list view, and a detailed view. As shown in Figure 7.2, each editor needs to interact with the process support component and the central data repository. The interfaces for these interactions are encapsulated in separate classes.

Figure 7.4 shows the code view of the second candidate architecture that was based on the PAC architectural pattern. Software architectures following the PAC pattern are structured as a tree-like hierarchy of interacting agents, as indicated by the dashed-line boxes in the figure. Each agent consists of three components: presentation, abstraction, and control. The presentation component implements the user interface of the agent, the abstraction component encapsulates the data model maintained by the agent and operations on this

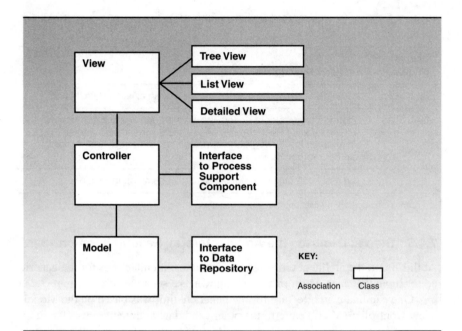

Figure 7.3   Code View of the MVC-Based Candidate Architecture of the Generic ATAT Editor

data model, and the control component connects presentation and control and manages the interactions with other agents.

The top-level PAC agent ATAT-Core implements the functional core of the ATAT system. Its presentation component provides a framework for the user interface of lower-level PAC agents, and its abstraction component maintains the global data model. One class of lower-level agents, ATAT-Entities, represent a self-contained semantic concept of the application domain (for example, a scenario, a requirement, or an architectural connector). The presentation component of the ATAT-Entities provides a user interface to invoke operations on the entities and can be plugged into the GUI framework provided by the top-level agent. The abstraction component of an ATAT-Entity maintains the internal data structure of the entity (for example, number, description, and priority of scenarios), and the control component maintains relationships to other ATAT-Entities (for example, a group maintains relationships to all its group members).

7.4.6   Step 3: Classify and Prioritize the Scenarios

In the next step, the analysis team grouped and prioritized the scenarios. The goal of scenario grouping is to identify related scenarios and to generalize them. We have found in practice that when an architecture is assessed relative

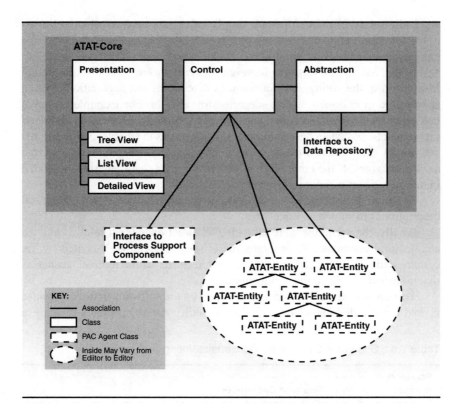

Figure 7.4   Code View of the PAC-Based Candidate Architecture of the Generic ATAT Editor

to a generalized scenario a broader set of concerns are addressed. In this SAAM evaluation a small number of scenario groups were proposed and defended by the stakeholders. For example, one stakeholder pointed out that scenarios 7, 22, and 35 were all about changing the underlying communication infrastructure. After some discussion it was decided that at least 22 and 35 were similar enough to be grouped (and voted on as a group). After all grouping was completed, we proceeded to prioritization.

In this SAAM exercise we had forty-one scenarios that needed to be prioritized. We gave each stakeholder 30 percent, or 12 votes, to allocate. Stakeholders may allocate as many or as few votes as they wish to each scenario; they might choose to give one vote each to 12 different scenarios, or to put 12 votes on one scenario, or to distribute any other combination that adds up to 12.

Once everyone has voted, we tally the votes and order the scenarios by the number of votes they have received. We then choose a cutoff point on the ordered list for detailed analysis. This may be at a particular number of votes, if there is an obvious place to cut (a significant discontinuity in the number of votes allocated), or the cutoff may simply be chosen because of time limitations. Ten to fifteen scenarios are typically the most that can be considered in a one-day analysis session.

In this SAAM exercise the top eight scenarios were scrutinized in detail. In addition to the voting, some amount of discussion and negotiation is often appropriate in choosing which scenarios to consider. For example, a stakeholder with a strong interest in a particular scenario can argue for its inclusion (as we mentioned when describing the ATAM process in Chapter 3, we call this making an "impassioned plea"), even if that scenario did not receive a large number of votes. If the other stakeholders agree, then that scenario is included in the subsequent mapping process.

The top eight scenarios we chose to map onto the candidate architectural descriptions are shown in Table 7.6.

Finally, the scenarios were classified as direct or indirect relative to each architectural candidate. To reiterate: direct scenarios can be executed by the system without modifications to the architecture, while indirect scenarios require modifications to the architecture.

This classification was done, in this case, by the software architect because he had the detailed knowledge of how to modify the architectures to achieve

Table 7.6 Scenarios Ordered by Consensus Voting

Scenario Number	Votes	Scenario Description
7	14	Change the underlying LAN for communication to a WAN.
8	11	Change the relationships between data items to be maintained (e.g., add the ability to associate scenarios with stakeholders).
13	11	Change the data structure of an entity (e.g., store a date with each scenario).
16	10	Add a new data item/data structure to the architectural description.
19	8	Change the user interface to a Web-based GUI.
20	8	Change the GUI toolset used to build the tool.
27	7	Create a stakeholder editor using the existing implementation of the utility tree editor as a basis. Both editors use a tree view, a list view, and a detailed view.
30	6	The relationships between data items have been changed in one editor (e.g., the ability to associate scenarios with stakeholders has been added to the stakeholder editor). Update all other editors so that they also reflect the changed relationship between data items.

the desired effect. Whether a scenario is direct or indirect depends on the software architecture under consideration; a scenario can be direct for one architecture and indirect for another one. To put it another way, whether a property is direct or indirect is a property of a scenario/architecture pair and not just the scenario alone. Hence, each scenario must be classified with respect to each candidate architecture. The number of direct scenarios is a first parameter that can be used to compare different candidate architectures.

All the scenarios turned out to be indirect for both candidate architectures except scenario 30, which is indirect for the MVC-based architecture and direct for the PAC-based architecture. This is not an accident: the stakeholders were focused on using the SAAM to measure the impact of anticipated changes, not to "walk through" the architecture or understand its functionality. The classification of scenarios is shown in Tables 7.7 and 7.8.

7.4.7 Step 4: Individually Evaluate Indirect Scenarios

The results of the scenario evaluation and effort estimates for the scenarios are shown in Table 7.7 for the MVC-based architecture and in Table 7.8 for the PAC-based architecture.

Table 7.7 SAAM Scenario Evaluations for the MVC-Based Architecture

Scenario Number	Scenario Description	Direct/ Indirect	Elements Requiring Change	Number of Changed/ Added Components	Effort for Changes (estimate)
7	Change the underlying LAN for communication to a WAN.	Indirect	Model, Interface to data repository	3	1 person-month
8	Change the relationships between data items to be maintained (e.g., add the ability to associate scenarios with stakeholders).	Indirect	Model, controller, view	3	1 person-week

(*continued*)

Table 7.7   SAAM Scenario Evaluations for the MVC-Based Architecture
(*continued*)

Scenario Number	Scenario Description	Direct/ Indirect	Elements Requiring Change	Number of Changed/ Added Components	Effort for Changes (estimate)
13	Change the data structure of an entity (e.g., store a date with each scenario).	Indirect	Model, controller, view, detailed view	4	1 person-week
16	Add a new data item/ data structure to the architectural description.	Indirect	Model, view, controller, tree view	4	1.5 person-weeks
19	Change the user interface to a Web-based GUI.	Indirect	View, tree view, list view, detailed view	4	2 person-weeks
20	Change the GUI toolset used to build the tool.	Indirect	View, tree view, list view, detailed view	4	2 person-weeks
27	Create a stakeholder editor using the existing implementation of the utility tree editor as a basis. Both editors use a tree view, a list view, and a detailed view.	Indirect	Model, view, controller, tree view, list view, detailed view of the new editor (reuse of commonalities via subclassing)	6	1 person-month

(*continued*)

Table 7.7 SAAM Scenario Evaluations for the MVC-Based Architecture (*continued*)

Scenario Number	Scenario Description	Direct/ Indirect	Elements Requiring Change	Number of Changed/ Added Components	Effort for Changes (estimate)
30	Relationships between data items have been changed in one editor (e.g., the ability to associate scenarios with stakeholders has been added to the stakeholder editor). Update all other editors so that they reflect the changed relationships.	Indirect	View, controller, model, and tree view of all affected editors	Depends on the number of affected editors	2 person-weeks to 1 person-month

Table 7.8 SAAM Scenario Evaluations for the PAC-based Architecture

Scenario Number	Scenario Description	Direct/ Indirect	Elements Requiring Change	Number of Changed/ Added Components	Effort for Changes (estimate)
7	Change the underlying LAN for communication to a WAN.	Indirect	Abstraction, interface to data repository	1	1 person-month
8	Change the relationships between data items to be maintained (e.g., add the ability to associate scenarios with stakeholders).	Indirect	The ATAT-Entity PAC agent for scenarios and stakeholders	2	2 person-days

(*continued*)

Table 7.8 SAAM Scenario Evaluations for the PAC-based Architecture (*continued*)

Scenario Number	Scenario Description	Direct/ Indirect	Elements Requiring Change	Number of Changed/ Added Components	Effort for Changes (estimate)
13	Change the data structure of an entity (e.g., store a date with each scenario).	Indirect	The ATAT-Entity PAC agent for the affected entity	1	1 person-day
16	Add a new data item/ data structure to the architectural description.	Indirect	The ATAT-Entity PAC agent for the new data item and the ATAT-Entity PAC agents for related data items	1 + the number of related data entities	2 person-days
19	Change the user interface to a Web-based GUI.	Indirect	The presentation component of ATAT-Core and the presentation components of all ATAT-Entity PAC agents	Depends on the number of ATAT-Entity PAC agents.	1.5 person-months
20	Change the GUI toolset used to build the tool.	Indirect	The presentation component of ATAT-Core and the presentation components of all ATAT-Entity PAC agents	Depends on the number of ATAT-Entity PAC agents	2 person-weeks

(*continued*)

Table 7.8 SAAM Scenario Evaluations for the PAC-based Architecture (*continued*)

Scenario Number	Scenario Description	Direct/ Indirect	Elements Requiring Change	Number of Changed/ Added Components	Effort for Changes (estimate)
27	Create a stakeholder editor using the existing implementation of the utility tree editor as a basis. Both editors use a tree view, a list view, and a detailed view.	Indirect	New ATAT-Entity PAC agent for stakeholders plus new abstraction and control classes (reuse of commonalities via subclassing)	3	2 person-weeks
30	Relationships between data items have been changed in one editor (e.g., the ability to associate scenarios with stakeholders has been added to the stakeholder editor). Update all other editors so that they reflect the changed relationships.	Direct	—	—	—

7.4.8 Step 5: Assess Scenario Interactions

This analysis gave us an estimate of per-scenario effort. In addition to this estimation, each of the scenarios in Table 7.6 was mapped onto the architectural representations provided by the architect so that we could see the areas of scenario interaction—portions of the architecture that are affected by multiple independent scenarios.

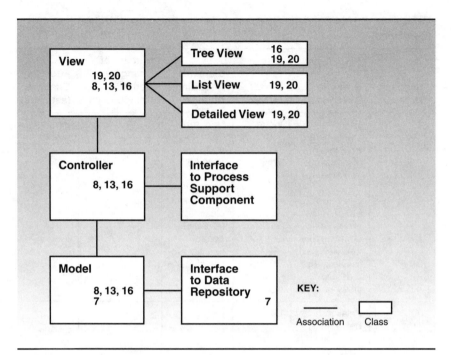

Figure 7.5   Annotated Code View of the MVC-Based Architecture

One such representation, of scenarios mapped onto the MVC-based architecture of the generic ATAT editor, is shown in Figure 7.5. Scenarios 19 and 20 as well as scenarios 8, 13, and 16 form groups of semantically related scenarios (as determined by the architect). As shown in Figure 7.5, the view, model, and tree views are affected by more than one scenario group. In other words, semantically *unrelated* scenarios interact in these components. Hence these components are potential problem areas—areas of predicted high future complexity. Of course, in any SAAM analysis a discussion among the stakeholders could allay or resolve such concerns. The SAAM simply highlights *potential* problem areas.

7.4.9   Step 6: Create the Overall Evaluation—Results and Recommendations

Table 7.9 compares the architectural candidates and shows how they support the analyzed scenarios. Recall that in such comparison tables a + means that this architecture is better (that is, it affects fewer components), a − means that this architecture is worse, and a *0* means that there is no significant difference, as determined by the architect.

Table 7.9 Evaluation Summary Table

Scenario Number	MVC	PAC
7	0	0
8	–	+
13	–	+
16	–	+
19	+	–
20	+	–
27	–	+
30	–	+

The result of this SAAM exercise was clear: the PAC-based architecture far outperformed the MVC-based architecture with respect to the high-priority scenarios.

However, this decision was not the only important result of this architectural evaluation. Other structural changes to the architectural design resulted from discussions that took place when the architect mapped the scenarios onto the proposed architectures. The most important results are listed below.

- To increase performance during updates of the GUI, the architect decided to add a change management component.
- To improve the reusability of the abstraction component, the architect decided to partition the central data repository into semantically related segments and create an abstraction component for each partition that could be reused without modifications in all editors that rely on this data segment.
- The architect decided to introduce an abstraction layer between Acme-specific functionality and ATAT core functionality so that a programmer could easily change the underlying data representation language or migrate to a new version of Acme.
- For performance reasons the architect decided that lower-level PAC agents are allowed to not only interact with the control component of higher-level agents but also directly call functionality in the presentation and abstraction components of higher-level agents.
- The architect decided to prototype whether it is feasible to introduce an abstraction layer between functionality provided by the GUI toolset and ATAT core functionality.

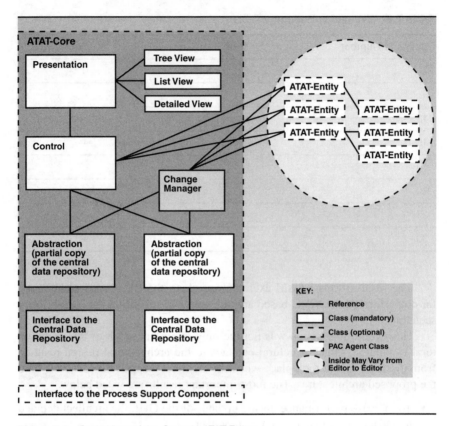

Figure 7.6   Code View of the Generic ATAT Editor

Figure 7.6 shows the architecture implemented after this SAAM exercise, indicating which components are mandatory, which components are optional, and which components may vary from editor instance to editor instance.

Overall, this SAAM exercise was extremely useful. It provided insights into the architecture that surprised both the stakeholders and the architect. It also improved stakeholder communication and buy-in tremendously. These are the main benefits of a SAAM-based evaluation.

7.5 Summary

The SAAM is a relatively simple architecture evaluation method that was created to operationalize the vague claims of modifiability, robustness, portability, and so forth that people typically make for their architectures. The SAAM achieves this by replacing claims of quality attributes with scenarios that operationalize those claims. The SAAM is a good place to begin incorporating architecture evaluation into your organization. It is easy to learn and easy to carry out.

A SAAM evaluation produces many important social and technical benefits. It forces an appropriate level of architectural documentation to be revealed and explained or, in some cases, to be created for the first time. It reveals the scenarios, and hence the underlying business goals, that are of greatest concern to the stake-holders and shows how the architecture, or architectures under consideration, respond to these scenarios. Finally, it causes the stakeholders to come together and discuss the architecture in a shared, mutually comprehensible language.

7.6 For Further Reading

The SAAM was first described by Kazman et al. [Kazman 94, 96] and later described in greater detail by Bass et al. [Bass 98], including several in-depth case studies. The evaluation presented in this chapter made use of several design patterns. For a general introduction to design patterns, the interested reader should consult Gamma et al. [Gamma 95]. The specific PAC and MVC patterns used in this chapter's case study are described in some detail in Busch-mann et al. [Buschmann 96].

The Dali toolkit, which was referenced as a potential integration target for the ATAT tool, is used for the reverse engineering of software architectures [Kazman 99].

7.7 Discussion Questions

1. What would it take for the SAAM to be adopted in your organization? Think about getting management buy-in, stakeholder buy-in, and buy-in from the architects. Would this be easier or more difficult than getting some other method, such as the ATAM, adopted?

2. For some hypothetical software system (or a real system you know about) write a scenario or two for a SAAM-based evaluation that expresses a spe-cific concern with one of the architecture's quality attributes:

   a. Modifiability, such as accommodating a change in one or more of its functions

    b. Portability across computing platforms

    c. Portability across operating systems

    d. Extensibility, or addition of function

    e. Scalability, or the ability to accommodate extreme growth in some aspect

    f. Subsetability, or the ability of the system to be fielded with partial or reduced functionality

    g. Functionality, or the ability of the system to deliver its promised capabilities

3. For each scenario you wrote above, identify a stakeholder for the system who might be interested in that scenario.

4. For each scenario you wrote above, determine whether it is a direct or an indirect scenario.

5. For each indirect scenario you identified above, walk through the architecture to measure its impact.

8

ARID—An Evaluation Method for Partial Architectures

People ask you for criticism but they want only praise.
—William Somerset Maugham
Of Human Bondage

Both the ATAM and the SAAM are comprehensive methods for evaluating full-blown software architectures. However, architectures do not spring into existence in final, polished form but often emerge slowly, in fits and starts. Architectures often comprise complicated subdesign problems that represent stepping stones on the path to the full architecture. If these intermediate designs are inappropriate, the entire architecture can be undermined. Therefore, reviewing a design in its prerelease stage provides valuable early insight into the design's viability and allows for timely discovery of errors, inconsistencies, or inadequacies. Further, most projects go through this preliminary stage for each and every one of their major components or subsystems.

What is called for at this stage is an easy, lightweight evaluation approach that concentrates on *suitability*, exposes a design to its stakeholders in a way that generates buy-in, and can be carried out in the absence of detailed documentation. This chapter introduces such a method: Active Reviews for Intermediate Designs (ARID). ARID lies at the intersection of two approaches. The first is scenario-based design review techniques, such as the ATAM or the SAAM that have already been described. The second is active design reviews (ADRs).

ARID is best suited for evaluating a partial design in its infancy. At this stage, the designer—perhaps he or she is not even the architect—merely wants to know, "Am I on the right track? Are the services I'm designing in this part of the architecture sufficient?" In other words, the designer wishes to know whether the design being proposed is suitable from the point of view of other

241

parts of the architecture that will be required to use it. Perhaps the potential adopter/reuser of a framework that is being designed wants to understand how the framework can be used.

8.1 Active Design Reviews

ADRs are an effective technique for ensuring quality, detailed designs in software. The method relies on actively engaging the reviewers by assigning them review tasks that are carefully structured to avoid asking yes/no questions. Such questions can undermine a review by making it easy for a reviewer to toss off a carelessly considered answer. In contrast, an ADR asks the reviewer to utilize the design in a series of exercises that test actual, not merely feigned, understanding.

For example, a conventional design review often begins with the chosen multitude of reviewers receiving stacks of read-ahead documentation, which they may or may not examine. The masses are then assembled in a central location on the appointed day. There is a presentation of the design being analyzed, and the design leader then opens the floor for discussion. A somewhat more structured review technique uses a checklist that asks reviewers to make sure that the design meets certain standards. Both of these are susceptible to reviewer boredom: even with the best of intentions, reviewers often find it easier to give designers the answer they desire, rather than the right one. And a high-pressure group setting compels some reviewers to say nothing at all.

Table 8.1 illustrates some of the differences that one might observe between an active design review and a conventional review.

ADRs are primarily used to evaluate detailed designs of coherent units of software, such as modules or components. The questions tend to address (1) quality and completeness of the documentation and (2) sufficiency, fitness, and suitability of the services provided by the design. The reviewers are chosen to represent consumers of both the design and its documentation.

Table 8.1   Conventional versus Active Design Review Questions/Instructions

Conventional Design Review Questions	Active Design Review Instructions
Are exceptions defined for every program?	Write down the exceptions that can occur for every program.
Are the right exceptions defined for every program?	Write down the range or set of legal values of each parameter. Write down the states under which it is illegal to invoke the program.

(continued)

Table 8.1   Conventional versus Active Design Review Questions/Instructions (*continued*)

Conventional Design Review Questions	Active Design Review Instructions
Are the data types defined?	For each data type, write down • An expression for a literal value of that data type • A declaration statement to declare a variable for that type • The greatest and least values in the range of that data type
Are the programs sufficient?	Write a short pseudo-code program that uses the design to accomplish (some defined task).
Is the performance of each program adequately specified?	For each program, write down its maximum execution time and list the shared resources that it may consume.

Origins of Active Design Reviews

In 1985, David Parnas and David Weiss wrote a paper entitled "Active Design Reviews: Principles and Practices" for that year's International Conference on Software Engineering [Parnas 85]. Parnas is well known for his foundational papers in software engineering, including the 1972 pioneering work that first described information-hiding as a design principle [Parnas 72]. Viewed as a body, Parnas's work (with colleagues such as Weiss) can be seen as bridging the gap between "theoretical" software engineering and practical application of sound engineering methods. (Parnas once said that "theoretically" is often a euphemism for "not really.") In their 1985 paper, Parnas and Weiss expressed the fundamental principle behind the architectural evaluation methods described in this book: undirected, unstructured reviews of software designs don't work. The common practice was—and still is—to identify a group of reviewers, drop a stack of read-ahead material on their desks a week or so prior to a meeting, haul them all into a conference room for a few tedious hours, ask if anyone has any comments about the materials they were given, and hope for the best.

The outcome of such a "review" is entirely predictable and entirely disappointing. Human nature being what it is, most of the participants will not have cracked the read-ahead material until the last minute, if at all. Perhaps they will have read just enough so that they can make an intelligent comment or two so that, if they're called upon, they won't have to stare at their shoes. The organizers of this ritual will as often as not fail to uncover any serious problems with the design under consideration but will happily check the "design review" box on their project plans. What problems actually do exist will, of course, lay dormant and undetected until the least opportune time imaginable, weeks or months downstream.

Parnas and Weiss prescribed a better way. An active design review is one in which the reviewers are carefully chosen because of their areas of expertise, not simply because of their availability. But more importantly, each reviewer is given a questionnaire to complete. That forces the reviewer to actually use the design documentation being reviewed to answer the questions. For example, a question might be, "How would you use the facilities provided by this module to send a message to the user and await a response?" The reviewer would then be obliged to sketch out the answer in pseudo-code, using the facilities described in the design.

The result is that the artifact being reviewed is actually exercised. To see if it is readable, the reviewers are compelled to read it. To see if it is usable, the reviewers are compelled to use it. The reviewers are forced to think hard about what they are reading, rather than skimming it for obvious errors. Their answers are then examined by the artifact owners to see if there are any surprises, and if there are, then the reviewers are interviewed to find out why. Another happy result is that the reviewers become engaged in the process.

All of the architecture evaluation methods in this book, not just ARID, are also active design reviews. They require the participation of experts selected for their specific stake in the architecture. They intentionally avoid open-ended questions such as, "Does anyone see any problems with this architecture?" Rather, they pursue a strict path of directed analysis, first eliciting a specific statement of the conditions that the architecture must satisfy to be acceptable, and then following a prescribed analytical path to compare the architecture to those conditions. They are also designed to give the reviewers a strong sense of participation.

The result of an active design review is of much higher quality than an open-ended feel-good session in which everyone sits around and shares whatever happens to be on their minds. The goals of the review—that is, what the organizers hope to learn—are explicitly made known to the participants. Thus, progress toward those goals can always be gauged. There is an identifiable point in the process when you know you're done, when the targeted information has been collected. Contrast this with an unstructured review, in which participants leave not really knowing if the important issues have been aired.

Active design reviews not only produce higher-quality results but also have a positive effect on the people who participate. As Parnas and Weiss put it, "Performing a good job as a reviewer is difficult work. It is important that the review be designed to give the reviewers a sense of participation and accomplishment. Lacking such a feeling they are unlikely to participate in future reviews." [Parnas 85] A directed review process in which the participants make identifiable contributions at each step along the way leaves them feeling that the exercise made good use of their (valuable) time. This translates to respect for the reviewers as a valuable resource. This respect will be repaid the next time you ask them to participate in a review.

—*PCC*

8.2 ARID: An ADR/ATAM Hybrid

ADRs and the ATAM both bring useful features to bear on the problem of evaluating preliminary designs, but neither is appropriate on its own.

In an ADR, stakeholders receive detailed documentation and then complete exercise questionnaires on their own. But in preliminary designs, there is often no detailed documentation. Further, while ADRs eschew central meetings by individually debriefing the reviewers, one of our goals is to achieve group buy-in, and purely individual work would not accomplish that.

On the other hand, the ATAM is geared toward evaluating a whole architecture, not a portion of it. Further, for preliminary designs we are interested only in whether the overall approach is suitable. So the elicitation of business drivers and utility trees and the gathering and analysis of architectural approaches are all obviated.

Clearly something else is needed. We were adamant about not falling back on the unimaginative technique of gathering the stakeholders in a room, presenting the design, and asking "What do you think?" We recognized that ADRs and the ATAM both had strong qualities that could be brought to bear on this problem. An ADR requires active reviewer participation, which we thought would be ideal on two fronts. First, ADRs assure high-fidelity responses on the part of the reviewers: they can't simply sit there and say nothing. Second, active participation would, we hoped, increase the likelihood of group buy-in. From the ATAM, we embraced the idea of stakeholder-generated scenarios that would form the basis of the exercise. Rather than having the designers tell the services' consumers what suitability meant, the consumers would tell the designers, thus setting the stage themselves for what it meant to pass the review. That, we reasoned, would also help with buy-in: if the reviewers set the conditions for the test, and the design passed the test, then surely that would signal that the design was suitable.

Thus was born Active Reviews for Intermediate Designs. By combining the best of ADRs and scenario-based architecture evaluation methods such as the ATAM, ARID fills a niche in the spectrum of design review techniques.

8.3 The Steps of ARID

Like the ATAM, ARID has nine main steps. The ARID steps are distributed over two main phases.

8.3.1   Phase 1: Rehearsal

First, a meeting between the lead designer and the review facilitator takes place to prepare for the exercise. This meeting usually lasts about a day. In this meeting, the first four steps are taken.

1. **Identify the reviewers.** The reviewers are the software engineers who will be expected to use the design. Because they have a vested interest in the quality of the design—a stake, if you will—they are the best people to judge its adequacy. So we merge the concept of ADR reviewers and ATAM stakeholders. In ARID, the reviewers are the design's stakeholders. We aim for approximately a dozen stakeholders, but this can vary depending on the size of the user community.

2. **Prepare the design briefing.** The designer prepares a briefing explaining the design. A rule of thumb is to aim for two hours' worth of material. Include examples of using the design to solve real problems. The goal is to present the design in sufficient detail so that a knowledgeable audience member could use the design. The designer gives a dry run of the presentation to the review facilitator, which serves several purposes. First, it lets the facilitator see the design and ask a set of "first order" questions that the reviewers would probably ask, thus helping the designer prepare. Second, it helps identify areas where the presentation could be improved. Third, it helps set the pace for the presentation itself, ensuring that the two-hour slot is not overrun. And fourth, it gives the designer practice in presenting the material to a critical audience.

3. **Prepare the seed scenarios.** The designer and the review facilitator prepare a set of seed scenarios. Like the scenarios in the ATAM and the SAAM, these are designed to illustrate the concept of a scenario to the reviewers, who have an opportunity to see a sample set. The scenarios may or may not be used in the actual evaluation; that will be up to the stakeholders present. Aim for roughly a dozen scenarios.

4. **Prepare the materials.** Copies of the presentation, seed scenarios, and review agenda are produced for distribution to the reviewers during the Phase 2 meeting. The meeting is scheduled, stakeholders are invited, and steps are taken to assure the presence of a quorum of reviewers at the meeting.

8.3.2   Phase 2: Review

Next, the stakeholders are assembled and the main activities of the review commence. Nominally this phase takes about a day and a half, during which the remaining five steps of the ARID analysis are completed.

5. **Present ARID.** The review facilitator spends 30 minutes explaining the steps of ARID to the participants.

6. **Present the design.** The lead designer presents the two-hour overview presentation and walks through the examples. During this time, a ground rule is that no questions concerning implementation or rationale are allowed, nor are suggestions about alternate designs. The goal is to see if the design is suitable, not to find out why things were done a certain way or to learn about the implementation secrets behind the interfaces. Questions of factual clarification are allowed and encouraged. The facilitator enforces this rule during the presentation.

   During this time, a scribe captures each question and each instance where the designer indicated that some sort of resource (usually a kind of documentation) is on its way but not yet available. The resulting list is summarized to show potential issues that the designer should address before the design could be considered complete and ready for production.

7. **Brainstorm and prioritize scenarios.** A session is held for scenario brainstorming and prioritization. Just as in the ATAM, stakeholders suggest scenarios for using the design to solve problems they expect to face. During brainstorming, all scenarios are deemed fair game. The seed scenarios are put into the pool with all the others. After a rich set of scenarios is gathered, a winnowing process occurs. Reviewers might suggest that two scenarios are versions of the same scenario or that one subsumes another and should be merged. After the pool of scenarios is winnowed, voting occurs. Each reviewer is allowed a vote total equal to 30 percent of the number of scenarios. Reviewers can allocate their votes to any scenario or scenarios they wish. The scenarios receiving the most votes are then used to "test" the design for suitability. After voting is complete, it is important to make the point that the reviewers have just defined at least a minimal specification of what it means for the design to be suitable: it performs well under the adopted scenarios, then it must be agreed that the design has passed the review. Buy-in has begun.

8. **Apply the scenarios.** Beginning with the scenario that received the most votes, the facilitator asks the reviewers, working as a group, to craft code (or pseudo-code) that uses the design services to solve the problem posed by the scenario. Reviewers make extensive use of the examples that were handed out as part of the designer's presentation. Code statements, captured by a scribe on a flipchart at the front of the room, are gathered that use the services to carry out the scenario. During this time, a ground rule is that the designer is not allowed to help or give hints. If, however, the group becomes stuck or begins to go off in the wrong direction, the facilitator can stop the proceedings and ask the designer to get the group moving again by providing whatever information is deemed necessary. However, each time this happens, the facilitator must ask the scribe to record as an issue where and why the group stalled since this indicates an area where the design or the materials handed out to represent it are insufficient to

allow a nonexpert to proceed. Any discrepancies uncovered during the review are also recorded as issues.

This step continues until one of the following events occurs.

- The time allotted for the review has ended.
- The highest-priority scenarios have been exercised. Often the voting scheme produces a set of scenarios at the high end, with several votes each, and a set of scenarios at the low end, with one or zero votes each. When the former set is completed, it is usually safe to declare the review complete.
- The group feels satisfied that a conclusion has been reached. Either (a) the design is deemed suitable, which is indicated by the group quickly seeing how each subsequent scenario can be carried out as a straightforward variation on either the designer's examples or previously exercised scenarios, or (b) the design is deemed unsuitable, which is indicated by the group finding some show-stopping deficiency.

9. **Summarize.** At the end, the facilitator recounts the list of issues, polls the participants for their opinions regarding the efficacy of the review exercise, and thanks them for their participation.

Like the ATAM, the two main phases of ARID can be preceded by a partnership and preparation phase, in which a statement of work is negotiated and a review team formed. For ARID, the minimum team complement is two: a facilitator and a scribe. The facilitator also carries out team leader duties; the scribe is usually asked to be timekeeper, process enforcer, and data gatherer as well. A process observer can be added to the team, or the two people can share that role's duties.

A completion phase wraps up an ARID exercise. The results of a participants' survey are catalogued, feedback is digested, and the results of the exercise (namely, the code produced and the issues raised) are transmitted to the client.

8.4 A Case Study in Applying ARID

Some time ago, we were asked to conduct a technical review of a design of a portion of a software system. This "portion" provided a cohesive, user-invocable service but did not correspond to any simple subset of the architecture: it spanned two of the architecture's layers and included parts of several different work assignments. The domain was real-time embedded vehicle control.

The designer wanted two things.

1. He wanted to know whether the design was tenable. That is, he wanted to know whether writers of applications that use it could do so effectively.

Did it provide the necessary services? Did it provide those services in a suitable manner? Was the design conceptually coherent? Would the services impose too high a performance penalty?

2. He wanted to unveil the design to the community of software writers who needed it to do their jobs. Assuming that the basic design was sound, he wanted the design review to serve as the debut of the design to its consumers. In short, he wanted the participants to be trained, and he wanted their buy-in.

The design was not yet well documented. The invocable programs constituting the services were partially designed, meaning that they had been named, their parameters' types had been listed, and a rough statement of their semantics had been sketched. But the details that would have been provided by complete documentation were missing, such as:

- What exceptions might be raised by each program
- What would happen if the programs were called in illegal states
- How to declare variables of some of the types
- How programs in different processes, or on different processors, communicated and shared data with each other

The object of this review was not an entire architecture, and it was clear that neither the ATAM nor the SAAM were appropriate tools. This was a job for ARID.

8.4.1 Carrying Out the Steps

For this application of ARID, we assembled a simple facilitator/scribe team.

Phase 1

For the Rehearsal phase, the facilitator met with the designer one-on-one for a full day. They brainstormed about the stakeholders who should be recruited to participate. The facilitator suggested roles; the designer connected names to the roles. Between them, they identified eleven stakeholders who would be invited. They included two application builders from each of four different projects who were planning to use this design; two designers of an older system that this design was intended to replace; and a member of an implementation team working on a subsystem that this design needed to use.

Next, the facilitator and designer worked on preparing the briefing the designer would give to the stakeholders. This consisted of a two-hour viewgraph presentation that explained the services available. It included six examples in which the services were used together to solve different problems. The designer gave a dry run, and the facilitator asked probing questions about apparent flaws in the design. These were addressed when the presentation was revised.

Finally, ten or so seed scenarios were drafted. About half were variations of the examples in the designer's presentation; the other half were based on knowledge of the applications that would be represented by the stakeholders present.

Phase 2

One week later, the eleven stakeholders, the designer, and the two-person ARID team assembled. The agenda used is shown in Table 8.2.

Steps 5 and 6 went as planned. The dress rehearsal of Step 6 paid off because three of the questions raised by stakeholders had already been anticipated during Phase 1.

In Step 7, the stakeholders crafted 20 scenarios, as in a SAAM or ATAM exercise. During the merger activity, 5 were deleted, leaving us with 15. After voting, 6 emerged as the scenarios warranting the most attention, and we were ready to begin Step 8.

The design we were reviewing was of a "virtual input/output" service suite whose purpose was to insulate application software from changes when, for example, a platform changed input/output channels or wiring harnesses or an application was ported to a different processor in the distributed system. The highest-priority scenario was this: "We move from a platform that uses two measured inputs to derive a third input to a platform that includes a sensor to measure that third input directly." The group worked out the code statements, captured by the scribe, that used the services to implement the first case, where the third input is derived from the first two. Then the group worked out what would have to change when the new platform was adopted. This first scenario,

Table 8.2   Sample Agenda for Phase 2 an ARID-Based Review

Time	Step
Day 1	
8:00–8:30	Present ARID (Step 5)
8:30–11:00	Present design (including break) (Step 6)
11:00–12:00	Brainstorm and prioritize scenarios (Step 7)
12:00–1:00	Lunch
1:00–5:00	Apply scenarios (breaks as needed) (Step 8)
Day 2	
8:00–11:00	Apply scenarios (continued; breaks as needed) (Step 8)
11:00–11:30	Summarize (Step 9)

being the most popular (and thus, it is hoped, most important) was also among the most complex to solve; it took the group almost three hours to finish it.

During Step 8, as we said, the designer is not allowed to help or give hints. In our exercise, we put the designer to work by asking him to "fly" the design's UML model on a direct-display projector, so that when participants had questions about a particular program's interface or interactions, he could quickly take us to the specification where the question could be answered. In Step 8, we were able to handle 5 of the 6 scenarios. The last one was seen to be straightforward variation of one of the other scenarios and was set aside for tackling at a later date.

8.4.2 Results of the Exercise

The scribe captured a list of about two dozen issues during this exercise. Most were about discrepancies in the design, but some were ancillary matters such as process-oriented questions related to using the design. These were technically outside the scope of the design's suitability, but they were captured anyway, just as they are in the ATAM (see the Issues sidebar). The enlisted reviewers reported that they were generally quite happy with the exercise. There was some initial concern about spending more than a day group-writing code, but in the end they seemed to enjoy the problem-solving challenge. By and large, they felt that the ARID exercise was a good use of their time. Our "client," the lead designer, was very pleased and felt that the exercise satisfied his goals of training, buy-in, and design review.

We made the following observations about this experience with ARID.

- Starting with the highest-priority scenario (the one receiving the most votes) is often going to mean starting with the most complicated one. Stakeholders are likely to key on what they understand the least. Recall that the ATAM prioritizes scenarios along the two dimensions of importance and difficulty. In ARID, however, importance is not likely to play as large a role: if a stakeholder understands how to carry out a scenario by looking at the design, then that scenario (no matter how important) is not likely to float to the top of the list. Working on this first scenario may take hours, and by the afternoon of the first day there can be a glazed look in the participants' eyes. It may be better to start with a simpler scenario to keep people's energy high. With luck, the complex scenario might then be seen as a variant of a scenario handled previously and can then be easily dispatched.

- Have the architect for the overall system attend. The architectural knowledge he or she will bring to the table is invaluable. Questions often come up about parts of the architecture that are not fully developed, and the reviewers need answers in order to solve a problem at hand. The architect will be able to help them make a reasonable assumption about the missing parts so that they can make progress.

- As in all reviews, the quality and expertise of the reviewers will determine the fidelity of the review results. For example, in this exercise the group determined the difficulty of changing an interface. This is a significant achievement and could not have been accomplished with novice reviewers.

- There is a risk that design documentation that is promised will not be delivered. After all, the design has passed the review, and application programmers are using it to build products—so what's the point? That is dangerous software engineering, or perhaps more precisely, it is not software engineering at all but something less. The devil is often in the details, and solving necessary details may sometimes precipitate changes in what was thought to be a stable design, even after the design is in the hands of the masses. That risk should be recognized and addressed by the organization conducting this kind of review.

8.5 Summary

Of the evaluation techniques presented in this book, ARID is the newest kid on the block, but all of its foundational ideas come with a rich pedigree and a long résumé of practical experience. ARID fills a useful niche in the spectrum of design review techniques. ARID is a lightweight method that can be used to assess the suitability of a design before all of the details are worked out. By combining the best aspects of active design reviews and scenario-based architecture evaluation methods such as the ATAM, ARID provides a way to evaluate those partial architectures or intermediate designs that all architectures must pass through on their way to fruition. It fills out an architect's repertoire of evaluation methods.

8.6 For Further Reading

Active design reviews, of which ARID is an example, were first described by Parnas and Weiss [Parnas 85]. A good introduction to technical reviews can be found in Freedman and Weinberg [Freedman 90], and more specific techniques can be found in two other sources [Johnson 94, Fagan 76].

8.7 Discussion Questions

1. If your organization uses any standard questions or checklists for its design reviews, rewrite them to become active design review instructions.

2. Suppose your organization has to choose among a set of competing COTS components for use in a software system it is developing. How would you use ARID to help decide which component to purchase?

3. Make a case that all of the evaluation team roles given for the ATAM in Table 3.3 are also useful in an ARID exercise. Try to allocate the roles to a team of two people, and then to a team of three people.

4. A recommended part of every architecture evaluation is the follow-up survey, sent to the development organization six months after the exercise to gauge its effectiveness. Craft such a survey specifically for ARID. How would it differ from a similar survey for the SAAM? For the ATAM?

5. Pick a design in your organization and walk through a small ARID exercise on it. Identify the designer who would represent it during the review. Choose the stakeholders you would want to review it. Craft a set of scenarios that exemplify its usage. Then, using only the documentation available for the design, try to apply a few of the scenarios. What issues did you discover?

6. Describe a component interface in sufficient detail so that ARID could be used to assess its suitability. Craft some scenarios to assess the interface. Write some pseudo-code to assess the interface vis-à-vis the scenario.

9

Comparing Software Architecture Evaluation Methods

The wise man does not permit himself to set up even in his own
mind any comparisons of his friends. His friendship is capable of
going to extremes with many people, evoked as it is by many
qualities.

—attributed to Charles Dudley Warner

This book has presented three architecture evaluation methods: the ATAM, the
SAAM, and ARID. This chapter shows how they relate to each other and by
extrapolation to other evaluation techniques that you may encounter or wish to
use to help analyze an architecture.

First, let's look at the three methods: Table 9.1 shows how the ATAM, the
SAAM, and ARID relate to each other.

In general, all evaluation methods (not just these three) use one or both of
the following techniques.

- *Questioning techniques* use questionnaires, checklists, and scenarios to
  investigate the way an architecture addresses its quality requirements.
  Questioning techniques for architecture evaluation usually involve carrying out some "thought experiment" to predict how the system will behave
  since the system itself may not actually exist yet.

- *Measuring techniques* apply some measurement tool to a software artifact.
  Measuring techniques include running a simulation of the system whose
  architecture is being evaluated to see, for example, its performance under
  certain workload profiles. Metrics fall under measuring techniques. Measures

Table 9.1   The ATAM, the SAAM, and ARID Compared[a]

	ATAM	SAAM	ARID
Quality attributes covered	Method is not oriented to any particular quality attributes, but historically an emphasis has been placed on modifiability, security, reliability, and performance.	Primarily modifiability and functionality.	Suitability of design approach.
Object(s) analyzed	Architectural approaches or styles; architectural documentation showing process, data-flow, uses, physical, or module views.	Architectural documentation, especially showing the logical or module views.	Components' interface specifications.
Project stage(s) when applied	After the architecture design approaches have been chosen.	After the architecture has allocated functionality to modules.	During architecture design.
Approach(es) used	Utility trees and brainstormed scenarios to articulate quality attribute requirements. Analysis of architectural approaches to identify sensitivities, tradeoff points, and risks.	Brainstormed scenarios to articulate quality attribute requirements. Scenario walk-throughs to verify functionality or estimate change cost.	Active design reviews, brainstormed scenarios.
Resources required	Nominally 3 days plus time for preparation and post-exercise summary. Participants include client, architect, stakeholders, and 4-person evaluation team.	Nominally 2 days plus time for post-exercise summary. Participants include client, architect, stakeholders, and 3-person evaluation team.	Nominally 2 days plus time for preparation and post-exercise summary. Participants include architect, designer, stakeholders, and 2-person evaluation team.

a. The rows of this table are based on an elegant taxonomy of software audit techniques proposed by Rivera, J.A. "Software Audits: A Taxonomy" (unpublished report), Pittsburgh, PA: CMU School of Computer Science, 1996.

of complexity are usually used to draw conclusions about modifiability, as are coupling and cohesion metrics. Data-flow metrics (measuring the size and frequency of data passed along communication channels) can be used to predict performance or performance bottlenecks.

The two classes of techniques are often used in tandem: measuring technique (such as building a simulation or taking a metric-based measurement) might be the way to authoritatively answer a question raised in a questioning-type evaluation. In fact, questions are the measuring techniques' reason for being. Measurements are not useful for their own sake; rather, measurements (such as CPU utilization under maximum workload) are taken to help answer some question about the system (such as "Will this system meet its performance goals?").

9.1 Questioning Techniques

Questioning techniques are the broadest category of review techniques. Unlike measuring techniques, which actually require the existence of some artifact to measure, questioning techniques can be used to investigate any area of a project in virtually any state of readiness. Questioning techniques can therefore be applied early and can be used to assess project management and process issues as well as design decisions. Questioning techniques include questionnaires, checklists, and scenarios, which are all used to elicit discussion about the architecture and to increase understanding of the architecture's fitness with respect to its requirements.

9.1.1 Questionnaires and Checklists

A questionnaire is a list of general and relatively open questions that apply to all architectures. Some questions might apply to the way the architecture was generated and documented (by asking, for example, if there is a designated project architect or if a standard description language was used). Other questions focus on the details of the architecture description itself (by asking, say, if all user interface aspects of the system are separated from functional aspects). The review team is looking for a favorable response and will probe a single question to a level of detail that is necessary to satisfy their concern. The utility of a questionnaire is related to the ease with which the domain of interest can be characterized and circumscribed.

A checklist is a detailed set of questions developed after much experience evaluating a common (usually domain-specific) set of systems. Checklists tend

Danger Signals to Look For

In 1996 the Software Engineering Institute held a small workshop for people who practice software architecture evaluation on a routine basis. One of the participants, Philippe Kruchten of Rational Corporation, showed a list of warning signs that he looks for when evaluating an architecture. The list was documented in the workshop report [Abowd 96] and also in the book *Software Architecture in Practice* [Bass 98]. Those warning signs are listed below.

- The architecture is forced to match the current organization. For example, is there a database built into the design because one is needed or because there is a database group that's looking for work?

- There are more than 25 top-level architecture components. This design will likely be too complex for the architects to maintain intellectual control over, let alone the developers to whom they hand it.

- One requirement drives the rest of the design. In one system we evaluated, the requirement for ultra-high availability was the primary impetus behind the architecture. When that requirement was eventually relaxed, the architecture was then much too complex for the task at hand. Focusing on a single requirement tends to give others short shrift.

- The architecture depends on alternatives in the operating system. This makes the architecture mortally vulnerable to inevitable operating system upgrades; this obvious design flaw occurs surprisingly often.

- Proprietary components are being used when standard components would do. This renders the architecture dependent on a single supplier.

- The component definition comes from the hardware division. Hardware changes as systems evolve, and hardware components tend to merge into more general-purpose processors or split into special-purpose devices. Keeping the software independent of the hardware organization insulates it from these changes.

- There is redundancy not needed for reliability. For instance, the presence of two databases, two start-up routines, or two error locking procedures suggests that the designers could not agree, resulting in unnecessary complexity and a system much harder to maintain.

- The design is exception driven; the emphasis is on the extensibility and not core commonalities.

- The development unit is unable to identify an architect for the system.

To this list, we add the following items.

- The architect or project manager has difficulty identifying the architecture's stakeholders. This might mean they haven't thought about them.

- Developers have a plethora of choices in how they code an interaction between two components. The architecture either provides this plethora or is silent on the issue. This means that the architecture is underdefined.

- The architect, when asked for architecture documentation, produces class diagrams and nothing else.

- The architect, when asked for architecture documentation, provides a large stack of documents automatically produced by some tool but which no human has ever seen.

- Documents provided are old and apparently are not kept up to date.

- A designer or developer, when asked to describe the architecture, is either unable to or describes a much different architecture than the architect presented.

As you gain experience evaluating software architectures, it is instructive to maintain your own list of danger signals that you come across.

—PCC

to be much more focused on particular functions or quality attributes of the system. For example, performance questions in a real-time information system ask whether the system is writing the same data multiple times to disk or whether consideration has been given to handling peak as well as average loads.

Questionnaires and checklists have an important aspect in common: both are stored repositories that reviewers use to illuminate issues that arise over and over again in software development.

The typical, perhaps best-of-breed, checklist technique is the method used by AT&T (and, after they split off, Lucent Technologies) to perform architecture audits. Because the systems they develop dwell in a common domain, it was possible to "grow" lists of questions into a checklist that can be applied with confidence to each new system in the domain. As reported by Avritzer and Weyuker:

Before scheduling an audit, the review team chairperson usually spends about two hours with the project's lead architect in order to identify the technological expertise that the review team will need to have. . . . During the audit, the project delivers presentations to the reviewers on important aspects of the architecture. The review identifies issues by making inquiries during the presentations, which are noted on cards. At the end of the audit, the review team meets and assigns categories and severities for each finding, and these results are then reported to the project. After the audit, the findings are also entered into a database for resolution tracking. A findings report is issued and distributed to the lead architect and the project's upper management. [Avritzer 98]

Although such audits have been carried out on hundreds of projects at AT&T, Avritzer and Weyuker compiled findings for a set of 50. They reported that the project-threatening management issues that arose most often were the following:

- The stakeholders are not clearly identified.
- No domain experts have been committed to the team.
- Project funding has not been formalized.
- No project manager/leader has been identified.
- No project plan/schedule is in place.
- Deployment date is unrealistic.
- Measures of success need to be identified.
- No software architects have been selected.
- Although each layer has an architect, no individual is responsible for the overall architecture.
- An overall architecture plan has not been written.
- No independent requirement writing team [exists].
- No hardware and installation schedule [exists].
- No independent performance effort is in place.
- No quality assurance organization is in place.
- No system test plan has been developed.

Other risk areas were identified as well. For example, the most common project-threatening performance issues were the following:

- End user has not established performance requirements.
- No performance data has been gathered.
- Performance budgets have not been established.
- Expected traffic rates have not been established.
- No mechanism for measuring transaction times or numbers of transactions has been established.
- No assessment has been made to assure that required throughput can be handled.
- No assessment has been made to assure that hardware will meet processing requirements.
- No performance model [exists].

Although Avritzer and Weyuker did not divulge the checklists that brought about these findings, the questions they include are easy to imagine. Checklists are prearranged lines of inquiry that are general enough to transcend any one system and thus apply to an entire class of systems.

Checklists can come from taxonomies of quality attributes that occur in the literature. (Recall from Chapter 5 that in the ATAM, attribute-specific questions are inspired from quality attribute characterizations.) For example, if your system has stringent security requirements, you might wish to construct a checklist to see how it is protecting itself from the threats shown in Table 9.2 [Landwehr 94].

9.1.2   Scenarios and Scenario-Based Methods

As we have already seen, a scenario is a short description of an interaction with the system from the point of view of one of its stakeholders. A user may pose a use case to see how the system would respond to a certain request and whether the architecture could deliver the required functionality. A maintainer might

Table 9.2   Taxonomy of Security Flaws by Genesis

Genesis				
	Intentional	Malicious	Trojan horse	Non-replicating
				Replicating (virus)
			Trapdoor	
			Logic/time bomb	
		Nonmalicious	Covert channel	Storage
				Timing
			Other	
	Inadvertent	Validation error (incomplete, inconsistent)		
		Domain error (including object reuse, residuals, and exposed representation errors)		
		Serialization/aliasing		
		Inadequate identification/authentication		
		Boundary conditions violation (including resource exhaustion and violable constraint errors)		
		Other exploitable logic error		

pose a change scenario to test how modifiable the system would be under its architecture.

Scenarios are usually specific to the system whose architecture is being evaluated. Experience reviewing a family of related systems can result in generalizing a set of commonly used scenarios, turning them into either domain-specific entries in a checklist or more general items in a questionnaire. Scenarios, since they are system specific, are developed as part of the review process itself, by the assembled stakeholders, for an individual project. Checklists and questionnaires are assumed to exist before a project begins.

As an example of the difference between scenarios and checklists, consider the following checklist item, adapted from a checklist used by a large corporation: "Is there error recovery code in a process to clean up after it detects an error?" The scenario form of this question is: "A division by zero occurs and the system must continue to operate." A scenario is typically more specific with respect to the type of error, and it is up to the reviewers to determine that cleanup is required. The checklist specifies that cleanup is required and asks the reviewers (and the architect) to verify that this function has been assigned a place in the design.

The ATAM, the SAAM, and ARID are all scenario-based evaluation methods, but they are not the only ones.

Survivable Network Analysis Method

Another scenario-based evaluation technique is the Survivable Network Analysis (SNA) method, developed by the SEI CERT Coordination Center. SNA is intended to permit systematic assessment of the survivability properties of proposed systems, existing systems, and modifications to existing systems. The SNA method helps organizations understand survivability in the context of their operating environments. What functions must survive? What intrusions could occur? How could intrusions affect survivability? What are the business risks? How could architecture modifications reduce the risks?

The SNA method is composed of four steps.

1. **System definition.** The first step focuses on understanding mission objectives, requirements for the current or candidate system, structure and properties of the system architecture, and risks in the operational environment.

2. **Essential capability definition.** Essential services (services that must be maintained during attack) and essential assets (assets whose integrity, confidentiality, availability, and other properties must be maintained during attack) are identified, based on mission objectives and failure consequences. Essential service and asset uses are characterized by use case scenarios, which are traced through the architecture to identify essential components whose survivability must be ensured.

3. **Compromisable capability definition.** Intrusion scenarios are selected based on assessment of environmental risks and intruder capabilities.

These scenarios are likewise mapped onto the architecture as execution traces to identify corresponding compromisable components (components that could be penetrated and damaged by intrusion).

4. **Survivability analysis**. The final step of the SNA method concentrates on essential but vulnerable components of the architecture identified in the previous steps. These so-called *softspot components* and the supporting architecture are then analyzed in the context of resistance, recognition, and recovery. *Resistance* is the capability of a system to repel attacks. *Recognition* is the capability to detect attacks as they occur and to evaluate the extent of damage and compromise. *Recovery*, a hallmark of survivability, is the capability to maintain essential services and assets during attack, limit the extent of damage, and restore full services following attack.

The analysis is summarized in a Survivability Map. The map enumerates, for every intrusion scenario and corresponding softspot effects, the current and recommended architecture strategies for resistance, recognition, and recovery. The Survivability Map provides feedback to the original architecture and system requirements and gives management a road map for survivability evaluation and improvement.

9.2 Measuring Techniques

Measuring techniques are used to answer specific questions about specific quality attributes. Unlike questioning techniques, they require the presence of a design or implementation artifact upon which to take their measures.

A review based on measuring techniques needs to focus not only on the results of the measurement but also on the assumptions under which the measurement was deemed useful. For example, a calculation of performance characteristics makes assumptions about patterns of resource utilization. How valid are these assumptions? If they are not particularly valid, then the measurement, while accurate, is not particularly helpful in drawing desired conclusions.

For example, complexity measures are almost always used to predict which parts of a software system are most likely to undergo change, if only through bug fixes. Thus, complexity measures embody the assumption that complex code is error-prone code. Is this necessarily true? A very complex module may have been built with the utmost care compared with simpler modules, and it may in fact be the most reliable. A measurement advocate will point out immediately, however, that it was the complexity measure that told the manager on which modules to exercise that utmost care, and that is probably true. But when using measurements, don't accept them at face value. Rather, seek to understand what it is they're trying to tell you and decide for yourself whether the assumptions they embody apply in your situation.

9.2.1 Metrics

Metrics are quantitative interpretations placed on particular observable measurements on the architecture, such as fan in/fan out of components. The most well-researched measuring techniques provide answers on overall complexity that can suggest the locations of likely change or where change will be difficult. For example, an arbitrary change is more likely to affect a highly coupled module, even if that change has nothing to do with the module's nominal area of concern.

The following is a set of metrics proposed to measure complexity (and hence, to predict areas of change) in a real-time telecommunications system built using object-oriented design [Arora 95]. These metrics are appealing because many can be collected by examining a detailed design, as opposed to code.

- *Number of events:* the number of synchronous and asynchronous calls to which an object reacts.
- *Number of synchronous calls:* the total number of synchronous calls made by an object to other objects, either to get or set some data/resource.
- *Number of asynchronous calls:* the total number of asynchronous calls made by an object to other objects.
- *Number of component clusters:* the number of component clusters of which an object is composed. For example, a car is made of wheels, steering mechanisms, transmission, and so forth, and these objects are in turn made of other objects.
- *Depth of structure:* the number of layers of encapsulation that define an object.
- *Depth of finite state machine (FSM):* if an object's behavior is described by an FSM, the states of which are also described by FSMs, this measures the depth of that indirection.
- *Number of data classes:* the total number of data classes used or referenced by an object.
- *Number of extended state variables:* the number of variables needed by an object's FSM to deal with the machine's synchronization aspects.
- *Depth of inheritance tree:* the total depth of an object (from the base class) in the system's inheritance tree.

Other metrics predict the source of faults. For example, below are two sets of metrics that were shown to be useful indicators of fault-prone modules in the telecommunications domain [Khoshgoftaar 96].

Call Graph Metrics

- *Modules used:* the number of modules that this module uses, directly or indirectly, including itself.
- *Total calls to other modules:* the number of calls to entry points in other modules.
- *Unique calls to other modules:* the number of unique entry points in other modules called by this module.

Control-Flow Graph Metrics

- *If–then conditional arcs:* the number of arcs that contain a predicate of a control structure but are not loops.
- *Loops:* the number of arcs that contain a predicate of a loop construct.
- *Nesting level:* the total nesting level of all arcs.
- *Span of conditional arcs:* the total number of arcs located within the span of conditional arcs.
- *Span of loops:* the number of vertices plus the number of arcs within loop control structure spans.
- *McCabe cyclomatic complexity:* arcs – vertices + number of entry points + number of exit points.

9.2.2 Simulations, Prototypes, and Experiments

Building a prototype or a simulation of the system may help to create and to clarify the architecture. A prototype whose components consist of functionless stubs is a model of the architecture. Performance models are often built as simulations. Creation of a detailed simulation or prototype just for review purposes is typically expensive. On the other hand, these artifacts often exist as a portion of the normal development process. In this case, using these artifacts during a review or to answer questions that come up during the review becomes a normal and natural procedure.

An existing simulation or prototype may be an answer to an issue raised by a questioning technique. For example, if the review team asks, "What evidence do you have to support this assertion?" one valid answer would be the results of a simulation.

9.2.3 Rate-Monotonic Analysis

Rate-monotonic analysis (RMA) is a quantitative technique for ensuring that a set of fixed-priority processes can be scheduled on a CPU so that no process ever misses its execution deadline. RMA is a way to assure that a system will meet its real-time performance requirements, and it has the powerful advantage that it can be performed in the absence of an implementation. Rather, all that is required is a set of process definitions, with timing and synchronization information about each. As long as the implementation does not violate the constraints given in the concurrency model—that is, as long as no process runs too long or introduces new synchronization constraints not accounted for in the model— the analysis will remain valid and the system will meet its performance goals. This means that RMA can be performed as the architecture (specifically, the process view) is being evolved and well before the implementation is under way.

RMA is well enough understood that its application is straightforward. By characterizing the context of a real-time system in predefined terms and by specifying the number and nature of the processes to be scheduled, a designer has available algorithms to compute the schedulability of those processes. If the algorithm produces an affirmation, then any faithful implementation of those processes will be schedulable so that no process misses its deadline. If the algorithm returns otherwise, then the design will have to be modified.

9.2.4   Automated Tools and Architecture Description Languages

Formal notations and languages to represent architecture are becoming much more common. The Unified Modeling Language (UML) is perhaps the most widely known and utilized architectural notation, but others exist as well. Several architecture description languages (ADLs) have emerged from the academic and industrial research communities: UniCon, Acme, Wright, Rapide, MetaH, and Darwin are but a few.

Each of these languages has its own supporting tool technology to help create, maintain, evolve, and analyze the architectures rendered in the language. If the ADL includes some way to describe the behavior of the system (as opposed to simply its structure), then its tool environment is almost certain to have a facility for generating a simulation of the system. The simulations will exhibit a fidelity consistent with the amount of information put into the specification of the architecture; if a key aspect is omitted (or is not representable in the language to begin with), then it will also not be taken into account by the simulation. But such simulations often provide early insight into design errors that lead to behavioral errors. They can also reveal performance bottlenecks. Some tools (such as MetaH and UniCon) feature schedulability analysis using RMA formulas. Some tools (such as Wright) can analyze connectors among components for potential deadlock situations. And many of the tool environments have at least a rudimentary code generation capability, turning architectural specifications into executable source code.

9.3 Hybrid Techniques

While the methods described previously fall fairly clearly into one of the two camps, some methods combine elements of both.

9.3.1 Software Performance Engineering

Software Performance Engineering (SPE) is a hybrid analysis technique used to examine an architecture to see whether the system as designed will meet its performance constraints. SPE delivers much more than a "yes" or "no" result. In the face of a performance discrepancy, the designers have many choices to make: the performance requirements can be relaxed, software functions can be omitted, or hardware capability can be increased. Quality of results can be weakened, or resource requirements can be reduced. The purpose of SPE is to help a designer illuminate and navigate among the tradeoffs that are available. By scheduling SPE evaluations early and often, the intent is to build in performance (rather than add it) to the system's design.

Although SPE is a generic term, the most comprehensive description of it has been given by Smith and Williams [Smith 01]. SPE methods include holding performance walk-throughs, constructing performance models that are applicable to the system's context and scope, gathering and analyzing performance data in light of the models, taking steps to compensate for uncertainties, and applying general principles for performance-oriented design.

SPE produces resource usage estimates by establishing a picture of the workload, a characterization of the computing environment, and a model of the software. The workload is captured by scenarios that describe typical usage under normal workloads; standard parameters such as the number of concurrent users and request arrival rates are also accounted for. The scenarios are applied against the software structure as it is then understood, and resource utilization is catalogued. Data calculated include quantities such as programs, procedures, and objects to be executed by a scenario; the probability that a software entity is executed; the number of repetitions; and the protocols exercised. From these, platform utilization estimates can be drawn: CPU usage, I/O rates, database calls, communication overhead, memory load, and so on.

At first, the models are all quickly and roughly drawn to get early best-guess estimates to see whether or not there is a catastrophic mismatch brewing between the software, its performance goals, and its computing platform. The models are all refined as the design progresses and more information becomes available.

In all cases, SPE strives to produce standard-case estimates plus lower and upper bounds. If no disaster is looming, then the upper bound of the resource utilization will be well within the performance bounds of the platform. The hallmark of a catastrophe-in-waiting is an average resource utilization that lies beyond the best capabilities of the platform. Of course, all combinations in between these two extremes are possible and denote areas of concern. They may be obviated by higher-fidelity models that will become possible when more detail becomes available, or they may be mitigated by taking remedial steps to alter the design, the requirements, or the platform right away.

9.3.2   The ATAM

The ATAM is a hybrid technique. It uses questioning techniques (both scenarios and preexisting questions based on architectural styles and quality attributes). It is also a measuring technique, using quantitative outputs from performance, security, and reliability models.

Quality Attribute Workshops

Mario Barbacci
Software Engineering Institute

A quality attribute workshop (QAW) is a method for assessing a system architecture's quality attributes through test cases. The QAW is derived from the ATAM but is used in situations where the ATAM is not the best choice. For example, the QAW can be applied during the acquisition of a large-scale system in which there are many vendors competing for the contract. In this case, each competing team is motivated to show off its proposed architecture in the best light and not motivated to generate scenarios that might stress the architecture. Also, during an acquisition phase, the architectures might not yet be sufficiently developed to support an ATAM. The QAW was invented to provide an objective way to compare competing proposals even when the architectures are not fully fleshed out.

The QAW process (see the following figure) is organized into four distinct segments, echoing the steps of an ATAM evaluation:

1. Scenario generation, prioritization, and refinement
2. Test case development
3. Analysis of test cases against the architecture
4. Presentation of the results

The first activity consists of scenario generation, prioritization, and refinement. The scenarios are generated during a brainstorming workshop attended by facilitators, stakeholders, and the architecture team. The stakeholders are provided in advance with a workbook containing several quality attribute characterizations, sample questions relating to these characterizations

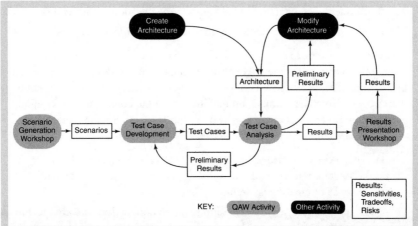

The Quality Attribute Workshop

(to assist in generating scenarios), example scenarios for each quality attribute, and examples of refined scenarios. During this activity, thirty to forty scenarios are typically generated and prioritized. The high-priority scenarios (usually the top three or four) are then refined by the stakeholders to provide a better understanding of their context and detail.

The next step is to transform each refined scenario from a statement and list of bullets into a precisely defined and documented test case. The test cases may combine and/or extend the scenarios, add assumptions and clarifications, define issues, and ask relevant questions. The test case has a context section outlining the important aspects of the case, an issues and questions section stating the various architectural concerns, and a utility tree summarize the issues and questions. The context section describes the mission, the assets involved, the operational setting, and the players. The issues and questions section defines the issues associated with each section of the context and proposes questions that connect these issues to quality attributes. To provide a complementary visual image of the collection of quality attributes questions and issues, each test case has a utility tree linking quality attributes to specific attribute issues to specific questions. This use of a utility tree differs slightly from the way it is used in the ATAM.

In the next step the architecture team analyzes the test cases against the architecture to

1. Review the capabilities of the assets in the test case context and determine how the system will react to the situation

2. Make and document any assumptions necessary for proceeding with the analysis

3. Determine which architectural views can best describe how the system addresses the issues and their associated questions

4. Refine the architecture to help answer the questions, if necessary

5. Document the answers to the questions as specifically as possible

In the final step, the test case analyses are presented to the stakeholders. It is an opportunity for the members of the architectural team to demonstrate that they completely understand the test cases, their architecture is able to handle these cases correctly, and the team members have the competence to continue analyzing important test cases as part of architecture development efforts.

There are a number of benefits to the QAW approach.

- The process provides opportunities for communication between the architecture team and the other stakeholders before incurring the expense of creating an architectural description.

- Scenario and test case generation can be done before the architecture is in place.

- The test cases provide a mechanism for the architecture team to analyze the consequences of architectural decisions.

- The results of the analysis provide a mechanism for architectural improvements before exposing the architecture to others.

- The test cases provide a means to halt further analysis and to move forward to presenting results.

- Additional scenarios can be developed into new test cases for further analysis.

- The process gives the sponsor and other significant stakeholders early insight into the architecture team's capabilities and approach to building the system.

The process for conducting QAWs is solidifying as we continue to hold them with additional organizations, in different application domains, and at different levels of detail. The approach appears to be promising. Acquiring organizations feel that they have much greater understanding and control of the systems that they are considering acquiring. Also the concept of "testing out" flaws in the architecture before committing to production reduces rework when building the system.

9.4 Summary

Table 9.3 summarizes the architecture evaluation techniques discussed in this chapter, using a set of criteria similar to those used in Table 9.1, which began this chapter.

Table 9.3 Evaluation Techniques Compared

Technique	Quality Attribute(s) Covered	Approach(es) Used	When applied
Questioning Techniques			
Questionnaires and checklists	Various	Predefined domain-specific questions	Can be used to prompt architect to take certain design approaches, or any time thereafter
Scenario-based methods	Various; either non-run-time attributes such as modifiability or run-time attributes such as security	System-specific scenarios to articulate specific quality attribute requirements; scenario walk-throughs to establish system's response	When architecture design is complete enough to allow scenario walk-throughs
SAAM	Modifiability, functionality		
ARID	Suitability of design		
SNA	Security		
Measuring Techniques			
Metrics	Various; often emphasize modifiability and reliability	Static analysis of structure	After architecture has been designed
Simulations, prototypes, experiments	Various; often emphasize performance, functionality, usability	Measurement of the execution of an artifact	After architecture has been designed
RMA	Performance oriented to real-time systems	Quantitative static analysis	After the process model has been built and process-to-processor allocations have been done

(*continued*)

Table 9.3   Evaluation Techniques Compared (*continued*)

Technique	Quality Attribute(s) Covered	Approach(es) Used	When applied
ADLs	Various; tend to concentrate on behavior and performance	Simulation, symbolic execution	When architectural specifications are complete
Hybrid Techniques			
SPE	Performance	Scenarios and quantitative static analysis	When performance constraints have been assigned to architectural components
ATAM	Not oriented to any particular quality attributes, but historically emphasizes modifiability, security, reliability, and performance	Utility trees and brainstormed scenarios to articulate quality attribute requirements; analysis of architectural approaches to identify sensitivities, tradeoff points, and risks	After the architecture design approaches have been chosen

Table 9.3 shows the generality of the ATAM. It can be targeted to any quality attribute, and it employs many of the approaches used by the other methods. Scenarios (which could evolve to checklists and questionnaires in the face of repeated application in a single domain) are used to articulate the quality attribute requirements up front and to establish the basis for evaluation. On the back end, the analysis portion of the ATAM is richly variable. For performance, it employs the kinds of modeling and calculations found in RMA and SPE. Any quality attribute that can appeal to a body of analytic work can be easily plugged into the ATAM; this includes any attributes for which simulations, prototypes, experiments, or ADL-based analysis capabilities may be brought to bear. For example, for security and availability the ATAM uses analysis models that are to those qualities what SPE is to performance.

Because of this generality and the flexibility with which it handles analysis, it is possible to consider the ATAM to be not just a method but rather a framework for architecture evaluation. It provides a way to articulate the quality attributes desired and to expose the architectural decisions relevant to those qualities. And any analytic capability that is appropriate for a quality attribute of interest can be inserted seamlessly into the method.

9.5 For Further Reading

While there is no single comprehensive overview of architecture evaluation methods, there are many resources to which you can turn for information on individual methods. A discussion of architecture evaluation best practices can be found in Abowd et al. [Abowd 96]. This is where the distinction between questioning and measuring techniques in architectural analysis methods originated. The home page for the Software Engineering Institute's Architecture Tradeoff Analysis initiative contains publications about the ATAM and the SAAM, as well as other software architecture topics [SEI ATA]. Finally, Zhao has compiled a bibliography on software architecture analysis [Zhao 99]. His Web site, where the list is kept up to date, is cited on the SEI's ATA page.

For further information on system survivability, peruse the SEI's Web site for Network System Survivability [SEI NSS] and the many useful links and references therein.

Smith's *Performance Engineering of Software Systems* [Smith 90] remains the definitive treatment of software performance engineering. It should be accompanied, and not replaced, by its excellent sequel, Smith and Williams's *Performance Solutions: A Practical Guide for Creating Responsive, Scalable Software* [Smith 01]. The authoritative reference for rate-monotonic analysis is Klein et al. [Klein 93].

Finally, an overview of ADLs can be found in Medvidovic and Taylor [Medvidovic 00]. Pointers to the Web pages for several of them can be found on the SEI's ATA page [SEI ATA].

9.6 Discussion Questions

1. How would you go about tailoring an architecture evaluation method for your organization? What are the qualities that you are commonly concerned with? What organizational support is there for creating and maintaining checklists or questionnaires?

2. Construct a checklist you believe would reveal the kinds of risks uncovered by Avritzer and Weyuker.

3. Under what conditions would you consider using a measuring technique? A questioning technique? A hybrid technique?

4. Checklists and questionnaires represent reusable assets that can be applied across a large number of systems. What reusable assets do each of the other kinds of evaluation methods produce?

10

Growing an Architecture
Evaluation Capability
in Your Organization

An empowered organization is one in which individuals have the
knowledge, skill, desire, and opportunity to personally succeed in a
way that leads to collective organizational success.
—attributed to Stephen R. Covey

Performing an architecture evaluation is one thing. Making architecture evaluation a repeatable, common practice within an organization is another. Instituting a program of architecture evaluation is a special case of a technology change project. Technology change projects are undertaken to help organizations prepare themselves to adopt a new technology or way of doing business. Successful technology change projects account for not only the specific new technology but also the human factors involved in the adoption.

This chapter shares guidance for setting up an architecture evaluation unit. Doing so entails building organizational buy-in, finding the right people and training them, and establishing a corporate memory: growing and maintaining repositories of artifacts and guidance.

10.1 Building Organizational Buy-in

If you are going to ask your organization's management to absorb the cost of setting up an architecture evaluation unit, you're going to need its buy-in. There are two primary strategies for achieving this: top-down and bottom-up.

The top-down strategy involves finding a champion within management who can fund the unit, defend its budget to other members of management, and help make sure that its services are utilized by projects under his or her purview. To make the champion's job easier, you'll need to collect cost and benefit data that show the evaluation unit to be a cost-effective use of resources (more on this shortly).

If you don't have an angel protector from above, then you'll have to start from below. Find a project manager who's willing to host an architecture evaluation. Then find another. And then another. Again, keep careful records about cost and benefit. Arrange a seminar or brown-bag lunch in which the project managers discuss the benefits to them and to the organization of the architecture evaluations. Grow the unit informally by finding qualified volunteers willing to work a little extra on something that is at the leading edge of mature architecture practice. And keep looking for ways to achieve management buy-in.

10.2 Growing a Pool of Evaluators

To establish an architecture evaluation capability within your organization, you must identify and target the most qualified people to become members of evaluation teams. Architecture evaluation shares a trait with software development (and, for that matter, most human endeavors): the best people do the best job. In this case, evaluators need to be perceived as impartial in their duties and thoroughly knowledgeable about software architecture. Engineers at AT&T, which makes architecture evaluation a standard part of its development process and has carried out many hundreds of them, have this to say about the issue:

> *All architecture audits are done by our best technical people, with the requirement that they do not belong to the project's development team. Reviewers are recognized as world class experts on the technologies and processes that are required for the projects to be successful. [Avritzer 98]*

Our advice is: start out with the best. A likely source of knowledge and expertise about architecture is, of course, in your organization's pool of best architects. If at all possible, establish your first team to include the best and most experienced architects you can find.

You may encounter resistance to the idea of the best architects spending their time reviewing instead of creating architectures. And the architects themselves will probably want to spend only a portion of their time evaluating rather than crafting. So it is essential to have an evaluation team mentoring process that brings on new members of the team, trains them, and slowly develops them into experienced evaluators. In this way, you can begin a rotation of individuals on and off the evaluation duty roster. The rotation cycle will depend on your organization and how many evaluations your group is called upon to perform in a given time period.

Junior designers are ideal candidates because they have at least a rudimentary understanding of architecture. You may also want to recruit experts on various quality attributes that play a role in your organization's systems, experts on commercial products, or experts in relevant domains. These people are very handy to have on the team during an evaluation exercise.

To "grow" new members, try the following suggestions.

- Have them read a book like this one.
- On their first evaluation, assign them to be timekeeper, scenario scribe, process observer, questioner, or some combination of these roles.
- Have them write the portions of the final report that describe the process and recount the activities in the evaluation. Prior final reports can serve as a model. Also have them write a portion of the section that recaps the analysis; perhaps assign each of them to write up the analysis based on one of the scenarios, using the other scenarios' write-ups as a guide.
- On a subsequent evaluation, have them facilitate the scenario prioritization step.
- On a subsequent evaluation, have them facilitate the portion of the discussion during which one of the scenarios is used to analyze the architecture. It should be one of the later ones since early scenarios often involve a fair amount of architecture discovery. Later scenarios tend to be somewhat more pro forma and hence easier to facilitate after the participants become familiar with the process.
- Have them write more and more of the final report.
- Choose an evaluation, perhaps one that resembles others in which they have participated, and use this as the first chance for one of them to lead.

It is essential to keep attracting the most talented people to the evaluation group. To do this requires the cooperation of your organization's management. Not only must they make it clear that they consider evaluation an important activity, they must also do what they can to make assignment to the evaluation group a career-enhancing step. And it should be. Very few organizations, if any, have formal architect training programs, and serving on evaluation teams is arguably the next best thing. The evaluators will see firsthand the best and the worst architectures and come to understand and be fluent about what makes them so. When it is their turn to create system designs, they can emulate the best and eschew the mistakes of others. They will have an innate appreciation of what makes an architecture successful, they will tend to seek out their stakeholders early, and they will orient their designs to pass the stress test of evaluation.

10.3 Establishing a Corporate Memory

As your organization conducts more and more architecture evaluations, the experience it gains from each one can be channeled into making each succeeding one more effective. Establishing a corporate memory is a matter of cataloging the experience and storing it so that it is accessible and useful to future evaluators. A corporate memory consists of:

- Cost and benefit data
- Method guidance
- Reusable artifacts

10.3.1 Cost and Benefit Data

Whether you set up the team as an evaluation unit in a consulting company to evaluate architectures for external customers or as a work group internal to a development organization to use as part of its standard development process, the clients for your evaluations are going to want to know what an evaluation will cost them and what quantitative benefits it will bring.

Chapter 2 listed approximate costs for ATAM exercises of varying degrees. You can construct similar tables for SAAM or ARID exercises assuming, say, a dozen stakeholders. Whatever method you choose, begin with a rudimentary table showing the approximate cost in person-days, including preparation and setup time. Your client will want to know how much effort will be required on the part of the architect and developers and for how much of your team's time the project will be billed.

At the end of each evaluation, compile the time spent by each team member.[1] Then survey the other participants in the exercise, and find out how much time they spent before and during the evaluation exercise. (Recall that in the ATAM, Step 9 of Phase 2 includes handing out a survey to collect this information.)

---

1. If travel time to and from the site of the evaluation is nonnegligible, you should factor that out of the effort data.

To catalog benefit data, we use a two-pronged approach. We circulate a survey among the participants at the end of the evaluation exercise asking whether the participants felt the exercise was of value. Figure 10.1 shows such a survey. Six months later, we send a follow-up survey to the client asking about the long-term benefits of the exercise. Figure 10.2 shows the part of the long-term benefits survey we use to gauge impacts to the surveyed project, and Figure 10.3 shows the survey we use to ask about the organizational impacts of an architecture evaluation.

Participants' End-of-Exercise Survey

Thank you for participating in the architecture evaluation. Please take a few moments now to tell us about your experience on the architecture evaluation. Your candid feedback will help us to improve the evaluation method for future applications.

1. Do you feel that you were sufficiently prepared to participate in the architecture evaluation? If no, please tell us the areas of the evaluation for which you felt unprepared.

2. How much time did you spend preparing for the evaluation? (Include time for preparation, studying read-ahead material, and setting up the exercise. Do not count travel time, if any.) How much time did you spend during the evaluation?

3. Did you receive read-ahead material for the evaluation? If so, what was it? For each document you received, please rate it from 1 (not useful) to 5 (very useful). Use 0 to mean "did not read." What read-ahead material would you like to have received but did not?

4. What risks, nonrisks, sensitivity points, and tradeoffs that were identified by the evaluation were you already aware of beforehand?

5. What risks, nonrisks, sensitivity points, and tradeoffs that were identified by the evaluation were you unaware of beforehand?

6. Do you feel you will be able to act on the results of the architecture evaluation? What follow-on actions do you anticipate?

7. What design decisions will you make differently as a result of the evaluation (if you are in a position to make design decisions on the project)?

8. Which parts of the method did you feel were the most useful? Please check those below and tell us why you feel these parts were the most useful.

Method Step	Not Useful	A Little Useful	Moderately Useful	Very Useful
Step 1: Present the ATAM				
Step 2: Present, business drivers				
Step 3: Present architecture				
Step 4: Identify architectural approaches				
Step 5: Generate quality attribute utility tree				
Step 6: Analyze architectural approaches				
Step 7: Brainstorrn and prioritize scenarios				
Step 8: Analyze Architectural approaches				
Step 9: Present results				
Other (please describe)				

9. Overall, do you believe the evaluation was worthwhile? Why or why not? What could we have done to improve the value or effectiveness of this exercise?

Figure 10.1 An ATAM End-of-Exercise Participant's Survey

Architecture Evaluation Follow-up Survey: Project Impacts

The following questions ask for information concerning the results and impact of the architectural evaluation or the owning project.

1. Name of system whose architecture was evaluated:

2. What, in your opinion, were the main findings of the architecture evaluation?

3. Which risks uncovered by the architecture evaluation have been addressed? How?

4. For each item listed above, what would the effects have been if the risk had gone unaddressed? Be as quantitative as you can. Estimate the impact in terms of schedule, cost, product quality, customer satisfaction, and future capability.

   Schedule:

   Cost:

   Product quality:

   Customer satisfaction:

   Future capability:

   Other:

5. Which risks uncovered by the architecture evaluation have not (yet) been addressed?

6. For each risk listed above, what has the impact been so far, if any? What is the anticipated impact?

7. Have new risks been discovered with the architecture since the evaluation?

   If yes, please describe each risk and say what system or project qualities the risk impacts.

   If yes, were they found as a result (either direct or indirect) of the architecture evaluation?

   If yes, why do you think that the risks were not identified during the evaluation?

   If yes, how do you think the evaluation method could be improved to find this type of risk?

8. At the time of the evaluation, were there decisions not yet made that were identified as a source of risk? If yes, please describe them briefly.

   If yes, have any of those decisions been resolved since then? If so, did you find that the evaluation was useful in helping make the decision?

   For any decisions still pending, are they still considered a source of risk?

9. Do you feel that the evaluation had a noticeable effect on the communication channels in the project, such as between architect and developers or between architect and stakeholders? Please describe.

10. Do you feel that the architecture documentation was improved as a result of the evaluation? If so, how? If not, why not?

11. Have you used any of the evaluation techniques on your own since the evaluation? If so, please describe.

12. As best you can, please estimate the net project savings attributable to the architecture evaluation, as a percentage of total project cost.

    0%____ 1–5%____ 6–10%____ 11–15%____ 16–20%____ 21–25%____ 25+%____

    Feel free to look back at your answers to question #4 to help you estimate the savings.

Figure 10.2   Follow-up Survey to Gauge Project Impacts of an Architecture Evaluation

Some architecture evaluators simply ask project managers to estimate the cost savings to their project associated with the evaluation, either as a percentage of the project's budget or in absolute terms. It's always hard to estimate the cost of the path not taken, but it's a question worth asking.

Architecture Evaluation Follow-up Survey: Organizational Impacts

The following questions ask about what, if any, impact the architectural evaluation had on the organization.

1. What, if any, do you think were the long-term effects of the evaluation on your project and your organization? Consider aspects such as improved communication, better awareness of architectural issues, addition of architecture reviews to the development process, establishment of a position of architect in the organization, establishment of architecture training or discussion groups, etc. Do you feel the benefit of the architecture evaluation exceeded its cost?

2. Do you feel that it would be of ongoing benefit to adopt architecture evaluation (or any parts thereof) as part of your standard development process? Why or why not? If yes, are there criteria that you would use to determine which projects should have architectural evaluations? Please describe the criteria or heuristics.

3. Do you have any comments concerning the conduct or value of architecture evaluations that have not been addressed?

Figure 10.3   Follow-up Survey to Gauge Organizational Impacts of an Architecture Evaluation

10.3.2 Method Guidance

This book is an example of a guidance repository, but as you carry out more and more evaluations, you will discover new heuristics, new steps, new advice to give team members, and new ideas for better evaluations. As you think of them, record them.

Chapter 6 shows checklists for each of the ATAM steps. These are part of a *process model* for the method. A process model shows

- A sequence of steps.
- The necessary entry conditions for a step to begin (for example, the step preceding it has been completed, or certain resources are available, or some necessary action has been taken).
- The actions carried out in the step.
- The results produced by the step (that may serve as inputs to another step).
- The next step in the process and, if there is a choice of next steps, the criteria for selection.

For the method or methods you employ, construct a process model and use it during each evaluation exercise. The process model should specify what activities are required of each role on the evaluation team: scribe, process observer, evaluation leader, and so on. Let the process model be your primary vehicle for describing how best to carry out an evaluation. As you accumulate experience, you can annotate the process model in appropriate places with suggestions about how to execute a step.

Making Analysis Methods Manageable

You have now learned about a number of architecture analysis methods. These methods range from simple, small, and informal to complex and highly structured. There are steps to think about, business drivers to elicit, architectural specifications to record, roles to manage, resulting issues to organize, architectural approaches to recognize and analyze. It can seem a bit overwhelming. You may be thinking, "Can I do one of these only if I have a big team of seasoned reviewers? Can I use the SAAM only if I am a modifiability expert? Or the ATAM only if I am an expert in performance or availability or security?" Of course not. While we have shown you the "gold" version of the ATAM, there are definitely silver and bronze versions as well. You can execute the method with an evaluation team as small as one or two people. You can lead an ATAM-based evaluation even if you have never designed a large system yourself. Or if the ATAM seems too daunting, you can easily start with a SAAM-based evaluation or any other simple scenario-based method.

And while you cannot expect to get the same results from an evaluation team of novices that you would get from a team of experienced architects and reviewers, each evaluation will bring results—often surprising results and unexpected insights. In a software architecture course that I teach regularly at Carnegie Mellon University, students form teams to design candidate architectures, and then they form teams to analyze the architectures that they designed. These teams typically have few, if any, seasoned architects. None of the students is an expert in performance or any other quality attribute. Few of the students have done substantial design work before. None of them have ever participated in an architectural evaluation. And their results are first-rate. They find important risks in their designs that cause them to go back and redesign. And we have obtained the same results in industry.

So how do you scale down a method? You can do several things. If your team is small, then each of the members can wear many hats. For example, an ATAM leader might also be a questioner and scenario scribe. A SAAM proceedings scribe can also be a questioner and process observer, and so forth. With any method you can limit the amount of time expended on each step, or you can limit the focus to a specific quality or a specific portion of the system. The point is that you can get value out of each of these methods even if you do not have a lot of experience, a lot of time, or a full complement of evaluators.

The process of getting together, talking about the architecture (and the business goals and requirements that motivated it) in a structured way, and recording the findings in a rigorous way will always bring benefit. So be brave.

—*RK*

Once you have established this baseline of methodological authority, you will need to update it as you perform more and more evaluations. You have several sources of improvement suggestions at your disposal.

- You can survey your evaluation team immediately after the exercise. In the ATAM, a postmortem meeting of the team members is a standard part of the method (Step 2 of the follow-up phase). At this meeting, we ask for impressions and ideas for improvement.
- You can use the process observer's report to identify improvements.
- You can use the process enforcer's experience during the exercise to identify parts of the method that appeared problematic because more stay-on-track reminders were required.
- You can survey the other participants at the end of the exercise. In the ATAM, our participants' end-of-exercise survey asks which parts of the exercise they found the most (and least) useful, and why.

You can, and should, use all of this input to update your process model. A word of caution, however. It is tempting to try to modify the method after each exercise based on the unique conditions of that exercise. If you do this, you may find yourself thrashing—that is, updating the process model after one exercise, only to undo those changes after the next. If in doubt, insert a change to the process model as a suggestion and leave its use to the discretion of the next evaluation leader.

10.3.3 Reusable Artifacts

Architecture evaluations produce tangible outputs, and these outputs represent a priceless inventory of experience that can be collected and reused. Your evaluation unit will be much more effective if they can draw from the following kinds of repositories.

- *Final reports.* You will want to scan these from time to time to see if patterns are emerging in the results you are uncovering or the way in which you present them. Much of a final report is pro forma, describing the method used, the people who were present, and a skeletal outline for filling in the results of each step. A well-formed template makes final report preparation a much less tedious chore.
- *Risks.* If your evaluation unit works its craft on many systems in the same organization or across the same domain or application area, you may find yourself uncovering the same kinds of risks over and over again. If so, you can improve the efficiency of your evaluation method by making sure to search for risks you have seen many times before.
- *Scenarios.* Again, if your evaluations cover similar systems, you may encounter similar scenarios. If you store them in a repository, your evaluation

team members can use them in preparation for the next evaluation. Vintage scenarios are especially useful to people filling the questioner role in an evaluation, for the scenarios help them to pose quality-attribute-related questions in a fashion meaningful to the system being evaluated.

- *Exemplary documentation.* If a development organization produces a high-quality architecture presentation, business drivers presentation, system overview, or read-ahead architecture documentation, you can use those artifacts for the next evaluation to show that client the kind of information you want. You may, of course, have to sanitize the documents to prevent disclosure of proprietary information. It is helpful to think about what makes the artifacts exemplary and to distill that into guidance for the next evaluation.

- *Quality attribute characterizations and evaluation questions.* In Chapter 5, we listed a set of evaluation questions associated with the quality attribute characterizations for performance, availability, and modifiability. These characterizations are necessarily incomplete; it is not feasible to expect to completely characterize a quality attribute. The evaluation questions they suggest are therefore also incomplete. As you flesh out the quality attribute characterizations to suit your needs for the systems that you encounter, additional evaluation questions will arise. Adding these to your artifact repository will help you prepare for the next evaluation in which that quality attribute plays a role. It will be fodder for the questioners assigned that quality attribute and will serve as training material for new evaluators.

- *ABASs.* In Chapter 5, we said that if you encounter the same architectural style or approach over and over again in your evaluation work, it may well be worthwhile to construct an ABAS for it. ABAS will let you re-use analytical reasoning about the quality attribute associated with that approach, and going over the ABAS will serve as an excellent preparatory exercise for the evaluation team. ABASs also serve as repositories of oft-repeated risks, sensitivities, and tradeoff points that are well known to occur and are well understood.

- *Other artifacts.* Your evaluation unit may produce standard letters to the client setting up an exercise or delivering results, or the contracts or statements of work used in your organization may be standard. As an example, the checklist of supplies shown in Figure 6.2 can be used from evaluation to evaluation (and updated as needed). You may wish to produce a standard set of viewgraphs that explains the method and then shows participants where the exercise is at any point in time. You may wish to produce a wall chart showing the steps of the method, pinning a marker to the chart to indicate the current step in progress. These and other artifacts, if created with reuse in mind and updated as the need arises, will save your teams incalculable time and energy.

Finally, assign someone the responsibility of maintaining and updating the artifact repositories. In our organization, we assemble a "portfolio" of evaluation artifacts from each evaluation exercise and have delegated to an administrative assistant the task of obtaining the artifacts from each exercise's team leader and installing them in the repository.

10.4 Summary

Growing a mature, high-quality architecture evaluation capability in your organization is different from simply carrying out a series of architecture evaluations. Growing a capability requires growing people skills and establishing a detailed and accessible corporate memory. Perhaps most of all, it requires a high degree of disciplined introspection to identify potential improvements and the dedication to carry them out.

10.5 Discussion Questions

1. Discuss a training curriculum that you would use to help someone become a software architecture evaluation expert. What talents or experience would be required of a person before beginning such training?

2. Experience, by itself, doesn't necessarily update a process model. The experience needs to be analyzed to figure out what has worked and what has not. Consider how you might go about capturing your experiences in a way that is reusable and transferable. Would you do it with a case study? Would you use a formal process notation?

3. Outline a memorandum or a presentation that you would take to a member of management in your organization to make a strong argument for establishing an architecture evaluation unit. Include cost/benefit arguments, suggest individuals who would lead and serve in the unit, propose some projects to serve as pilots, and address training and rotation issues.

4. Craft a process model for the SAAM or ARID.

5. Think about how you could collect cost and benefit data in your organization and how you would use the data to create a compelling argument for using (or not using!) architecture evaluations in your organization.

11

Conclusions

11.1 You Are Now Ready!

You are now ready to carry out an architecture evaluation. We have described three methods in full detail: the ATAM, the SAAM, and ARID. We have narrated several case studies that illustrate the methods in action. We have compared several evaluation methods and discussed organizational considerations. We have offered practical aids such as templates, checklists, and process guidance.

Even with all of this information, you might be thinking that just reading about a method is not enough to be ready to use it. Certainly we appreciate this concern. However, even if you have never performed an architecture evaluation, there is enough information in this book to try using any of the methods for the first time. Undoubtedly your second experience will be better than your first, and your tenth experience better yet. You'll learn something from every evaluation that you carry out—we certainly have—but this book has prepared you for your first.

After trying the ATAM, the SAAM, or ARID for the first time you should reflect on your observations (and those of your process observer and others involved) and then re-read selected portions of this book. Perhaps some of the sidebars will really resonate with you after some experience. Perhaps you will have a deeper appreciation for the purpose of each of the steps after you have had a chance to see the steps in action.

It is also safe to say that we were much less prepared to carry out an evaluation using any of the methods for *our* first time (and probably our second and third times as well) than you will be after having read this book. We have done our best to codify our collective experience in using all of the methods, and we think this gives you a great head start.

11.2 What Methods Have You Seen?

You have seen three software architecture evaluation methods in this book: the ATAM, the SAAM, and ARID. All rely on scenarios as a vehicle for making concrete what is meant by quality attribute requirements.

The SAAM was developed to help architects understand how their designs would react to evolutionary pressures that lead to modifications, as well as how well the designs provided the functionality demanded by their users. The SAAM is notable for its simplicity: brainstorm and prioritize some scenarios and then see how the architecture reacts to the most important ones. The SAAM could be used during an afternoon to gain some key insights into your architecture.

Scenarios were the point of departure for the development of the ATAM. The ATAM raised to the fore the notion of tradeoffs among multiple quality attributes. The ATAM also added several other dimensions to architecture evaluation. Utility trees provide a top-down structured vehicle for generating scenarios. This ensures coverage of key quality attributes. The ATAM also takes advantage of the fact that architectural decisions should work synergistically to achieve quality attribute goals. Analysis via mapping scenarios onto the architecture in the SAAM evolved to the explicit elicitation and analysis of architectural approaches used in the ATAM. The ATAM also explicitly relates architectural risks and tradeoffs to business drivers.

ARID was born out of the need to probe an architecture in ways that the ATAM was not designed for. After an architecture evaluation, one of the participants told us, "As an application developer, the ATAM evaluation did not help me determine if I will be able to use the services provided by the architecture." He was right, and ARID was created to serve this purpose. ARID uses scenarios to allow application developers to specify their expectations for the set of services provided by the architecture. ARID also borrows an idea from active design reviews by having the reviewers craft pseudo-code that exercises the architecture's services to solve the problem posed by the highest-priority scenarios.

The three methods are related, but each serves its own niche. Together, they provide a formidable repertoire for a software architecture organization to draw upon to ensure high-quality, successful architectures.

11.3 Why Evaluate Architectures?

At this point we hope that you feel architecture evaluation is an important software development activity and, moreover, that you are not only able to perform an evaluation, but also willing to perform one.

Near the outset of this book we stated that architectures allow or preclude nearly all of the system's quality attributes. If software architectures are important, then so are software architecture evaluations. If you can reason in some way about the efficacy of a design in a low-cost, reliable manner, why wouldn't you?

A major goal of an evaluation is to elicit architectural risks. During an evaluation, we often feel like detectives, following clues until—"Aha!"—a risk is uncovered. Mildly elated by this mini-victory, we start on the trail of the next risk. At the end of a typical evaluation we may have amassed forty to fifty risks, and we usually feel pretty good about this. After one evaluation, however, we were told that about 75 percent of the risks we had uncovered were already known. This felt a little deflating at the time, but in fact no single stakeholder (including the project manager) was aware of every elicited risk. Everyone learned something. And even those stakeholders who knew 75 percent of the risks beforehand were still surprised to discover the other 25 percent. Moreover, writing down and sharing known risks was important, motivating, and the first step in mitigating those risks in a controlled, managed fashion.

After the final presentation in another evaluation, a manager said, "Congratulations on discovering those key risk themes. Those are certainly the right ones." This occurred in front of 30 key stakeholders, which lent immediate credibility to our results. Unknown to us at the time, we were not the first group of outsiders to come in, evaluate their situation, and make a recommendation. The previous group's results, however, left something to be desired, and this organization was wary of outside "experts." With effective methods we were able to find in a relatively short period of time what others knew only from living with the system over a long period of time. The results of the evaluation gave their architecture group an agenda, and the manager's statement gave them the authority to act on the risks. These risks were never written down before in such a concrete manner. Before the evaluation the collection of risks was abstract, diffuse, and amorphous. After the evaluation the risks were concrete, documented, and actionable.

Members of another organization found having a specific list of actionable risks so important that they put together a risk-tracking system to monitor progress in mitigating the risks.

While sometimes the elicited risks are not surprising to many of the stakeholders, quite often the elicited risks are completely unknown and sometimes shocking. The evaluation of the Battlefield Control System recounted in Chapter 4 produced previously unknown risks that were so significant that the architecture team went back to the drawing board to redesign the system.

Another reaction we often hear is, "This is the first time that business perspectives and technical perspectives were discussed at the same time. Moreover, this was the first time that technical risks were linked back to business drivers." One of the central themes of the ATAM is to start with business drivers and end with business drivers. The business drivers motivate the quality attribute goals that focus the architecture evaluation. The evaluation produces risks which are then tied back to the business drivers they potentially impact. To be able to conclude that a particular collection of architectural risks will potentially jeopardize the achievement of an important business goal is powerful because it simultaneously motivates managers to empower action and engineers to act.

We have also seen organizations take conscious advantage of the social effects brought about by an evaluation. One organization used the architecture evaluation experience as a team building experience, fostering synergy and creating a common knowledge base for a new architecture team (see the sidebar But It Was OK.) Another organization described their process of preparing for an architecture evaluation as a process of conducting "mini-ATAMs." They use scenarios and abbreviated analyses to elicit information from the system's architects in order to help the architects prepare for the full evaluation. Finally, NASA is using the ATAM as the basis for maintaining and evolving the EOS-DIS Core System that we discussed in Chapter 6.

In summary, for many organizations, for many different reasons, employing architecture evaluations has been a worthwhile addition to the development process.

11.4 Why Does the ATAM Work?

Since the ATAM is arguably the most sophisticated of the three methods we have presented, we would like to say a few words about the reasons behind its success.

While the ATAM was developing and evolving we constantly wondered if the ATAM was really a method or if the same results could be gathered by a bunch of experienced, bright people asking unstructured but insightful questions to find problematic architectural decisions. Our conclusion: There is little doubt that experienced evaluators bring value to an architecture evaluation; however, the ATAM mobilizes the experience of both the evaluation team and the architecture team and produces a synergy whose value exceeds the sum of its parts. The ATAM has properties that make its use more than an enlightened chat session. What are those properties?

Recall the ATAM's conceptual flow, as shown in Figure 11.1. The ATAM is designed to elicit quality attribute requirements that are important for achieving the business goals the system is intended to support. The concrete expressions of those goals are the quality attribute scenarios that appear as leaves of the utility tree, some of which are deemed as being most important.

But It Was OK

Years of experience have taught us that no architecture evaluation exercise ever goes completely by the book. And yet for all the ways that an exercise might go terribly wrong, for all the details that can be overlooked, for all the fragile egos that can be bruised, and for all the high stakes that are on the table, we have never had an architecture evaluation exercise spiral out of control. Every single one has been a strong success, as measured by the feedback we gathered from clients.

While they all turned out successfully, there were a few memorable cliff-hangers.

More than once, we began an architecture evaluation only to discover that the development organization had no architecture to be evaluated. Sometimes there was a stack of class diagrams or vague text descriptions masquerading as an architecture. (We weren't always so prudent about pre-exercise preparation and qualification. Our current diligence evolved because of experiences like these.) Once we were promised that the architecture would be ready by the time the exercise began, but in spite of good intentions, it wasn't. But it was OK. In cases like these, the evaluation's main results were the articulated set of quality attributes plus a set of documentation obligations on the architect. In all cases, the client felt that the detailed scenarios, plus the recognition of what needed to be done, more than justified the evaluation exercise.

A couple of times we began an evaluation only to lose the architect in the middle of the exercise. In one case, the architect resigned between preparation for and execution of the evaluation. This was an organization in turmoil and the architect simply got a better offer in a calmer environment elsewhere. Normally we don't like to proceed without the architect, but it was OK. In this case the architect's apprentice stepped in. A little additional prework to prepare him, and we were all set. The evaluation went off as planned, and the preparation that the apprentice did for the exercise helped mightily to prepare him to step into the architect's shoes.

Once we discovered halfway through an ATAM exercise that the architecture we had prepared to evaluate was being jettisoned in favor of a new one that nobody had bothered to mention. During Step 6 of Phase 1, the architect responded to a problem raised by a scenario by casually mentioning that "the new architecture" would not suffer from that deficiency. Everyone in the room, stakeholders and evaluators and client alike, looked at each other in the silence that followed. "What new architecture?" I asked blankly, and out it came. The developing organization (a contractor for the U.S. military, which had commissioned the evaluation) had prepared a new architecture for the system to handle the more stringent requirements that would be coming in the future. But it was OK. We called a time-out, conferred with the architect and the client, and decided to continue the exercise using the new architecture as the subject instead of the old. We backed up to Step 3, but everything else on the table—business drivers, utility tree, scenarios—still were completely valid. The evaluation proceeded as before, and at the conclusion of the exercise our military client was extremely pleased at the knowledge gained.

In perhaps the most bizarre evaluation in our experience, we lost the architect midway through Phase 2 of an ATAM exercise. The client for this exercise was the project manager in an organization undergoing massive restructuring. The manager was a pleasant gentleman with a quick sense of humor, but there was an undercurrent about him that said he was not to be crossed. The architect was being reassigned to a different part of the organization in the near future, and the manager said he wished to establish the quality of the architecture before his architect's untimely departure. When we set up the ATAM exercise, the manager suggested that the junior designers attend. "They might learn something," he said. We agreed. As the exercise began, our schedule (which was very tight to begin with) kept being disrupted. The manager wanted us to meet with his company's executives. Then he wanted us to have a long lunch with someone who could, he said, give us more architectural insights. The executives, it turned out, were busy just then, so could we come back and meet with them a bit later? At this point, Phase 2 was so far off schedule that the architect, to our horror, had to leave to fly back to his home in a distant city. He was none too happy that his architecture was going to be evaluated without him. The junior designers, he said, would never be able to answer our questions. Before his departure, our team huddled. The exercise seemed to be teetering on the brink of disaster. We had an unhappy departing architect, a blown schedule, and questionable expertise available. We decided to split our team. Half of the team would continue with Phase 2 using the junior designers as our information resource. The second half of the team would continue with Phase 2 by telephone the next day with the architect. Somehow we would make the best of a bad situation.

Surprisingly, the project manager seemed completely unperturbed by the turn of events. "It will work out, I'm sure," he said pleasantly and then retreated to confer with various vice presidents about the reorganization.

I led the team interviewing the junior designers. We had never gotten a completely satisfactory architecture presentation from the architect. Areas of concern highlighted by the documentation provided were dismissed with a breezy, "Oh, well, that's not how it really works." So I decided to start over with the presentation of the architecture. We asked the half dozen or so designers what their view of the architecture was. "Could you draw it?" I asked them. They looked at each other nervously, but one said, "I think I can draw part of it." He took to the whiteboard and drew a very reasonable component-and-connector view. Someone else volunteered to draw a process view. A third person drew the architecture for an important off-line part of the system.

As we looked around the room, everyone was busy transcribing the whiteboard pictures. None of the pictures corresponded to anything we had seen in the documentation so far. "Are these diagrams documented anywhere?" I asked. One of the designers looked up from his busy scribbling for a moment to grin. "They are now," he said.

To analyze the architecture using the scenarios previously captured, the designers did an astonishingly good job of working together to answer our questions. Nobody knew everything, but everybody knew something. Together in a half day, they produced a clear and consistent picture of the whole architecture that was much more coherent and understandable than anything the architect had been willing to produce in two whole days of pre-exercise discussion. And by the end of Phase 2, the design team was transformed. This erstwhile group of information-starved individuals with limited, compartmentalized knowledge became a true team. The members drew out and recognized each others' expertise. This expertise was revealed and validated in front of everyone—and most importantly, in front of their project manager, who had slipped back into the room to observe. There was a look of supreme satisfaction on his face. It began to dawn on me that—you guessed it—it was OK.

It turned out that this project manager knew how to manipulate events and people in ways that would have impressed Machiavelli. The architect's departure was not because of the reorganization but merely coincident with it. The project manager had orchestrated it. The arvhitect had, the manager felt, become too autocratic and dictatorial, and the manager wanted the junior design staff to be given the opportunity to mature and contribute. The architect's mid-exercise departure was exactly what the project manager had wanted. And the design team's emergence under fire had been the primary purpose of the evaluation exercise all along. Although we found several important issues related to the architecture, the project manager knew about every one of them before we ever arrived. In fact, he made sure we uncovered a few of them by making a few discrete remarks during breaks or after a day's session.

Was this exercise a success? The client could not have been more pleased. His instincts about the architecture's strengths and weaknesses were confirmed. We were instrumental in helping his design team, which would guide the system through the stormy seas of the company's reorganization, come together as an effective and cohesive unit at exactly the right time. And the client was so pleased with our final report that he made sure the company's board of directors saw it.

These cliffhangers certainly stand out in our memory. There was no architecture. But it was OK. It wasn't the right architecture. But it was OK. There was no architect. But it was OK. The client didn't really want an architecture evaluation. But it was OK.

Why? Why, time after time, does it turn out OK? I think there are three reasons.

First, the people who have commissioned the architecture evaluation really want it to succeed. The architect, developers, and stakeholders assembled at the client's behest also want it to succeed. As a group, they help to keep the exercise marching toward the goal of architectural insight. Second, we are always honest. If we feel that the exercise is derailing, we call a time-out and confer among ourselves (and usually with the client too). While a small amount of bravado can come in handy during an exercise, we never, ever try to bluff our way through an evaluation. Participants can detect that instinctively, and the evaluation team must never lose the respect of the other participants. Third, the methods are constructed to establish and maintain a steady consensus throughout the exercise. There are no surprises at the end. The participants lay down the ground rules for what constitutes a suitable architecture, and they contribute to the risks uncovered at every step of the way.

The theme of this chapter is that you are ready to begin architecture evaluation. This sidebar is intended to back that up. Do the best job you can. Be honest. Trust the methods. Trust in the goodwill and good intentions of the people you have assembled. And it will be OK.

—PCC

The ATAM is also designed to elicit the architectural approaches used to achieve quality attribute goals. Scenarios and approaches come together when we ask how the important scenarios are supported by the architecture. The result is a set of architectural decisions. If the decisions are potentially problematic or especially important, or if they affect more than one attribute, then they are recorded as risks, sensitivity points, and/or tradeoff points. The risks are consolidated into risk themes, which are then examined relative to their effect on achieving business drivers. Therefore, in a nutshell:

The ATAM exposes architectural risks that potentially inhibit the achievement of an organization's business goals.

The properties of the ATAM that enhance its ability to find significant architecture-related risks are listed below:

1. *Self-scoping based on business drivers.* Recall one of the quotes above where several of the participants in a recent architecture evaluation astutely observed that this was the first time that they had heard the system discussed from both the business and the technical perspectives and, furthermore, in terms of how those two perspectives were related. The ATAM focuses the evaluation on those aspects of the architecture that can have the most significant impact on achieving business goals.

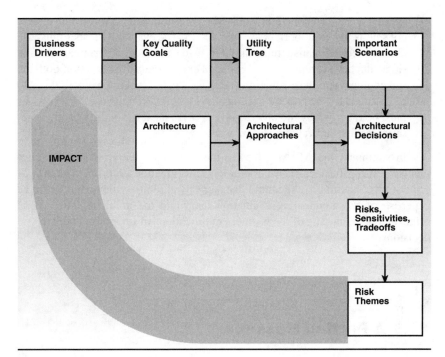

Figure 11.1 Conceptual Flow of the ATAM

2. *Self-scaling based on the number of scenarios analyzed.* The ATAM can be carried out in a relatively short period of time or over an extended period of time. The difference will be reflected in the number of scenarios that are analyzed.

3. *Full utilization of stakeholders.* The ATAM is designed to elicit information from all relevant stakeholders, exploiting their talents and perspectives. Phase 1 of the ATAM caters to the architect's perspective, eliciting the quality requirements the architect designed to and how he or she built to those requirements. Phase 2 elicits perspectives (in terms of scenarios) from all of the other stakeholders using a technique that fosters interaction and creative thinking. The ATAM combines these two perspectives to reach its conclusions.

4. *Evaluation team roles mirror the ATAM's strengths.* To realize the benefits of the depth and breadth of stakeholder experience during an architecture evaluation requires efficient elicitation of information, skillful management of social interactions, process introspection, and documentation of the results. The ATAM calls out team roles to manage these responsibilities. Questioners with some level of quality attribute expertise will gracefully force refinement of scenarios and ask probing questions about the

architecture. Questioners must also be careful listeners; sometime what is not said is just as important as what is said. The evaluation leader must use classic meeting management skills to foster interaction, terminate discussions that have reached a dead end, and ensure the participation of both the stakeholders and the evaluation team. To benefit from the method, it has to be enforced by the process enforcer, and to learn from its use, observations must be recorded by the process observer. To ensure credibility and to preserve results, several scribes are used.

In summary, the ATAM drives to the essential quality attribute requirements by using business drivers as a key prioritization criterion. The ATAM drives to the essential architectural decisions by exploiting the quality attribute expertise of the architecture evaluation team and the architect. The ATAM offers an understanding of the business ramifications of important architectural decisions.

11.5 A Parting Message

We started this chapter by conveying that we believe you are now ready to carry out an architecture evaluation. However, our parting message is a little stronger. We also believe that you are now ready to customize the methods for your own specific situation. We have tried not only to convey the steps of several evaluation methods but also to convey the purpose of the techniques used in each of the methods. For example, we can imagine that you might combine the ATAM and ARID. The ATAM is used to determine key quality attribute requirements, leading the evaluation to focus on a key subset of the architecture. However, at some point you might be interested in determining the suitability of the services provided by a part of the architecture for application builders, which is ARID's forte. You certainly can imagine other ways to combine the methods.

We're not advocating that you deviate from following the methods on a whim. On the other hand, we recognize that every situation is different, and you now have the tools at your disposal to cater to your specific situations.

We hope you have found this book informative and useful, but we are even more hopeful that it serves as a point of departure for your future success in architecture evaluation. Good luck! We encourage you to share your experiences with us.

A

An Example Attribute-Based Architectural Style

This appendix contains an example of an attribute-based architectural style (ABAS). The following sections illustrate the four parts of an ABAS:

1. Problem description
2. Stimulus/response
3. Architectural style
4. Analysis

This example, the Performance Synchronization ABAS, describes multiple processes requiring mutually exclusive access to a shared resource.

A.1 Problem Description

For the Performance Synchronization ABAS, we consider a single processor on which multiple processes reside, each of which performs computations on its own input data stream and produces final system outputs. Inputs arrive directly to each process and outputs must be produced within a specified time interval after the arrival of each input and, of course, after all the process's computations have been performed. We will refer to the input data as a *message*. The requirement then is to completely process each message with a specified, bounded end-to-end latency—a deadline.

The interesting feature of the Performance Synchronization ABAS is that this requirement must be met in the face of contention for a shared resource, for which the multiple processes must compete. The central properties of this ABAS for reasoning purposes is how contention for the shared resource is handled and how this contention affects performance, in particular, end-to-end latency. The Performance Concurrent Pipelines ABAS discussed in Klein and Kazman [Klein 99] is a related ABAS. The Performance Concurrent Pipelines ABAS focuses on multiple processes contending for a single processor using a preemptive scheduling discipline, whereas this ABAS focuses on multiple processes requiring *mutually exclusive access to a shared resource* such as shared data.

We assume the use of a priority-based preemptive scheduler.

A.2 Stimulus/Response

We characterize the important stimuli and their measurable, controllable responses as follows:

- *Stimuli:* two or more periodic or sporadic input streams of arrivals
- *Response:* end-to-end, worst-case latency

End-to-end refers to a measure beginning at the point of message input through all stages of computation until the associated output is produced.

A.3 Architectural Style

The synchronization style is shown in Figure A.1. In this ABAS, there is a single processor and a set of 2 or more periodic processes. (We illustrate this in Figure A.1 with three processes, P1–P3.) Some of these processes need to synchronize to share a resource controlled by S, the server process. We assume that a fixed-priority preemptive scheduling discipline is being used. The priorities of processes P1, P2, and P3 are distinct and denoted as high, medium, and low, respectively. The priority of process S is left unspecified (and will be discussed later in the analysis section of this ABAS).

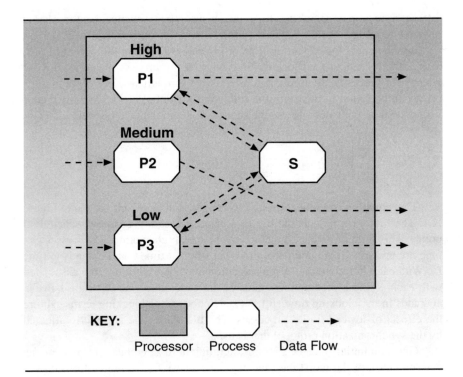

Figure A.1 Performance Synchronization ABAS, Showing Process Priorities

A.4 Analysis

In this section we present both a formal analysis, showing how to predict the end-to-end, worst-case latency in this ABAS, and an informal qualitative analysis, telling the designer what issues to be aware of when creating and evaluating any design of a Performance Synchronization ABAS.

A.4.1 Reasoning

There are three types of time that contribute to the latency of an arbitrary process under these circumstances: preemption, execution, and blocking time. *Preemption time* is the contribution to latency attributable to higher priority processes. *Execution time* is the amount of time it would take for the process to complete its computation if it had exclusive use of the processor. *Blocking time* is the contribution to latency due to having to wait for low-priority processes to release a resource. Blocking time arises as a consequence of the shared resource topology.

Let C_i denote the execution time of process i, T_i denote the period of process i, and B_i denote the blocking time incurred by process i. The worst-case latency for process i, assuming that processes 1 through $i - 1$ are of higher priority, can be found by iterating the following formula [Klein 93] until it converges (that is, the value of L_n is the same as L_{n+1} in the formula below).

$$ L_{n+1} = \sum_{j=1}^{i-1} \left\lceil \frac{L_n}{T_i} \right\rceil C_j + C_i + B $$

This equation is a reflection of the architectural decisions shown in Figure A.1. The first term reflects the use of a priority-based, preemptive scheduling policy. This term computes the number of times higher-priority processes can preempt process i in a window of time that starts at time 0 and extends to time L_n. With each iteration, the formula accumulates the execution time associated with each of these preemptions, adds in the execution time of process i (C_i), and adds in the blocking time (B_i). As stated above, the blocking terms capture the effects of lower-priority processes. The blocking time is directly affected by the synchronization protocol that is used.

Given an initial value of L_n for C_i, iterating until L_n equals L_{n+1} results in a determination of the worst-case latency for process P_i. If the iterations do not converge or they converge beyond the process's deadline, this is an indicator of potential timing problems. The lack of convergence signals an unbounded latency. Equation 1 illustrates the potential sensitivity of latency to higher-priority processes and blocking time.

A.4.2   Priority Assignment

One potential pitfall of the synchronization style is the prioritization strategy. It is possible to have very low levels of CPU utilization and still miss deadlines if an inappropriate prioritization strategy is used. Consider the situation in which there are two processes with the following characteristics:

- Process 1: High priority; execution time is 10 and period is 100.
- Process 2: Low priority; execution time is 1, period and deadline are 10.

If the two processes are initiated at the same time, process 2 will miss its deadline and yet the utilization of this set of processes is only 20 percent. The deadline monotonic priority assignment is a strategy for avoiding this problem in the context of fixed-priority scheduling [Leung 82]. This strategy assigns priorities as a monotonic function of deadline, with the shortest deadline receiving the highest priority.

A.4.3 Priority Inversion

This ABAS is a classical situation in which priority inversion and potentially unbounded priority inversion can arise. Consider the following situation. Assume that process P1 has a high priority, P2 has a medium priority, and P3 has a low priority (for now the priority of S, the server process, is unspecified). While the low-priority process is synchronizing with process S, the high-priority process will have to wait if it also needs to synchronize with S. This is priority inversion in the sense that the high-priority process is waiting while the low-priority process is executing (or strictly speaking, while process S is executing on behalf of the low-priority process). This could happen easily if the high-priority process preempts process S while it is executing at a low priority on behalf of the low-priority process. The medium-priority process could further exacerbate the situation by preempting the critical section and causing even further delay for the high-priority process. This is unbounded priority inversion in the sense that the high-priority process could be delayed arbitrarily by adding other medium-priority processes. This problem illustrates the sensitivity of the high-priority process's latency to the priority of the server process.

A.4.4 Blocking Time

While blocking time is a seemingly innocuous term in Equation 1, blocking is a significant and sometimes insidious contributor to latency. In general, blocking occurs whenever an architectural design permits a low-priority process to execute when a higher-priority process is also ready to execute.

In some cases, blocking is unavoidable. In other cases, as in the priority inversion discussion, blocking can be managed much more effectively. Several common sources of blocking are listed below.

- *Critical section.* As discussed above, a critical section is a source of blocking. An improper server priority can result in an unnecessarily large amount of blocking. The key to circumventing unbounded priority inversion is to ensure that medium-priority processes do not have an opportunity to preempt the critical section that is blocking the high-priority process. One such prevention technique is to set the priority of process S to be at least as high as the highest-priority client process. Another technique is to use a *priority inheritance protocol* [Rajkumar 91], which raises the priority of S to the highest-priority process that is blocked waiting for the services of process S.

- *Deadlock.* Deadlock is an extreme form of blocking in which processing comes to a halt. It occurs when two or more processes need mutually exclusive access to two or more of the same resources. Deadlock is discussed in most books on operating systems.

- *FIFO queue.* A first-in-first-out (FIFO) queue is another common source of blocking. If a high-priority process is stuck in a FIFO queue behind a lower-priority process, the blocking time can be arbitrarily long.

- *Nonpreemptable section.* Sections of lower-priority processes that are nonpreemptable can delay a higher-priority process since the higher-priority process is prevented from preempting when it is time for it to execute and the lower-priority process is in its nonpreemptable section.

- *Interrupt.* Strictly speaking, interrupts are not a source of blocking, but rather a source of preemption. However, often a lower-priority thread is initiated by an interrupt. Since the interrupt is executing on behalf of the lower-priority process, it can be viewed as a source of blocking to other higher-priority processes.

- *Threads and processes.* Some operating systems support threads, which are lightweight units of concurrency that execute within a single, shared address space (whereas each process executes in its own address space). Sometimes in this situation, a two-level scheduler is used. In other words, processes are first scheduled, and then threads within the process are scheduled. A thread's high priority can be virtually ineffective if the thread resides in a process that has been assigned a relatively low priority.

A.5 For Further Reading

The notion of an ABAS was inspired from two points of view: topological and analytical. Shaw and Garlan noticed that a relatively small number of topological patterns or styles are commonly used across many systems. They coined the term *architectural style* [Shaw 96]. The rate-monotonic analysis handbook shows that a close relationship exists between many styles and their associated performance analyses [Klein 93].

To read more about architectural styles and patterns, see Buschmann et al. [Buschmann 96] and Shaw and Garlan [Shaw 96]. To read more about rate-monotonic analysis, read Klein et al. [Klein 93]. For a detailed treatment of synchronization protocols, see Rajkumar [91].

References

[Abowd 96]   Abowd, G.; Bass, L.; Clements, P.; Kazman, R.; Northrop, L.; & Zaremski, A. "Recommended Best Industrial Practice for Software Architecture Evaluation." Technical Report CMU/SEI-96-TR-025. Software Engineering Institute, Carnegie Mellon University, 1996.

[Arora 95]   Arora, V.; Kalaichelvan, K.; Goel, N.; & Munikoti, R. "Measuring High-Level Design Complexity of Real-Time Object-Oriented Systems." *Proc. Annual Oregon Workshop on Software Metrics*, Silver Falls, OR, June 1995.

[Avritzer 98]   Avritzer, A., & Weyuker, E. J. "Investigating Metrics for Architectural Assessment." *Proc. IEEE Fifth International Symposium on Software Metrics*, Bethesda, MD, Nov. 1998: Los Alamitos, CA: IEEE Computer Society Press.

[Bachmann 00]   Bachmann, F.; Bass, L.; Chastek, G.; Donohoe, P.; & Peruzzi, F. "The Architecture Based Design Method" (CMU/SEI-2000-TR-001). Pittsburgh, PA: Software Engineering Institute, Carnegie Mellon University, 2000.

[Bass 98]   Bass, L.; Clements, P.; & Kazman, R. *Software Architecture in Practice*. Reading, MA: Addison-Wesley, 1998.

[Boehm 76]   Boehm, B. W.; Brown, J. R.; & Lipow, M. "Quantitative Evaluation of Software Quality." *Proceedings, 2nd International Conference on Software Engineering*, San Francisco, CA, Oct. 1976, Long Beach, CA: IEEE Computer Society; pp. 592–605.

[Bosch 00]   Bosch, J. *Design and Use of Software Architectures*. Boston, MA: Addison-Wesley, 2000.

[Buschmann 96]   Buschmann, F.; Meunier, R.; Rohnert, H.; Sommerlad, P.; & Stal, M. *Pattern-Oriented Software Architecture, Volume 1: A System of Patterns*. New York: Wiley & Sons, 1996.

[Chung 00]   Chung, L.; Nixon, B.; Yu, E.; & Mylopoulos, J. *Non-Functional Requirements in Software Engineering*. Boston, MA: Kluwer Academic, 2000.

[Clements 01]   Clements, P. & Northrop, L. *Software Product Lines: Practices and Patterns*. Boston, MA: Addison-Wesley, 2001.

[Conway 68]   Conway, M. "How Do Committees Invent?" *Datamation*, April 1968, 28–31.

[Dijkstra 68]   Dijkstra, E. W. "The Structure of the 'T.H.E.' Multiprogramming System." *CACM* 18(8):453–457, 1968.

[Fagan 76]   Fagan, M. E. "Design and Code Inspections to Reduce Errors in Program Development." *IBM Systems Journal*, 15(3):182–211, 1976.

[Freedman 90]   Freedman, D. P. & Weinberg, G. M. *Handbook of Walkthroughs, Inspections, and Technical Reviews: Evaluating Programs, Projects, and Products,* 3d ed. New York: Dorset House, 1990.

[Finnigan 97]   Finnigan, P.; Holt, R.; Kalas, I.; Kerr, S.; Kontogiannis, K.; Muller, H.; Mylopoulos, J.; Perelgut, S.; Stanley, M.; & Wong, K. "The Software Bookshelf." *IBM Systems Journal* 36(4):564–593, 1997.

[Gamma 95]   Gamma, E.; Helm, R.; Johnson, R.; & Vlissides, J. *Design Patterns—Microarchitectures for Reusable Object-Oriented Software*, Reading, MA: Addison-Wesley, 1994.

[Gamma 95]   Gamma, E.; Helm, R.; Johnson, R.; & Vlissides, J. *Design Patterns, Elements of Reusable Object-Oriented Software*. Reading, MA: Addison-Wesley, 1995.

[Garlan 97]   Garlan, D.; Monroe, R. T.; & Wile, D. "Acme: An Architecture Description Interchange Language." *Proceedings of CASCON 97*, November 1997.

[Hofmeister 00]   Hofmeister, C.; Nord, R.; & Soni, D. *Applied Software Architecture*. Reading, MA: Addison-Wesley, 2000.

[Iannino 94]   Iannino, A. "Software Reliability Theory." In *Encyclopedia of Software Engineering,* John Marciniak, Ed. New York: Wiley, 1237–1253.

[Jacobson 97]   Jacobson, I.; Griss, M.; & Jonsson, P. *Software Reuse: Architecture, Process, and Organization for Business Success*. New York, NY: Addison-Wesley, 1997.

[Jalote 94]   Jalote, P. *Fault Tolerance in Distributed Systems*. Upper Saddle River, NJ: Prentice Hall, 1994.

[Jazayeri 00]   Jazayeri, M.; Ran, A.; & van der Linden, F. *Software Architecture for Product Families: Principles and Practice*. Boston, MA: Addison-Wesley, 2000.

[Johnson 94]   Johnson, P. M. "An Instrumented Approach to Improving Software Quality through Formal Technical Review." *Proceedings of the 16th International Conference on Software Engineering*, Sorrento, Italy, May 1994, 113–122.

[Kazman 94]   Kazman, R.; Abowd, G.; Bass, L.; & Webb, M. "SAAM: A Method for Analyzing the Properties of Software Architectures." *Proceedings of the 16th International Conference on Software Engineering* (Sorrento, Italy), May 1994, 81–90.

[Kazman 96] Kazman, R.; Abowd, G.; Bass, L.; & Clements, P. "Scenario-Based Analysis of Software Architecture." *IEEE Software* 13(6):47–55,1996.

[Kazman 99] Kazman, R., & Carriere, S. J. "Playing Detective: Reconstructing Software Architecture from Available Evidence." *Automated Software Engineering* 6(2):107–138, 1999.

[Kazman 01] Kazman, R.; Asundi, J.; & Klein, M. "Quantifying the Costs and Benefits of Architectural Decisions." *Proceedings of the 23rd International Conference on Software Engineering (ICSE 23)*, (Toronto, Canada), May 2001, pp. 297–306.

[Khoshgoftaar 96] Khoshgoftaar, T. M.; Allen, E. B.; Kalaichelvan, K. S.; & Goel, N. "Early Quality Prediction: A Case Study in Telecommunications." *IEEE Software*, vol. 26, no. 3, January 1996, 65–71.

[Klein 93] Klein, M.; Ralya, T.; Pollak, B.; Obenza, R.; & Gonzales Harbour, M. *A Practitioner's Handbook for Real-Time Analysis.* Boston, MA: Kluwer Academic, 1993.

[Klein 99] Klein, M., & Kazman, R. "Attribute-Based Architectural Styles," CMU/SEI-99-TR-22. Pittsburgh, PA: Software Engineering Institute, Carnegie Mellon University, 1999.

[Krikhaar 99] Krikhaar, R.; Postma, A.; Sellink, A.; Stroucken, M.; & Verhoef, C. "A Two-Phase Process for Software Architecture Improvement." *Proceedings of ICSM '99* (Los Alamitos: IEEE CS Press), September 1999.

[Kruchten 98] Kruchten, P. *The Rational Unified Process: An Introduction.* Reading, MA: Addison-Wesley, 1998.

[Landwehr 94] Landwehr, C. E.; Bull, A. R.; McDermott, J. P.; & Choi, W. S. "A Taxonomy of Computer Program Security Flaws." *ACM Computing Surveys* 26(3):211–254,1994.

[Leung 82] Leung, J. L. T., & Whitehead, J. "On the Complexity of Fixed-Priority Scheduling of Periodic, Real-Time Tasks." *Performance Evaluation* 2(4):237–250, 1982.

[Lyu 96] Lyu, M. R. (ed.) *Handbook of Software Reliability Engineering.* New York; McGraw Hill: Los Alamitos, CA: IEEE Computer Society.

[Malveau 01] Malveau, R., & Mowbray, T. *Software Architect Bootcamp.* Upper Saddle River, NJ: Prentice Hall PTR, 2001.

[Medvidovic 00] Medvidovic, N., & Taylor, R. "A Classification and Comparison Framework for Software Architecture Description Languages." *IEEE Transactions on Software Engineering* 26(1):70–93, 2000.

[Parnas 72] Parnas, D. "On the Criteria to Be Used in Decomposing Systems into Modules." *Communications of the ACM* 15(12):1053–1058, 1972.

[Parnas 74] Parnas, D. "On a 'Buzzword': Hierarchical Structure." *Proceedings IFIP of Congress 74*, 336–339, Amsterdam: North Holland Publishing, 1974.

[Parnas 85]   Parnas, D. L., & Weiss, D. M. "Active Design Reviews: Principles and Practice." *Proceedings, Eighth International Conference on Software Engineering,* 132–136, Washington, DC: IEEE Computer Society Press, 1985.

[Rajkumar 91]   Rajkumar, R. *Synchronization in Real-Time Systems: A Priority Inheritance Approach.* Boston, MA: Kluwer Academic Publishers, 1991.

[Schmidt 00]   Schmidt, D.; Stal, M.; Rohnert, H.; & Buschmann, F. *Pattern-Oriented Software Architecture, Volume 2: Patterns for Concurrent and Networked Objects.* New York: Wiley & Sons, 2000.

[SEI ATA]   URL: http://www.sei.cmu.edu/ata/ata_init.html

[SEI NSS]   URL: http://www.sei.cmu.edu/organization/programs/nss/

[Shaw 96]   Shaw, M., & Garlan, D. *Software Architecture: Perspectives on an Emerging Discipline.* Upper Saddle River, NJ: Prentice Hall, 1996.

[Smith 90]   Smith, C. *Performance Engineering of Software Systems.* Reading, MA: Addison-Wesley, 1990.

[Smith 01]   Smith, C. & Williams, L. *Performance Solutions: A Practical Guide for Creating Responsive, Scalable Software.* Boston, MA: Addison-Wesley, 2001.

[Sullivan 99]   Sullivan, K.; Chalasani, S.; & Jha, S. "Software Design as an Investment Activity: A Real Options Perspective." In *Real Options and Business Strategy: Applications to Decision Making*, L. Trigeorgis (ed.). London: Risk Books, 1999.

[Yeh 97]   Yeh, A.; Harris, D.; & Chase, M. "Manipulating Recovered Software Architecture Views." *Proceedings of ICSE 19* (Boston, IEEE Computer Society Press), May 1997, pp. 184–194.

[Zhao 99]   Zhao, J. "Bibliography on Software Architecture Analysis." *Software Engineering Notes* 24(3):61–62, 1999.

Index

Note: Italicized page locators indicate figures/tables.

continued

continued

The SEI Series in Software Engineering

Software Engineering Institute | **Carnegie Mellon**

CERT® Resilience Management Model

CMMI for Development

TSP

Documenting Software Architectures

Reflections on Management

★ Addison-Wesley

Visit **informit.com/sei** for a complete list of available products.

The **SEI Series in Software Engineering** represents is a collaborative undertaking of the Carnegie Mellon Software Engineering Institute (SEI) and Addison-Wesley to develop and publish books on software engineering and related topics. The common goal of the SEI and Addison-Wesley is to provide the most current information on these topics in a form that is easily usable by practitioners and students.

Books in the series describe frameworks, tools, methods, and technologies designed to help organizations, teams, and individuals improve their technical or management capabilities. Some books describe processes and practices for developing higher-quality software, acquiring programs for complex systems, or delivering services more effectively. Other books focus on software and system architecture and product-line development. Still others, from the SEI's CERT Program, describe technologies and practices needed to manage software and network security risk. These and all books in the series address critical problems in software engineering for which practical solutions are available.

Carnegie Mellon
Software Engineering Institute

SEI℠
Classroom
Training

Based on decades of experience and supported by four widely acclaimed practitioner books in the SEI Addison-Wesley Series, the SEI offers the Software Architecture Curriculum and the Software Product Lines Curriculum.

Software Architecture Curriculum

Collection of six courses, three certificate programs, and a field exercise that equip software professionals with state-of-the-art practices so they can efficiently design software-intensive systems that meet their intended business and quality goals.

Courses:

Software Architecture: Principles and Practices

Documenting Software Architectures

Software Architecture Design and Analysis

Software Product Lines

Architecture Tradeoff Analysis Method (ATAM) Evaluator Training

ATAM Facilitator Training

ATAM Coaching and Observation

Certificate Programs:

Software Architecture Professional Certificate Program

ATAM Evaluator Certificate Program

ATAM Lead Evaluator Certificate Program

Software Product Lines Curriculum

Collection of five courses and three certificate programs that equip software professionals with state-of-the-art practices so they can efficiently use proven product lien practices to achieve their strategic reuse and other business goals.

Courses:

Software Product Lines

Adopting Software Product Lines

Product Line Technical Probe Training

Developing Software Product Lines

Product Line Technical Probe Facilitator Training

Certificate Programs:

Software Product Lines Professional Certificate

Product Line Technical Probe Team Member Certificate

Product Line Technical Probe Leader Certificate

For current course information visit: *www.sei.cmu.edu/products/courses/*
To register for courses call: **412.268.7388**
or email: *courseregistration@sei.cmu.edu*

In addition to the curricula and certificate programs, the SEI has developed software architecture and product line methods and approaches to assist organizations in achieving their technical and business objectives.

To learn more, visit: *www.sei.cmu.edu/programs/pls/*

Software Engineering Institute
4500 Fifth Avenue
Pittsburgh, PA 15213

412.268.5800   www.sei.cmu.edu

℠ SEI is a service mark of Carnegie Mellon University

The SEI Series in Software Engineering

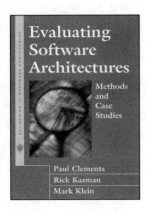

Evaluating Software Architectures
Methods and Case Studies
Paul Clements, Rick Kazman, and Mark Klein

This book is a comprehensive, step-by-step guide to software architecture evaluation, describing specific methods that can quickly and inexpensively mitigate enormous risk in software projects. The methods are illustrated both by case studies and by sample artifacts put into play during an evaluation: viewgraphs, scenarios, final reports—everything you need to evaluate an architecture in your own organization.
0-201-70482-X • Hardcover • 240 Pages • ©2002

Software Product Lines
Practices and Patterns
Paul Clements and Linda Northrop

Building product lines from common assets can yield remarkable improvements in productivity, time to market, product quality, and customer satisfaction. This book provides a framework of specific practices, with detailed case studies, to guide the implementation of product lines in your own organization.
0-201-70332-7 • Hardcover • 608 Pages • ©2002

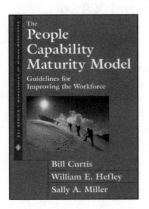

The People Capability Maturity Model
Guidelines for Improving the Workforce
Bill Curtis, William E. Hefley, and Sally A. Miller

Employing the process maturity framework of the Software CMM, the People Capability Maturity Model (People CMM) describes best practices for managing and developing an organization's workforce. This book describes the People CMM and the key practices that comprise each of its maturity levels, and shows how to apply the model in guiding organizational improvements. Includes case studies.
0-201-60445-0 • Hardback • 448 Pages • ©2002

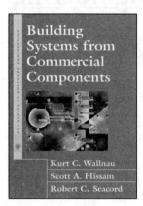

Building Systems from Commercial Components
Kurt C. Wallnau, Scott A. Hissam, and Robert C. Seacord

Commercial components are increasingly seen as an effective means to save time and money in building large software systems. However, integrating pre-existing components, with pre-existing specifications, is a delicate and difficult task. This book describes specific engineering practices needed to accomplish that task successfully, illustrating the techniques described with case studies and examples.

0-201-70064-6 • Hardcover • 432 pages • ©2002

CMMI^{SM} Distilled
A Practical Introduction to Integrated Process Improvement
Dennis M. Ahern, Aaron Clouse, and Richard Turner

The Capability Maturity Model Integration (CMMI) is the latest version of the popular CMM framework, designed specifically to integrate an organization's process improvement activities across disciplines. This book provides a concise introduction to the CMMI, highlighting the benefits of integrated process improvement, explaining key features of the new framework, and suggesting how to choose appropriate models and representations for your organization.

0-201-73500-8 • Paperback • 336 pages • ©2001

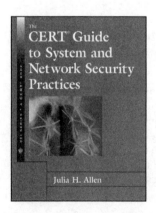

The CERT® Guide to System and Network Security Practices
By Julia H. Allen

The CERT Coordination Center helps systems administrators secure systems connected to public networks, develops key security practices, and provides timely security implementations. This book makes CERT practices and implementations available in book form, and offers step-by-step guidance for protecting your systems and networks against malicious and inadvertent compromise.

0-201-73723-X • Paperback • 480 pages • ©2001

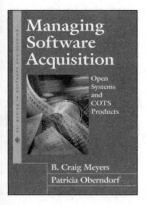

Managing Software Acquisition
Open Systems and COTS Products
B. Craig Meyers and Patricia Oberndorf

The acquisition of open systems and commercial off-the-shelf (COTS) products is an increasingly vital part of large-scale software development, offering significant savings in time and money. This book presents fundamental principles and best practices for successful acquisition and utilization of open systems and COTS products.

0-201-70454-4 • Hardcover • 400 pages • ©2001

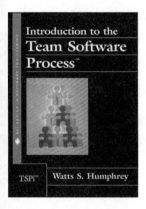

Introduction to the Team Software Process^{SM}
Watts S. Humphrey

The Team Software Process (TSP) provides software engineers with a framework designed to build and maintain more effective teams. This book, particularly useful for engineers and students trained in the Personal Software Process (PSP), introduces TSP and the concrete steps needed to improve software teamwork.

0-201-47719-X • Hardcover • 496 pages • ©2000

CMM in Practice
Processes for Executing Software Projects at Infosys
Pankaj Jalote

This book describes the implementation of CMM at Infosys Technologies, and illustrates in detail how software projects are executed at this highly mature software development organization. The book examines the various stages in the life cycle of an actual Infosys project as a running example throughout the book, describing the technical and management processes used to initiate, plan, and execute it.

0-201-61626-2 • Hardcover • 400 pages • ©2000

Measuring the Software Process

Statistical Process Control for Software Process Improvement

William A. Florac and Anita D. Carleton

This book shows how to use measurements to manage and improve software processes within your organization. It explains specifically how quality characteristics of software products and processes can be quantified, plotted, and analyzed, so that the performance of software development activities can be predicted, controlled, and guided to achieve both business and technical goals.

0-201-60444-2 • Hardcover • 272 pages • ©1999

Cleanroom Software Engineering

Technology and Process

Stacy Prowell, Carmen J. Trammell, Richard C. Linger, and Jesse H. Poore

This book provides an introduction and in-depth description of the Cleanroom approach to high-quality software development. Following an explanation of basic Cleanroom theory and practice, the authors draw on their extensive experience in industry to elaborate the Cleanroom development and certification process and show how this process is compatible with the Capability Maturity Model (CMM).

0-201-85480-5 • Hardcover • 416 pages • ©1999

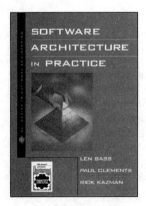

Software Architecture in Practice

Len Bass, Paul Clements, and Rick Kazman

This book introduces the concepts and practice of software architecture, not only covering essential technical topics for specifying and validating a system, but also emphasizing the importance of the business context in which large systems are designed. Enhancing both technical and organizational discussions, key points are illuminated by substantial case studies.

0-201-19930-0 • Hardcover • 480 pages • ©1998

Managing Risk
Methods for Software Systems Development
By Elaine M. Hall

Written for busy professionals charged with delivering high-quality products on time and within budget, this comprehensive guide describes a success formula for managing software risk. The book follows a five-part risk management road map designed to take you from crisis to control of your software project.

0-201-25592-8 • Hardcover • 400 pages • ©1998

Software Process Improvement
Practical Guidelines for Business Success
By Sami Zahran

This book will help you manage and control the quality of your organization's software products by showing you how to develop a preventive culture of disciplined and continuous process improvement.

0-201-17782-X • Hardcover • 480 pages • ©1998

Introduction to the Personal Software Process
By Watts S. Humphrey

This workbook provides a hands-on introduction to the basic discipline of software engineering, as expressed in the author's well-known Personal Software Process (PSP). By applying the forms and methods of PSP described in the book, you can learn to manage your time effectively and to monitor the quality of your work, with enormous benefits in both regards.

0-201-54809-7 • Paperback • 304 pages • ©1997

Managing Technical People
Innovation, Teamwork, and the Software Process
By Watts S. Humphrey

Drawing on the author's extensive experience as a senior manager of software development at IBM, this book describes proven techniques for managing technical professionals. The author shows specifically how to identify, motivate, and organize innovative people, while tying leadership practices to improvements in the software process.

0-201-54597-7 • Paperback • 352 pages • ©1997

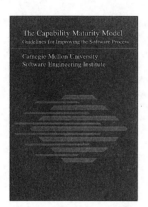

The Capability Maturity Model
Guidelines for Improving the Software Process
By Carnegie Mellon University/Software Engineering Institute

This book provides the authoritative description and technical overview of the Capability Maturity Model (CMM), with guidelines for improving software process management. The CMM provides software professionals in government and industry with the ability to identify, adopt, and use sound management and technical practices for delivering quality software on time and within budget.

0-201-54664-7 • Hardcover • 464 pages • ©1995

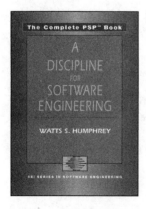

A Discipline for Software Engineering
The Complete PSP Book
By Watts S. Humphrey

This book scales down to a personal level the successful methods developed by the author to help managers and organizations evaluate and improve their software capabilities—methods comprising the Personal Software Process (PSP). The author's aim with PSP is to help individual software practitioners develop the skills and habits needed to plan, track, and analyze large and complex projects, and to develop high-quality products.

0-201-54610-8 • Hardcover • 816 pages • ©1995

Software Design Methods for Concurrent and Real-Time Systems

By Hassan Gomaa

This book provides a basic understanding of concepts and issues in concurrent system design, while surveying and comparing a range of applicable object-oriented design methods. The book describes a practical approach for applying real-time scheduling theory to analyze the performance of real-time designs.

0-201-52577-1 • Hardcover • 464 pages • ©1993

Managing the Software Process

By Watts S. Humphrey

This landmark book introduces the author's methods, now commonly practiced in industry, for improving software development and maintenance processes. Emphasizing the basic principles and priorities of the software process, the book's sections are organized in a natural way to guide organizations through needed improvement activities.

0-201-18095-2 • Hardcover • 512 pages • ©1989

Other titles of interest from Addison-Wesley

Practical Software Measurement

Objective Information for Decision Makers
By John McGarry, David Card, Cheryl Jones, Beth Layman, Elizabeth Clark, Joseph Dean, and Fred Hall

A critical task in developing and maintaining software-intensive systems is to meet project cost, schedule, and technical objectives. This official guide to Practical Software Measurement (PSM) shows how to accomplish that task through sound measurement techniques and the development of a software measurement process. It provides a comprehensive description of PSM's techniques and practical guidance based on PSM's actual application in large-scale software projects.

0-201-71516-3 • Hardcover • 256 pages • ©2002

Making the Software Business Case
Improvement by the Numbers
By Donald J. Reifer

This book shows software engineers and managers how to prepare the *business* case for change and improvement. It presents the tricks of the trade developed by this well-known author over many years, tricks that have repeatedly helped his clients win the battle of the budget. The first part of the book addresses the fundamentals associated with creating a business case; the second part uses case studies to illustrate cases made for different types of software improvement initiatives.
0-201-72887-7 • Paperback • 304 pages • ©2002

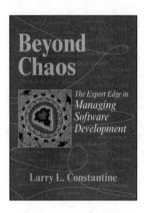

Beyond Chaos
The Expert Edge in Managing Software Development
Larry L. Constantine

The essays in this book, drawn from among the best contributions to Software Development magazine's Management Forum, reveal best practices in managing software projects and organizations. Written by many top names in the field—including Larry Constantine, Karl Wiegers, Capers Jones, Ed Yourdon, Dave Thomas, Meilir Page-Jones, Jim Highsmith, and Steve McConnell—each piece has been selected and edited to provide ideas and suggestions that can be translated into immediate practice.

0-201-71960-6 • Paperback • 416 pages • ©2001

Component-Based Software Engineering
Putting the Pieces Together
By George T. Heineman and William T. Councill

This book provides a comprehensive overview of, and current perspectives on, component-based software engineering (CBSE). With contributions from well-known luminaries in the field, it defines what CBSE really is, details CBSE's benefits and pitfalls, describes CBSE experiences from around the world, and ultimately reveals CBSE's considerable potential for engineering reliable and cost-effective software.

0-201-70485-4 • Hardcover • 880 pages • ©2001

Software Fundamentals
Collected Papers by David L. Parnas
By Daniel M. Hoffman and David M. Weiss

David Parnas's groundbreaking writings capture the essence of the innovations, controversies, challenges, and solutions of the software industry. This book is a collection of his most influential papers in various areas of software engineering, with historical context provided by leading thinkers in the field.

0-201-70369-6 • Hardcover • 688 pages • ©2001

Software for Use
A Practical Guide to the Models and Methods of Usage-Centered Design
by Larry L. Constantine and Lucy A. D. Lockwood

This book describes models and methods that help you deliver more usable software-software that allows users to accomplish tasks with greater ease and efficiency. Aided by concrete techniques, experience-tested examples, and practical tools, it guides you through a systematic software development process called usage-centered design, a process that weaves together two major threads in software development: use cases and essential modeling.

0-201-92478-1 • Hardcover • 608 pages • ©1999

CMM Implementation Guide
Choreographing Software Process Improvement
by Kim Caputo

This book provides detailed instruction on how to put the Capability Maturity Model (CMM) into practice and, thereby, on how to raise an organization to the next higher level of maturity. Drawing on her first-hand experience leading software process improvement groups in a large corporation, the author provides invaluable advice and information for anyone charged specifically with implementing the CMM.

0-201-37938-4 • Hardcover • 336 pages • ©1998

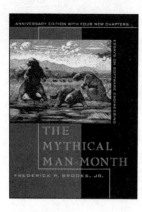

The Mythical Man-Month, Anniversary Edition

Essays on Software Engineering
By Frederick P. Brooks, Jr.

Fred Brooks blends software engineering facts with thought-provoking opinions to offer insight for anyone managing complex projects. Twenty years after the publication of this influential and timeless classic, the author revisited his original ideas and added new thoughts and advice, both for readers already familiar with his work and for those discovering it for the first time.

0-201-83595-9 • Paperback • 336 pages • ©1995